TRANSOCEANIC STUDIES
Ileana Rodriguez, Series Editor

National Consciousness and Literary Cosmopolitics

Postcolonial Literature in a Global Moment

WEIHSIN GUI

THE OHIO STATE UNIVERSITY PRESS · COLUMBUS

Copyright © 2013 by The Ohio State University.
All rights reserved.

Library of Congress Cataloging-in-Publication Data

Gui, Weihsin, 1978–
 National consciousness and literary cosmopolitics : postcolonial literature in a global moment / Weihsin Gui.
  p. cm. — (Transoceanic studies)
 Includes bibliographical references and index.
 ISBN 978-0-8142-1230-1 (cloth : alk. paper) — ISBN 978-0-8142-9332-4 (cd)
 1. Nationalism and literature. 2. Nationalism in literature. I. Title. II. Series: Transoceanic studies.
 PN56.N19G85 2013
 809'.93358—dc23
                          2013017115

Cover design by James A. Baumann
Text design by Juliet Williams
Type set in Adobe Minion Pro
Printed by Sheridan Books, Inc.

♾ The paper used in this publication meets the minimum requirements of the American National Standard for Information Sciences—Permanence of Paper for Printed Library Materials. ANSI Z39.48-1992.

9 8 7 6 5 4 3 2 1

CONTENTS

Acknowledgments vii

INTRODUCTION	Constellations, Critical Nationality, and Literary Cosmopolitics	1
CHAPTER 1	Articulating Adorno with Postcolonial Critique: Fanon, Said, Spivak	15
CHAPTER 2	"More English than English": Kazuo Ishiguro's Negation of National Nostalgia	38
CHAPTER 3	"The Possibilities of the New Country We Are Making": Transnational Fragments and National Consciousness in Derek Walcott's Writing	78
CHAPTER 4	"Not Monological but Multilogical": Gender, Hybridity, and National Narratives in Shirley Geok-lin Lim's Writing	121
CHAPTER 5	Ethnographic Tactics and the Cosmopolitical Aesthetic in Contemporary Malaysian Fiction	162
CONCLUSION	Nation, Narration, Negation	198

Works Cited 201
Index 211

ACKNOWLEDGMENTS

THIS book grew out of a dissertation written for my PhD at Brown University where I had the pleasure and privilege of being taught and mentored by Olakunle George, Timothy Bewes, and Rey Chow. Nancy Armstrong, Leonard Tennenhouse, and Khachig Tölölyan also offered invaluable advice and encouragement during my years at Brown, and I am especially grateful to John Marx, who read almost every word of this book's early drafts and gave direct and trenchant critiques. My fellow graduate students Jacqueline Wernimont, Wendy Lee, Emily Steinlight, Asha Nadkarni, Chris Lee, David Babcock, Daniel Block, Raymond Sultan, and Chris Holmes made my time there much more sociable and enjoyable. The collegiality and friendship of Charles Wharram and Suzie Park saw me through a rather difficult time in a strenuous environment. At the University of California Riverside, I am thankful for the guidance and support of my department chair Deborah Willis and the intellectual and social exchanges I have had with my colleagues Susan Zieger, Traise Yamamoto, Vorris Nunley, Carole-Anne Tyler, George Haggerty, Mariam Lam, Henk Maier, and Annmaria Shimabuku. UCR's Center for Ideas and Society, directed by Georgia Warnke, awarded me a residential fellowship in the spring of 2012, during which I completed this book and formulated a new intellectual project. My parents, Gui How Meng and Aik Poh Hong, and my sister, Crystal Gui, have always supported me half a world away in Singapore. Last but certainly not least, I am extremely grateful for the affection and companionship of Connie Chow and those "woofingtons" Holly and Milton.

INTRODUCTION

Constellations, Critical Nationality, and Literary Cosmopolitics

> Distance is not a safety-zone but a field of tension. It is manifested not in relaxing the claim of ideas to truth, but in delicacy and fragility of thinking.
>
> —Theodor Adorno, *Minima Moralia* 127

THIS book is concerned with the conjunctions of national consciousness and literary cosmopolitics in a global moment rather than making a case for or against the nation from political, economic, or anthropological perspectives. Drawing on the aesthetic theory and negative dialectical thinking of Frankfurt School critic Theodor Adorno, I argue that postcolonial literary form and style negates the homogenizing and exclusionary impulse of a unitary national identity and helps us recognize nationalism as a critical constellation of political, economic, and cultural forces that make up a social formation. Even with the increase in flows of people, capital, and culture around the globe, nations have not withered away. This is nothing new; as the editor of a recent anthology on nationalism remarks rather tiredly, "by now it is practically axiomatic that obituaries of the nation are premature" (Burton 1). This book takes a different tack by arguing that, after the heyday of anticolonial independence in the Third World and the establishment of postcolonial literature and its academic corollary—postcolonial studies—as distinct fields of writing and research, literary texts and their authors in the late twentieth and early twenty-first centuries evince a critical national consciousness particular to their individual sociocultural contexts, and that in a global moment this national consciousness is dynamically engaged with both local cultural formations and transnational cultural flows. This engagement with what lies beyond the nation's symbolic and territorial boundaries is a literary cosmopolitics—the imagination and representation of sustained political engagement between local and translocal cultural particularities through fiction and poetry. In using the term *global moment* as opposed to globalization, I wish to connote a spatial and temporal conjunction rather than an existing economic process or condition. A moment is both a rotational force as well as an instant in time, and it is against the backdrop of a sweeping force field of narratives of cultural and economic globalization that we see the intersections of national consciousness and literary cosmopolitics rather than the establishment of a triumphantly postnational moment in literature, culture, and world politics. Narratives of cultural and economic globalization, or globalism, may reveal spaces of minority discourses and counternarratives and refigure the national imaginary as a complex weave of negotiations and multiple identifications, but they do not lead to a definitive repudiation of the nation either as a unit of analysis or as a social formation. The persistence of tropes and figures of national consciousness in literary texts, together with the loosening of the hyphen between nation and state in contemporary world politics, suggests that nationalism is a salient cultural and political movement and that the nation remains a contested space worth thinking, feeling, and writing about.

A cosmopolitical perspective on nationalism considers how "the tightness or laxity of the hyphen between nation and state is an important historical factor in the evaluation of the aims of nationalism and their compatibility with normative cosmopolitanism" (Cheah, "The Cosmopolitical—Today" 31). Thus, in contrast to the normative cosmopolitanism of radical, global culture espoused by proponents of globalism, cosmopolitics asks us "to turn our critical focus on the mutating global field of political, economic, and cultural forces in which nationalism and cosmopolitanism are invoked as practical discourses" (31). This critical focus on the mutual imbrication of national and transnational forces in a constantly changing global framework helps us recognize that while globalization is a useful concept with which to broaden interpretations of national and postcolonial literatures, it "doesn't displace or replace existing institutions and practices once and for all; too much of the discourse on globalization has failed to remember the force and power of the residual at every moment of the dominant" (O'Brien and Szeman 609). By rethinking nationalism not as national identity but as political consciousness and cultural critique constituted through and inextricably bound with cosmopolitical engagement, postcolonial literature goes against the grain of celebratory narratives of cultural and economic globalization or globalism.

Globalism and Postnationalist Discourse

In the last two decades, scholars in the social sciences and humanities have argued against the nation as a framework for critical analysis and emphasized the priority of global cultural flows and their corresponding transnational intersections with social and cultural formations at the local or subnational level. I call such arguments that foreground the global in cultural and literary studies "globalism," as distinct from social and economic theories of globalization that observe and analyze the workings of information technology, the movement of migrant and diasporic populations, and the flexible accumulation of finance capital across the borders of nation-states. I distinguish between these two strands of thinking about the global to more clearly delineate the specific focus of this book, which is an examination of national consciousness and literary cosmopolitics rather than a study of economic and demographic flows and movements.

Drawing on the ideas of traveling cultures and routes of exchange developed in anthropology by James Clifford (1997), scholars both in the social sciences and in literary studies have challenged the authority of the nation-state and nationalism by emphasizing the decentralizing force of cultural fluidity through concepts such as diaspora, transnationalism, and postnationalism. These arguments often rely on a conceptualization of culture as everyday practice in the anthropological or sociological sense, thus eliding the significance of nationalism and national consciousness as a sociocultural concept that is continually contested and redefined. Proponents of globalism conceptualize culture as a set of everyday processes encompassing whole ways of life, and these quotidian processes and experiences are always already in opposition to and exceed the symbolic and territorial boundaries of the nation-state. For scholars of globalism, the terms diaspora, migration, and transnationalism not only denote population flows across inter- and intranational borders but also connote social and symbolic exchanges and intermixings across such borders in defiance of the regulation of nation-states. Focusing on the hybridity and ambivalence of migrant and diasporic subjects in colonial and postcolonial societies, Homi Bhabha uses "the disjunctive temporality of the nation" resulting from the slippage between what he calls the pedagogical and performative aspects of nationalism to reread the monolithic nation-state as "the liminal figure of the nation-space" where "no political ideologies could claim transcendent or metaphysical authority for themselves" (299). Bhabha's thinking deconstructs nationalism as an anticolonial project, whereby the *différance* of culture introduces a temporal slippage into and thus a deferral of nationalism's "transcendent or metaphysical authority" as a political ideology. But Bhabha's case against nationalism as a political ideology is predicated on an opposition of the nation's "historical certainty and settled nature" against "culture's transnational dissemination" (292, 320). Bhabha's redefinition of the homogenizing, totalizing project of the nation-state into a nation-space of contesting narratives may destabilize the hyphen between nation and state, but his argument misses the persistent and residual national connections that diasporic and postcolonial individuals or communities maintain, because it equates such figures with transnational culture or cultural practices that must always transcend or cross over the nation. Arjun Appadurai's ethnography of border-crossing cultural flows also attempts to "think ourselves beyond the nation" (158). Arjun Appadurai coins the term "postnational" to describe a decentralized global system, and in this system "while nations might continue to exist, the steady erosion of the capabilities of the nation-state to monopolize loyalty will encourage the spread of national forms that are largely divorced from territorial states" (169). But Appadurai's critique of nationalism in the form of the territorial state is premised upon a deterritorialized national consciousness; Appadurai, like Bhabha, challenges nationalism in the form of the nation-state but wants to retain the idea of nationalism as a nation-*space*, because he ultimately favors the "extraterritorial nationalism of populations who love America but are not necessarily attached to the United States" (171). While Appadurai opposes the dominant narrative of "monopatriotism," he reinstates the United States as the privileged site of postnationalism because "America may yet construct another narrative of enduring significance," and "in this narrative, bounded territories could give way to diasporic networks, nations to transnations, and patriotism itself could become plural, serial, contextual and mobile" (176). Thus, despite his emphasis on the transformation of patriotism into a plural and mobile concept, Appadurai's postnationalism is actually located and territorialized in the one remaining country that is also a superpower state. If, so the argument goes, we must transgress or bypass the nation-state, then it stands to reason that our next horizon of reading must now be the changing space of diaspora, migration, and trans- or postnationalism—in other words, the entire world or globe in its totality and fluidity.

The fluidity of transnational identities is emphasized by Stuart Hall, who uses the idea of diaspora to destabilize national and ethnic identities. Stuart Hall's metaphorization of Caribbean hybridity into a cultural identity that exemplifies our globalized world assumes that the diasporic condition is an already accomplished fact and elides the nationalist sentiments of the diasporas he uses as his examples, notably that of the Palestinians. Hall's anti-imperialist criticism is simultaneously anti-nationalist; he identifies "the people of

Palestine" as a population defined by their flight from a geographical location that is rightly theirs ("Cultural Identity" 235). The competition for that territory and the Israeli population that currently governs it offers, by contrast, a "backward-looking conception of diaspora" as Israeli nationalism stands for the atavistic mode of patriotic nationalism that is complicit with "the old, the imperialising, the hegemonising" Western power (235). In place of the singular and statist concepts of ethnicity and nationalism, Hall offers diaspora as an "experience" of productive cultural identities "which lives with and through, not despite, difference; by *hybridity*" (235, original emphasis). But Hall misses the national consciousness of the Afro-Caribbean and Palestinian diasporic peoples by reframing identity in exclusively cultural terms, such that "the issue of cultural identity now constitutes one of the most serious global problems at the start of the twenty-first century" ("Negotiating" 25). By using diaspora as a metaphor for cultural identity and framing cultural identity within a global framework, Hall tries to portray nationalism as a restrictive and limited container of identity, because "instead of thinking of national cultures as unified, we should think of them as constituting a *discursive device* which represents difference as unity or identity. They are cross-cut by deep internal divisions and differences, and 'unified' only through the exercise of different forms of cultural power" ("The Question of Cultural Identity" 617, original emphasis). Hall's insight that "*Modern nations are all cultural hybrids*" (617, original emphasis) is an argument against the unification of national identity through race or ethnicity performed by the suturing power of national culture. But the discursive nature of national culture, its power as "a *discourse*—a way of constructing meanings which influences and organizes our actions and our conceptions of ourselves" by "producing meanings about 'the nation' with which we can *identify*" (613, original emphasis)—suggests that national culture may not always serve a homogenizing national identity promulgated by the sovereign state. In the hands of postcolonial writers, national culture may even be used to envision or construct alternative meanings or definitions of the nation that interrogate, contradict, or deviate from the dominant national identity. Despite his contention that diaspora as a metaphor helps us to think of "identity as a 'production,' which is never complete, always in process, and always constituted within, not outside, representation" ("Cultural Identity" 222), Hall does not consider how the discursive and productive force of national culture may be in dialogue or tension rather than in lockstep with national identity and state power.

The transnational, postnational, and diasporic arguments put forward by Bhabha, Appadurai, and Hall all emphasize the potential of culture as lived experience and transnational flow to subvert nationalist discourse and transgress national boundaries. Furthermore, the figure who embodies and represents these transgressions is the diasporic or migrant subject, a subject whose mobility and deterritorialized condition foregrounds a radical cultural identity that resists the homogenizing force of nationalism. But this strategic move that sets culture (represented by the ethnicized, diasporic subject) against the nation-state is itself inscribed within a larger, global framework that may contain or undermine culture's radical heterogeneity. As Khachig Tölölyan observes, the increasing valorization of the term "diaspora" causes "a reduction of or an inattention to the complexity of the past and present of diasporic social formations [. . .] which occurs when the ideas of identity and subjectivity produced by a theory-inflected investigation of texts is projected upon the *social* text of diaspora life" ("Rethinking Diaspora(s)" 28–29, original emphasis). From a different angle, Slavoj Žižek and Rey Chow have trenchantly examined how deterritorialized cultural and ethnic identities that offer the possibility of agency and change may be complicit with the logic of global capital. Žižek draws disturbing parallels between nineteenth-century as well as present-day Western cultural imperialism and multiculturalism, emphasizing how multiculturalism can repeat a colonial form of "racism with a distance," "a privileged universal position" that "'respects' the Other's identity [. . .] as a self-enclosed 'authentic' community" (44). Chow considers how the dominant articulations of cultural, ethnic, and diasporic identities may be "already firmly inscribed with the economic and ideological workings of capitalism" such that the radical challenge put forward from these identity positions "constitutes the economically logical and socially viable vocation for them to assume" (*Protestant Ethnic* 48). In short, the valorization of diasporic and ethnic cultures against nation-states creates a dichotomy that aligns itself with the logic of global capital. It creates a culture effect that hypostasizes the dynamic plurality of cultures: the identities and positions resulting from such objectification have predetermined ends mapped out for them, or become ends in themselves instead of allowing for an active politics. Culture's mobility, heterogeneity, and radicalism are encompassed by globalization and become symptoms of its administration.

Literature and the Nation:
Corporeal, Discursive, and Spectral Theories

The hypostatization of culture by global capital can be understood as a modern version of the mobilization of culture as national character in eighteenth-century European theories of literary nationalism. The concept of literature as an expression of a unified and unique national character originates in European Romantic ideas of language and collective identity, and this organicist or corporeal form of literary nationalism has been contested by postcolonial critics who argue for a cultural discursive as well as a spectral linkage between literature and nation. In this corporeal aspect, literature written in the national language is a crucial element in the national *Bildung* as it both embodies and expresses the spirit of the *Volk*, or the people. Johann Gottfried Herder, in his *Essay on the Origin of Language* (1772), observes that if "a fiery people reveals its boldness in its metaphors" (150), then "no step can be taken, no new word can be invented, no new felicitous form can be put to use which does not carry the imprint of the human soul" (164–65). Three decades later, Johann Gottlieb Fichte extends Herder's philosophy about language and national character in his *Addresses to the German Nation* (1807–8), exhorting his listeners "to mould the Germans into a corporate body, which shall be stimulated in all its individual members by the same interest" (15). The sinews of this corporate body are, in a Herderian fashion, formed out of a common language, such that anyone who speaks the German language "could consider himself as in a double sense a citizen, on the one hand, of the State where he was born and to whose care he was in the first instance commended, and, on the other hand, of the whole common fatherland of the German nation" (147). Language and literature, endowed with such organicist and corporeal powers, incorporates disparate individuals into a larger language-based identity; they also quicken and give voice to the national character that lies dormant in the collective body.

But concepts of linguistic and racial purity that seem to shape the modern nation in the eighteenth century are more closely bound to the biopolitical power of the state and its racialization of both individual bodies and the larger body politic. During the eighteenth and nineteenth centuries, there arose in European theories of nation and culture a slippage between nationalism defined as and through literary and cultural *Bildung* and nationalism as a social and political consciousness, and the latter formulation will be revisited by anti- and postcolonial critics in the second half of the twentieth century. In *"Society Must Be Defended,"* Foucault points out that "racism is born at the point when the theme of racial purity replaces that of race struggle" and in the shift "from the emancipatory project [of political struggle] to a concern with purity, sovereignty was able to invest and take over the discourse of race struggle and reutilize it for its own strategy. State sovereignty thus becomes the imperative to protect the race" and the State becomes "the protector of the integrity, the superiority, and the purity of the race" (81). Foucault analyzes the slippage between the State and the nation, the latter defined by contemporary jurists and politicians in social and civic rather than sovereign and racial terms, such that "the nation, or rather 'nations,'" are "collections, societies, groupings of individuals who share a status, mores, customs, and a certain particular law" understood as "regulatory statutes rather than Statist laws" (134). Even though the corporatist theories of literary nationalism become part of a discourse of state sovereignty premised on racial and cultural homogenization and the exclusion of what is other and nonidentical, there is still "something else that speaks in history and takes itself as the object of its own historical narrative," which "is the sort of new entity known as the nation" (142).

The organicist relationship between literature and nation has been taken to task by critics who examine the social formation of postcolonial nations as cultural discourse rather than natural development. Instead of regarding literature as emanating out of an already existing national character or organic body, they focus on the narrative and discursive dimensions of culture in dynamic tension with the nation-state. Literature as cultural discourse is no longer isomorphic with the nation, but becomes part of a people's collective lived experience and therefore does not have a specially defined mission to edify and corporatize the national body. Instead of articulating and performing a nation's particular character through affective language and narrative structure, literature as cultural discourse informs and reforms the nation. Benedict Anderson discusses the connection between literature and nationalism in terms of print-capitalism out of which the nation emerges as an "imagined political community" (6) thanks to cultural media such as the novel and the newspaper. Anderson's emphasis that the imagined nation is a political and not only a cultural community reminds us that the apparent fixity of the national body in ideas of racial, ethnic, and linguistic identity is not at all natural and is thus open to contestation. As he observes in terms that bring to mind Foucault's analysis of biopolitics and the state, "the fact of the matter is that nationalism thinks in terms of historical destinies, while racism dreams of eternal contaminations, transmitted from the origins of time through an endless sequence of loathsome copulations: outside history" (Anderson 145). The novel and the newspaper are part of a larger cultural discourse that imagines the nation as a political community, and they reimagine the nation's destiny as political and social circumstances change over historical time. As Timothy Brennan argues, the nation is "a gestative political structure which the Third World artist is consciously building or suffering the lack of" (46–47), and rather than reinforcing a preexisting national character, the novels written by these artists "often attempt to assemble the fragments of national life and give them a final shape" (61). Following Anderson's and Brennan's thinking, the symbolic and cultural space of the nation marked out in its totality by the state is always cross-hatched and crossed over by literature's textuality as a cultural discourse.

This tension between the centripetal and authoritarian power of the state, the symbolic and imagined contours of the nation, and the fluid, centrifugal cultural discourse of literature opens up a spectral or haunted reading of the nation. Pheng Cheah argues for a spectral nationality in literature from and about postcolonial societies, which involves "a mutual haunting of the popular organism and the state: the nation tries to reappropriate the state from authoritarian and global forces" (*Spectral Nationality* 11). This haunting of the state by the nation and vice versa is especially evident in literary narratives such as the postcolonial *Bildungsroman*, because, in Cheah's terms, "such novels do not only reflect or thematize the nation's *Bildung*. They are themselves intended to be part of it. They are meant to have an active causal role in the nation's genesis as they supply the occasion and catalyst for their implied reader's *Bildung* as a patriotic subject" (240). Spectral nationality marks a return to organicist theories of European Romantic literary nationalism, which Cheah considers a liberating and not totalizing project. But within the framework of late twentieth-century global capitalism, literary projects of "radical nationalist *Bildung*" fail more often than they succeed, and this failure to "organicize the foreign prosthesis of the neo-colonial state [. . .] points to a certain ghostliness within the living body" of the nation (246). Ghostliness as a productive dilemma and the uncanniness of the spectral nation is further developed by Vilashini Cooppan, who considers how literary narratives represent nations as "fantasmic objects knotted together by ambivalent forces of desire, identification, memory, and forgetting" (xvii). Cooppan stages an encounter between psychoanalysis, nationalism, and deconstruction, in which the nation itself becomes "a spectralized flow" rather than "a spirit of collective identity and zone of governmentality" because, "like ghosts, they keep *coming back* in the course of the still unfinished long twentieth century" (7, original emphasis). Like Cheah, who reads postcolonial literature as an incarnation of the mutual haunting of the nation and the state, Cooppan treats literature as a mode of interpellation, hailing melancholic national subjects who "live their nationalism in the mode of loss, for all must contend with the difficult process of identifying with something that is not entirely there, that exists in the present yet recedes into the deep past of national history" (32). In postcolonial and contemporary world literature, there is no escape from the specter of the nation, but at the same time subjects who are so haunted can "recognize [the nation] not as something to be worked through but as something we live after, and with, in the hopes of another kind of future" in which "states do not terrorize citizens and nations do not act alone or constitute their polity as purity" (274). According to Cheah and Cooppan, literature in its ghostly guise does not narrate or constitute the nation but instead marks its shallow grave around which the imagined community tries, however unsuccessfully, to weep and mourn both its incompleteness and its passing.

Adorno and the Negative Dialectics of Literature and Nation

In contrast to these organic, cultural, discursive, and spectral theories of literary nationalism, the critical theory of Frankfurt School philosopher Theodor Adorno offers an alternative framework to analyze the relationship between literature and nation in the context of postcolonial societies grappling with transnational flows in a global moment. The importance of Adorno and other Frankfurt School critics for thinking about postcolonial cultural politics, discourses of subjectivity, and acts of dissent has been discussed at length by other critics (Lazarus, Varadharajan, Spencer). My focus lies instead on the ways Adorno's thought helps us explicate the relationship between the cultural object of literature and the sociopolitical concept of nationalism as one of negative dialectics. Whereas dialectical thought as described by, say, Hegel and Marx tends toward a synthesis that resolves contradictory sociopolitical and intellectual forces, Adorno insists on the necessity of dwelling on the negative moments in dialectics between the concept of knowledge or the subject who knows and the object that is being recognized and apprehended. The tense but reciprocal and transformative dynamic between concept-subject and object is for Adorno inherent in the form and structure of works of art, including literature. Nationalism as a concept that defines the collective subject of a postcolonial people can be opened up to nonidentical objects or the multiplicities of objective reality through a rational critique of art and literature. In contrast to corporeal theories in which literature is either an emanation or an imitation of national character, Adorno argues that "rather than imitating reality, artworks demonstrate this displacement to reality" (*Aesthetic Theory* 132). Artworks displace not only elements of objective reality but also components of concepts into their own formal structure rather than identifying them with one another or aligning them with or around a pre-given essence or primordial attribute. Within artworks, "truth content presents itself in art as a multiplicity, not as a concept that abstractly subordinates artworks" (131), and new, forgotten, or elided relationships between concepts and objects emerge: "the fact that artworks exist signals the possibility of the nonexisting. [. . .] The object of art's longing, the reality of what is not, is metamorphosed in art as remembrance" (132). Adorno's comments here recall the ideas of critics who discuss literature's relationship to nationalism as cultural discourse and spectral haunting: the truth content that artworks make visible is one of multiplicity rather than of isomorphism between culture and the nation-state; conceptual order and objective reality undergo a metamorphosis in artworks and become filled with longing and remembrance, haunted by the undeath and incompleteness of nationalism. However, radical culture and spectral haunting are not the culmination of Adorno's thinking. Adorno's aesthetic theory allows us to connect the cultural discursive and spectral critiques of literary nationalism, and this connection is "strictly negative. Artworks say what is more than the existing, and they do this exclusively by making a constellation of how it is" (133). What Adorno means by constellation is "a juxtaposed rather than integrated cluster of changing elements that resist reduction to a common denominator, essential core, or generative first principle" (Jay, *Adorno* 14–15). Literary texts, as artworks, form a constellation out of the objective reality of cultural life, the conceptual elements of nationalism, the discourse of radical culture, and the spectral afterlife of the nation. Literature becomes part of an intellectual and artistic project of *critical* rationality motivated by a national consciousness that reveals, resists, and reconceptualizes the hypostasizing effects of *instrumental* rationality expressed through the determinate constructions of national identities. Literature, in summary terms, evinces a *critical nationality* open to what is nonidentical to it as it becomes imbricated with cosmopolitical and transnational cultural forms, in contrast to an *instrumental nationality* that insists on identifying an exclusively determined and extensively defended territory and population. In chapter 1, I explain these terms—critical nationality and instrumental nationality—through a further discussion of how Adorno's negative dialectics allows us to consider anew the role of national consciousness in anticolonial and postcolonial criticism; in the remainder of this introduction, I focus on comparisons and contrasts between Adorno's discussions of aesthetics and literature and the corporeal, cultural discursive, and spectral theories of literary nationalism.

Adorno's analyses of specific literary forms and genres foreground a critical, reflective rationality and an aesthetics of literary style as a way of thinking through and against the instrumental rationality of modern life, which helps us better understand the dynamic tension between nationalism and postcolonial literature. Instead of reading both nations and literary texts as artifacts that embody or reflect the particularities of various cultures, Adorno suggests that literature analyzes the conditions of possibility and the limitations of national identity through a rational critique. This critique is performed through an aesthetic revision and reversal of key tropes and cultural symbols associated with a particular national culture in order to distinguish between a national identity constructed by the postcolonial state as a racial, linguistic, or religious mode of collective belonging, and a national consciousness connected to the people as a social collective and a mode of political resistance and empowerment. By foregrounding literature as an artwork through his aesthetic and political theory, Adorno turns us away from a reading of the nation as a specter and of literature as melancholia toward an understanding of literature as a rational critique of instrumentalized national identity. Literature as artwork may be thought of as enacting the negative dialectic between national consciousness, given culture, and "the mutating global field of political, economic, and cultural forces" that is the cosmopolitical (Cheah, "The Cosmopolitical—Today" 31) rather than as affirming either a unified national identity or a transcendent cosmopolitan subjectivity. Cheah's description of the cosmopolitical as a global field in which "neither cosmopolitanism nor nationalism can be seen as the teleologically necessary and desired normative outcome of past and present globalizing processes" (31) is consonant with Adorno's explication of the artwork as "a process essentially in the relation of its whole and parts" that is not "reducible to one side or the other" and "is not a structure that integrates the sum of its parts" (*Aesthetic Theory* 178); the artwork is "an immanent, crystallized process at a standstill" (*Aesthetic Theory* 180). Different literary genres evince this nonreductive and nonintegrative crystallized process through their specific style and formal organization. In his reflections on the essay as a literary form, Adorno points out that "since the airtight order of concepts is not identical with existence, the essay does not strive for closed, deductive or inductive, construction" ("The Essay as Form" 98). The essay's openness and free-flowing structure, which might at first glance appear to be "fragmentary and random" (99), is actually the result of "the reciprocal interaction of its concepts in the process of intellectual experience. In the essay, concepts do not build a continuum of operations, thought does not advance in a single direction, rather the aspects of the argument interweave as in a carpet" (101). What is important here is that the essay structures the conceptual, intellectual experience of objective reality as "a constellation" (105) rather than as a subordinated or teleological relationship of cause and effect, or concept over object. Because "the essay is determined by the unity of its object, together with that of theory and experience which have migrated into the object" (105), it is the particulars of the object that have precedence in the essay and that shape and define its conceptual arguments and overall literary form. But lest we assume that the object's specificities have the final say in the interpretation of a literary text, Adorno reminds us that these specificities are always interwoven with an existing set of ideas and concepts and with social forces that make the object possible to begin with. In a lecture on lyric poetry Adorno argues that this most individualistic and subjectively expressive of poetic forms paradoxically highlights with great clarity the imbrication of the personal with the social, the objective or individual with the conceptual or the general, because "the descent into individuality raises the lyric poem to the realm of the general by virtue of its bringing to light things undistorted, ungrasped, things not yet subsumed" ("Lyric Poetry and Society" 156). The lyric poem, like the essay, organizes and galvanizes the specificities of objective reality and individual expression, and since "a poem's indigenous material, its patterns and ideas, cannot be exhausted through mere static contemplation," therefore "they ask to be thought through, and a thought once set into motion by a poem cannot be cut off at the poem's behest" (156). If the essay interweaves concepts and objects into its form like a carpet, then the lyric poem enables a similar reciprocal interaction: it motivates conceptual thought through the indigenous, objective material arranged in a pattern by the lyric, and this thought in turn reflects upon and revises the objective material since it cannot be cut off by the textual limitations of the poem. This reciprocity allows "the historical relation of subject to object, of individual to society within the realm of subjective spirit" to be "precipitated" and "crystallized involuntarily from within the poem" (160). In the context of the connection between literature and nationalism, the literary form of the lyric poem reveals the historical relationship between the nation-state and the individuals who make up its body politic, between national identity and the various cultures that are assimilated into it. Since, as Adorno argues in *Aesthetic Theory*, "history in artworks is not something made," and "truth content is not external to history but rather its crystallization in the works" (133), artworks resist the instrumentalization of history and truth as conceptual buttresses for national identity. Furthermore, as the "artwork is nothing fixed and definitive in itself, but something in motion," and "its immanent temporality is communicated to its parts and whole in such a fashion that their relation develops in time" (178), the relationship between nationalism, culture, and the global force field of literary cosmopolitics is open to revision and redefinition as social and political circumstances change over time, and these revisions can be represented and apprehended through literature.

The implicit and explicit connections between Adorno's thought and postcolonial criticism is the topic of chapter 1, which examines how negative dialectics helps us understand how Frantz Fanon, Edward Said, and Gayatri Chakravorty Spivak interrogate colonialism and imperialism in their specific ways while advocating a critical national consciousness. Chapter 2 discusses the fiction of British writer Kazuo Ishiguro and his critique of both a coercive mimeticism that instrumentalizes ethnic identity and a patriotic nostalgia revived by the booming heritage industry in late twentieth-century Britain. Chapter 3 looks at Derek Walcott's essays, lyric poems, and longer verse and argues that the Nobel Laureate's transnational travels and poetic imagination are interwoven with a national consciousness connected locally to his home country of Saint Lucia and regionally to the Caribbean islands. Chapter 4 further explores this negative dialectic between diaspora and nation in the literary criticism, poetry, and fiction of Shirley Geok-lin Lim, who moves between the United States, Malaysia, and Singapore. Lim's writing offers a feminist negation of patriotic nationalism's heroic masculinity and imagines an alternative social bond between women within the nation. Chapter 5 focuses on the politics of literary and cultural nationalism in contemporary Malaysia and examines how Preeta Samarasan and Twan Eng Tan combine ethnography and historical realism in their novels to challenge the anthropological exotic inherent in both the global literary marketplace for postcolonial writing and the Malaysian state's official multicultural policies. Finally, I conclude with an assessment of recent scholarship calling for a greater focus on state power and sovereignty instead of nationalism and the nation; I argue that this turn toward state sovereignty need not rely on a narrow and identitarian definition of nationalism because the critical nationality and literary cosmopolitics I explore in this book can offer equally salient, if not more productive, analyses of state power in a global moment.

CHAPTER 1

Articulating Adorno with Postcolonial Critique

FANON, SAID, SPIVAK

NATIONALISM is an inevitable phenomenon of global modernity, and its emergence and consolidation go hand in glove—or more appropriately, hand on globe—with European conquest and colonization of peoples the world over and with the struggles against colonialism and for self-determination by these formerly colonized peoples from the late nineteenth to mid-twentieth centuries. Therefore, a thorough understanding of nationalism as it takes shape after World War II can be achieved not only by examining the works of anti- and postcolonial thinkers writing in and from the postcolonies themselves, but also by turning to one of Europe's most trenchant self-critics, Theodor Adorno, who, with his colleagues in the Frankfurt School of Critical Theory, was appalled by the degradation and destruction wrought by the relentless rationalization of society and culture, of which the colonial enterprise was one important facet. Aimé Césaire, an early twentieth-century Martinician poet and politician with firsthand experience of French colonialism, argues that in European colonial regimes there was "no human contact, but relations of domination and submission which turn the colonizing man into a classroom monitor, an army sergeant, a prison guard, a slave driver, and the indigenous man into an instrument of production" (42). Colonialism is both a material and an intellectual and instrumental project involving a brutal conquest and binary categorization of colonizer and colonized in a

Manichean opposition of dominating and submissive subject positions. The latter became instruments of production, either lifeless cogs in or mere chattel gobbled up by a vast machinery of material extraction; the former turned into instruments of policing and punishment, the better to service the colonial engine of production. Hence Césaire's pithy summation: "My turn to state an equation: colonization = 'thingification'" (42). Now, if one were to take Césaire's polemic at face value, then he is not incorrect in identifying colonization as a process of turning people into things, but by setting the word in quotation marks—"'thingification'"—Césaire intimates that there is more at stake in the idea of thingification and in the state of being a thing than a reductive identification with colonization. The simple equation of two things runs precisely along the channels laid out by the instrumental logic of colonialism, something Césaire, with the astute craft of a politician and a poet, would surely not concur with. Instead, he "state[s]" the pithy equation not to summarize or repeat this dominating logic but, with all the irony expressed by a set of quotation marks, to highlight the irrationality of colonialism's identitarian and instrumental structures.

Writing in West Germany shortly after the end of World War II and at the beginning of a Cold War that sundered his home country in two, employing a vocabulary that is more philosophical and less anticolonial than Césaire's, Theodor Adorno critiques the identitarian and instrumentalizing demands of administered life in the late twentieth century as capitalism moves from an industrial toward a financial mode of accumulation. This critique appears in several venues, most notably in *Dialectic of Enlightenment*, but my focus is on a later essay, "Culture and Administration." By administered life, Adorno means the management of not only our everyday existence but also our entire cultural and political structures of social relations for the maximum extraction of value and the efficient conversion of that value for the purposes of exchange or accumulation of surplus. Culture, both as the quotidian customs and practices of social life ("low" or "ordinary" culture) and as the intellectual and artistic achievements and endeavors ("high" or "elite" culture), is confronted by an administration consisting of the authoritarian state and business corporations in league with or co-opting state power. Administration demands that culture "be measured by norms not inherent to it and which have nothing to do with the quality of the object, but rather with some type of abstract standards imposed from without" (Adorno, "Culture and Administration" 113). Culture and cultural producers are instrumentalized by state and corporate power, just as Césaire describes colonized people turning into instruments of production within Europe's colonial-capitalist system. Adorno also points out that this dominating relationship does not leave administration itself untouched: "at the same time the administrative instance—according to its own prescriptions and nature—must for the most part refuse to become involved in questions of immanent quality which regard the truth of the thing itself," just as Césaire observes European colonial officials transforming into the very instruments for policing and punishment they prescribed as necessary for maintaining the colonial politico-economic order ("Culture and Administration" 113). Adorno, like Césaire, does not construe the instrumentalizing relationship between administration and culture as absolute even as he highlights its irrationality; at the end of his essay he cautions that "no matter how reified both categories are in reality, neither is totally reified; both refer back to living subjects" ("Culture and Administration" 130). This suggests that if we were to become involved in and broach questions about the truth of things themselves or thingification itself (as Césaire would have it), we might disclose other aspects of the relationship between administration and culture besides that of instrumentalization. While Césaire equates with quotation marks, Adorno gestures with question marks: Césaire's pithy equation is partly an ironic summation of the identification between colonization and thingification but also a hint toward other possibilities inherent in the process of thingification and in things; Adorno's concluding remark is doubtless a condemnation of administrative domination but also a reminder that we discard or dismiss the things and thingness produced by administered life at our peril, for other nonadministered, nonidentical possibilities can be traced in the products of administration where culture has been identified with exchange value.

This book regards nationalism and the postcolonial nation-state as things emerging from the encounter between European colonialism and anticolonial, self-determining liberation struggles and between the administrative power of modern states and corporations and the lived experience and literary expositions of postcolonial cultures. My objective in the first section of this chapter is to connect Theodor Adorno's critique of instrumental rationality and administered life to that of anti- and postcolonial thinkers such as Frantz Fanon, Edward Said, and Gayatri Chakravorty Spivak, all of whom take issue with colonialism, imperialism, and (especially for Said and Spivak) globalism. My comparison of Aimé Césaire's and Theodor Adorno's perspectives on thingification paves the way for situating Adorno within a postcolonial framework, rather than casting him as postcolonial theorist *avant la lettre* or suggesting that postcolonial theory is purely derivative of European philosophy. Adorno's refusal of identitarian and instrumental thinking (what he famously calls "negative dialectics") has important connections to the ways in which key critics of colonialism and imperialism Fanon, Said, and

Spivak approach the problems and possibilities of nationalism in a global moment. While discourses of globalism tend to construe nationalism and the nation-state as obsolete social and political formations, I argue that we should not dismiss them so swiftly, for in a global moment we must revise our understanding of nationalism and postcolonial nations as multivalent objects situated in a force field of cosmopolitical relations rather than reject them outright as self-enclosed concepts, subjects, or identities, or refuse the possibility that they might contain a liberatory promise of political consciousness and cultural critique. Given the close connections between literature and nationalism outlined in my introduction, the questions I ask in this book are literary ones in that they are as much concerned with what Adorno calls the immanent quality or the formal and stylistic strategies of literary writing as they are with reconsidering the objective bases of nationalism as cultural critique and political consciousness instead of as identities premised on race, ethnicity, religion, or other primordial attributes. I argue that it is only through attention to the formal and stylistic turns of postcolonial writing by Kazuo Ishiguro, Derek Walcott, Shirley Geok-lin Lim, Preeta Samarasan, and Twan Eng Tan that we are able to grasp the quality of the object or the truth of the thing that is national consciousness in a global moment, and we are better able to grasp these truths disclosed and mediated through fiction and poetry by bringing Adorno's thinking to bear on postcolonial theory and literary criticism.

Connecting Theodor Adorno's critical theory with nationalism might seem at first glance counterintuitive, as Adorno is not the first name that comes to mind when we think about nationalism. However, in his last lectures on Hegel and in the final section of his book *Negative Dialectics,* Adorno takes up the question of nationality as part of a critique of Hegel's idea of world history and interrogates the concept of the nation through his elaboration of negative dialectics. For Adorno, negative dialectics extends Hegel's dialectic of philosophy and world history while also negating the assumption of synthesis or reconciliation that forms the third moment of the dialectical tension between concepts and objects. Whereas for Hegel the dialectic leads up to the synthesizing moment that involves an identification between concept and object, Adorno's negative dialectics challenges this identity thinking, by which he means the identifying and equating of objects and objective reality with concepts and conceptual categories by a rationality that is no longer reflective and critical but instead instrumental and dominating. Writing together with Max Horkheimer in *Dialectic of Enlightenment,* Adorno argues that far from "liberating human beings from fear and installing them as masters," instrumental rationality has caused "the wholly enlightened earth [to be] radiant with triumphant calamity" (1). Horkheimer and Adorno's cautionary pronouncement comes out of a specific historical experience with European fascism as well as the commodity culture of the United States during the mid-twentieth century. Both German philosophers understood that although the European Enlightenment of the eighteenth century attempted to overcome the iron grip of myth and religion on human existence, its deployment of instrumental rationality had, in the twentieth century, become so extreme that "in the preemptive identification of the thoroughly mathematized world with truth, enlightenment believes itself safe from the return of the mythical" (Horkheimer and Adorno 18) when it has actually turned itself into a kind of myth and "a thing—a tool, to use its own terms" (19). In such circumstances, the concept of knowledge, "a product of dialectical thinking, in which each thing is what it is only by becoming what it is not," is arrested, hypostasized, and "defined as the unity of the features of what it subsumes" (11).

The significance of Adorno's critique of Enlightenment thought is that it enables us to perceive state-sponsored narratives of patriotism—official state projects of nation-building and the formation of a homogeneous national identity—as evidence of instrumental reason at work. Individuals literally need to stand up and be counted in order for the state to create the quantitative identity of the nation, which (contra Fichte) does not give humanity the "freedom to make itself what it really is originally" (46) and instead makes itself appear to be a natural condition of human existence that must be absolutely defended against intrusion and contamination by those who are qualitatively different or nonidentical. For Adorno and his Frankfurt School colleagues, instrumental reason, as a foundational principle of the Enlightenment with its scientific organization and technological innovation, is a driving force behind Europe's colonization of the rest of the world and culminated in the mass destruction and atrocities of the twentieth century, because "it was closely related to the exchange principle in which everything was reduced to an abstract equivalent of everything else in the service of universal exchange" such that "the qualitatively different and non-identical was forced into the mould of quantitative identity" (Jay, *Adorno* 37). Following the logic of the exchange principle and quantitative identity, the instrumentalization of the world also led to "the domination of nature," which meant not only the "scientific control" and shaping of the natural world to meet humanity's needs and desires or "the subjective domination of objects," but also "the comparable domination of subjects" or humans either as individuals or as collectives (37–38). Therefore, "domination of the external natural world led to control of man's internal nature and ultimately of the social world as well.

[. . .] 'Progress' turned out to spawn its antithesis, a barbarism all the more brutal because of its use of modern techniques of control" (38). The same techniques of control were used by European powers in their conquest of the New World through the creation of colonial states and, in the aftermath of various decolonization movements, still exist today in their independent but authoritarian and neocolonial counterparts. This dominating and homogenizing nationalism can be encapsulated in the term *instrumental nationality*, which highlights its roots in instrumental rationality or reason, and distinguishes it from a radical national consciousness which appears in the writings of anti- and postcolonial intellectuals.

The radical bent of anticolonial and postcolonial national consciousness can be further explicated in terms of negative dialectics. In his 1964 lecture on Hegel and the principle of nationality, Adorno argues that the Hegelian idea of world history incarnated in particular national spirits leads to "fetishization of the concept of the nation" (*History and Freedom* 111), and the European Romantic vision of national character "culminates in the delusions of racism," such that "a form of association that is essentially dynamic, economic, and historical misunderstands itself as a natural formation" (106). In terms that recall Stuart Hall's analysis of the suturing effect of national culture on different particular identities in the service of a unified national identity, Adorno observes that "precisely because the nation is not nature, it has ceaselessly to proclaim its closeness to nature, its immediacy and the intrinsic value of the national community" (107). In other words, the misrecognition of nationalism as a unified identity rather than a social and political consciousness brings about the need to foreground race or another apparently naturally binding primordial force as the basis for community. What Adorno elucidates here is the process by which instrumental reason identifies the nation as a concept defined by an essential national character or spirit and presents itself as an encapsulation of a natural condition of lived experience when it actually elides or reduces the objective reality of a people's cultural life. Adorno argues that Hegel's "theory of history in terms of national spirits is now outdated" and that "it is no longer possible to say that the world spirit inhabits a particular nation as Hegel could in his day" (110), because in the late twentieth century "nations, or many nations, are transforming themselves [. . .] into something like huge companies, vast economic entities," thus revealing how the nation as a "historical form of progressive rationalization has ceased to be the most rational way of doing things and it survives only in the interests of the existing relations of production" (105, 111). Yet despite its failings, Adorno does not completely dismiss the nation as a form of social organization and political consciousness, but suggests that turning away from the fetishization of the nation may enable "something that would change the form of society itself and put an end to the abstract organization that acts so repressively towards its members" (111). What Adorno suggests here may also be thought of as a transition from a national identity stitched together by state-sponsored patriotism toward a national consciousness that is responsive to and interwoven with cosmopolitics. This transition requires a critical rationality that can detect and challenge the abstract organization of instrumental nationality that represses the objective reality of popular sociocultural formations.

The importance of negative dialectics to the relationship between the concept of nationalism and the objective reality of culture is that, in contrast to the binary opposition of transnational culture and the monolithic nation-state in most discourses of globalism, we begin to see the nation–culture relation as fraught with tension but also as allowing reciprocity and transformation. If, as Adorno avers, "to think is to identify," and "conceptual order is content to screen what thinking seeks to comprehend," then what we need to move past the epistemological screen and to begin comprehending the particularities of objective reality is the "disenchantment of the concept" (*Negative Dialectics* 5). To perform this disenchantment, negative dialectics focuses on the traces and residues of objective reality in concepts so as to illuminate the dynamic tension between concepts and objects that was stabilized or hypostasized by instrumental rationality, because "objects do not go into their concepts without leaving a remainder [. . .] they come to contradict the traditional norm of adequacy" (5). Since "to change this direction of conceptuality, to give it a turn toward nonidentity, is the hinge of negative dialectics" (12), Adorno's disenchantment of the concept is a negation and a reversal of the subordinating relationship between the concept over the object that both retains and connects the concept and object together like a hinge. It does not dismiss or reject concepts outright as false consciousness in favor of a complete embrace of objects or objective reality, nor does it claim that a total understanding of objective reality is possible without any form of conceptual mediation. As one commentator on Adorno's philosophy observes, "for Adorno, experience is the process in which ideally, that is, in its fullest possibility, one (a subject) is affected and somehow changed by confrontation with some aspect of objective reality (an object). Experience has, in a sense, a structure of reciprocity and transformation" (O'Connor 2). If the lived experience of radical culture, which is much vaunted by proponents of globalism, is, in Adorno's terms, "the constant adjustment of concept to other ideal material," and if such "valid knowledge can be nothing other than a rationally compelling arrangement of these concepts" (O'Connor 35), then negative dialectics points to an arrangement or a reconfiguration of national consciousness and cosmopolitics as intertwined concepts as opposed to the triumph of postnational globalism in which transnational flows render nations moribund and obsolete.

Frantz Fanon:
The Crystallization of National Consciousness

Despite the European or Eurocentric context of Adorno's philosophy, both his work and that of the Frankfurt School have important implications for anticolonial discourse and postcolonial criticism. In the preface to the 1969 edition of *Dialectic of Enlightenment,* Horkheimer and Adorno draw connections between the crisis of Enlightenment thought, the Cold War, and anticolonial movements. "In the period of political division into immense blocs driven by an objective tendency to collide, horror has been prolonged. The conflicts in the Third World and the renewed growth of totalitarianism are not mere historical interludes" in "the transition to the administered world," and Horkheimer and Adorno argue for a "critical thought" that will "take up the cause of the remnants of freedom, of tendencies toward real humanity, even though they seem powerless in face of the great historical trend" (xi). Their emphasis on the need for critical rationality even when the world situation seems hopeless accords with the sentiments of anticolonial and anti-imperial critics such as Frantz Fanon, Edward Said, and Gayatri Chakravorty Spivak, critics whose works form the cornerstone of anticolonial thought and postcolonial criticism.

Fanon's analysis of colonial racism in the Caribbean and Africa along with the struggle for national liberation against the French colonial government and the Algerian neocolonial state has often been read through the lens of psychoanalysis and Jean-Paul Sartre's existential critique of the Hegelian dialectic of recognition between master and slave, self and other. However, there is a case to be made for Fanon's thinking as a form of negative dialectics that goes beyond psychoanalysis and Sartre's existentialism. As Nigel Gibson points out, Fanon's "recasting of Hegel's dialectic in *Black Skin, White Masks* is negative, because, for the Black, dialectical development is blocked off in non-reciprocity; the Black is frozen by the gaze of the white" (32). Fanon's reframing of Hegel's dialectical recognition also departs from Sartre's own quarrel with Hegel, because "unlike Sartre, for whom the idea of mutual recognition is a tragic farce [. . .] Fanon believes in its possibility" (Gibson 32). Sartre's tragically farcical gloss on mutual recognition comes from the instrumentalization of the slave or colonized other by the colonial master, but Fanon reads this relationship as one of critical rationality, because "'the native's' certainty during the modern period of decolonization is not really a return but a leap to a reason far more critical than the White master's" (Gibson 39). It is this critical leap of reason, a negative or "an untidy, open-ended dialectic" (Gibson 41), that I will trace in Fanon's analysis of the white-black/master-slave/self-other dialectic in *Black Skin, White Masks* and his discussion of national consciousness and national culture in *The Wretched of the Earth*. As Fanon explains, in the conventional Hegelian dialectic of recognition, "man is human only to the extent to which he tries to impose himself on another man in order to be recognized by him. [. . .] His human worth and reality depend on this other and his recognition by the other" (*Black Skin* 191). This recognition is supposed to be reciprocal, but in the racialized colonial situation, the white master "shut off the circuit," making "the two-way movement unachievable," thereby "keep[ing] the other within himself" (192) and turning the black, colonized other into an "animal-machine man" who, after the formal end of colonialism, becomes "a slave who was allowed to assume a master's attitude" (194).

Employing Adorno's critical terminology, one would say that the objective reality of the black colonized other is instrumentalized by the identity thinking of the white colonial master's conceptual apparatus embodied in colonial society and its institutions. Just as "the concept in itself, previous to any content, hypostasizes its own form against the content" and "objectifies by the logical identity" what is nonidentical to itself (*Negative Dialectics* 154), the black colonized other is imposed upon by the white colonial master whose own human worth and reality depend not on recognition received from the colonized other but rather on the subjugation of the other as a productive object in the colonial economy—a slave or worker in the plantations or factories. "The black man was acted upon" by the largesse of the white master both in servitude and after emancipation, and "went from one way of life to another, but not from one life to another" (Fanon, *Black Skin* 194, 195). Faced with this impasse, Fanon argues, "in order to achieve certainty of oneself, one has to integrate the concept of recognition" instead of waiting for recognition to come from an external subject such as the colonial master (192). Since the concept of recognition is withheld, instead of dismissing recognition as false consciousness the colonized other must integrate it into and fall back upon his or her own objective resources in order to begin a process self-recognition that will ultimately move beyond the limits of the self—in Fanon's words, "I go beyond life toward an ideal which is the transformation of subjective certainty of my own worth into a universally valid objective truth" (193).

This paradoxical integration of conceptual recognition into a process of self-definition without another being who bestows recognition and then departs from the subjective certainty of self-worth toward an objective truth points to the connections between Fanon's recasting of the Hegelian dialectic of recognition and Adorno's negative dialectics and aesthetic theory. The artwork is "a thing that negates the world of things" and is thus "helpless when called on to legitimate itself to this world" when the terms are defined by the world at large (Adorno, *Aesthetic Theory* 119), and it is paradoxically because of "the substance of personal experience" built into the artwork that "the elements of art" are not "abandoned but secured when art is fundamentally challenged by its experience" of the administered world that seeks to make the work a commodity (120). "The aim of artworks is the determination of the indeterminate," and this determination is different from the instrumentalization of the object through concepts because the "organization" of the personal or objective experience in the artwork allows them to "become more than they are" (124). This recalls the task undertaken by Fanon's colonized other who "ask[s] to be taken into consideration on the basis of [his or her] desire" rather than the one-sided recognition imposed by the colonial master, and emerges from self-recognition to declare that "I am not only here-now, locked in thinghood. I desire somewhere else and something else" (*Black Skin* 193). Far from being narcissistic or solipsistic, the colonized subject's self-recognition of the substance of objective personal experience clears the way for a negation of the tyranny of the colonial master and the disenchantment of the concept of recognition in the colonial situation.

Fanon, in his final work, *The Wretched of the Earth*, extends this negation and disenchantment from individual self-consciousness to the level of national consciousness and the problem of instrumental nationality in newly independent countries, and it is in this collection of essays that we see the dialectical tension between European modernity and the Third World that motivates Fanon's radical vision of an anticolonial politics and culture writ large on a national and an international scale. In the opening essay Fanon emphasizes that the struggle for decolonization involves a violence that, far from being a result of simple *ressentiment* and hatred of the white colonial master, is the expected reaction in a dialectics of colonialism which is itself "the encounter between two congenitally antagonistic forces that in fact owe their singularity to the kind of reification secreted and nurtured by the colonial situation" (*Wretched of the Earth* 2). The reification Fanon has in mind here—the process through which the colonizer "*fabricated* and *continues to fabricate* the colonized subject" (2, original emphasis)—is the instrumental rationality of the European Enlightenment interrogated by Adorno that creates "a colonial world" that is "compartmentalized, Manichaean and petrified, a world of statues" (*Wretched of the Earth* 15). Violence, both symbolic and physical, will continue to plague the newly independent societies unless the Manichaean "term-for-term correspondence between the two arguments" (50)—European colonial mastery and native colonized subjectivity—can be dialectically negated and new possibilities envisioned. If the Manichaean binary is not reconfigured, as Fanon cautions in his discussion of the "The Trials and Tribulations of National Consciousness," then the collective struggle for liberation will become instrumentalized in the hands of the local bourgeoisie, who merely fill the shoes of the European colonizers such that the newly independent nation fails at "organizing the state on the basis of a new program of social relations," and instead allows "the transfer into indigenous hands of privileges inherited from the colonial period" (100), thereby culminating in a reactionary movement "from nationalism to ultranationalism, chauvinism, and racism" (103) in which the neocolonial masters no longer wear white masks but have black skin. A critical national consciousness must avoid the instrumentalization of the nation into a chauvinistic, racialized identity to be used as a template for molding the individuals under its dispensation. On the contrary, Fanon urges the leaders of the new nation to consider how, "since individual experience is national, since it is a link in the national chain, it ceases to be individual, narrow, and limited in scope, and can lead to the truth of the nation and the world," and on these terms the project of "nation building" must be understood as the capability and responsibility of "every citizen [. . .] to embrace the nation as a whole, to embody the constantly dialectical truth of the nation" (140–41) as a social formation rather than as an absolute or homogenized racial identity.

The social reconfiguring of the colonial Manichaean binary is carried out on a literary level by the native intellectual or writer, who can no longer depend on a precolonial past to preserve a vision of native cultural authenticity and must, according to Fanon's arguments about national culture, recognize "that modes of thought, diet, modern techniques of communication, language, and dress have dialectically reorganized the minds of the people" (*Wretched of the Earth* 161). Although Fanon's injunction that "the first duty of the colonized poet is to clearly define the people" might appear at first glance to encourage a didactic and determining function for literature, he elaborates the artistic task set before the native writer in terms that recall Adorno's analysis of the modern artwork and its relationship to its social and political conditions of possibility: "It is not enough to reunite with the people in a past where they no longer exist. We must rather reunite with them in their recent counter move which will suddenly call everything into question; we must focus on that zone of hidden fluctuation where the people can be found, for let there be no mistake, it is here that their souls are crystallized and their perception and respiration transfigured" (*Wretched of the Earth* 163). What Fanon describes as the counter move of the people is a movement of negative dialectics rather than the antithesis or second movement in a conventional dialectical structure, since Fanon's counter move does not fit neatly into a binary or ternary structure but instead "call[s] everything into question." The people for Fanon are both a collective body and a social formation, and native writers and their literary works should not try to reunite with the people in a halcyon, nonexistent past by creating a nativist identity based on cultural authenticity. Instead, writers and their texts should represent and engage with the people as a social formation emerging gradually through transfiguration and crystallization of their political and cultural consciousness, and "the crystallization of the national consciousness will not only radically change the literary genres and themes but also create a completely new audience. Whereas the colonized intellectual started out by producing work exclusively with the oppressor in mind [. . .] he gradually switches over to addressing himself to his people" (Fanon, *Wretched of the Earth* 173)—or, as Adorno would say, "the historical relation of subject to object, of individual to society" is "precipitated" and "crystallized" ("Lyric Poetry" 160) in literature. With this aesthetic register in mind, it becomes clear that the relationship between literature, culture, and nationalism Fanon has in mind differs greatly from the European Romantic concept of literature as cultural *Bildung* for the nation. National consciousness is the self-recognition and political awareness of a colonized people unfolding in a negatively dialectical fashion against European colonialism, and national culture "is the collective thought process of a people to describe, justify, and extol the actions whereby they have joined forces and remained strong" and not a "folklore where an abstract populism is convinced it has uncovered the popular truth" (*Wretched of the Earth* 168).

Although Fanon wrote his essay "On National Culture" as a speech delivered in 1959, his remarks are still salient today in light of the various claims of globalism that the nation is obsolete and untenable: "Humanity, some say, has got past the stage of nationalist claims. The time has come to build larger political unions, and consequently the old-fashioned nationalists should correct their mistakes. We believe on the contrary that the mistake, heavy with consequences, would be to miss out on the national stage. If culture is the expression of national consciousness, I shall have no hesitation in saying, in the case in point, that national consciousness is the highest form of culture" (*Wretched of the Earth* 179). If "the nation is not only a precondition for culture, its ebullition, its perpetual renewal and maturation[, i]t is a necessity" (177), then in a situation where instrumental nationality predominates and national culture is hypostasized as national identity, the function of literature as an artwork of critical rationality must be to recall and represent this critical connection between nationalism and culture through a negation of figures and tropes associated with the patriotic ideal of identity thinking. Literature's crucial role in negating consolidated identities and negotiating between national consciousness and global currents is explored by Edward Said and Gayatri Chakravorty Spivak, who in their discussions of contrapuntal reading and transnational literacy respectively extend Fanon's famous exhortation that "national consciousness, which is not nationalism, is alone capable of giving us an international dimension" and that "it is at the heart of national consciousness that international consciousness establishes itself and thrives" (*Wretched of the Earth* 179, 180).

Edward Said:
COUNTERPOINTS OF NATIONALITY, NATIONALISM, AND NATIVISM

Inasmuch as Frantz Fanon was important to Edward Said's formation as an anticolonial thinker and as an advocate of Palestinian nationalism, Adorno too is a key figure, who informs Said's position as a professional critic of culture and literature and as an intellectual in exile. While Said's name and work are recognized as foundational to the field of postcolonial literary criticism, Said in his later years distanced himself from this field, dismissing the term postcolonialism itself because "there is a quality of reification in a label, of a school, a dogma, an orthodoxy" ("Conversation with Bill Ashcroft" 88). Despite Said's repeated claims to being a humanist rather than a theorist, of practicing a criticism based on secular worldliness rather than wordy sophistry, and his insistence on a contrapuntal reading of literary and cultural texts rather than a deconstructive analysis, there is in Said's invocations of Adorno a profound critique of imperialism and patriotism in the United States of America that is in the spirit of critical theory, if we understand that secular criticism and critical theory are both engaged in a similar intellectual exercise of mapping the workings of power, tracing its effects, and marking its limitations while imagining alternative ways of thinking and being. Said is professing what Adorno calls an "immanent analysis" (*Aesthetic Theory* 180) or critique of imperial power and patriotic identity not only from the standpoint of an outsider but as an exile working as a scholar and teacher of the humanities at a prestigious university within the United States, which, as Said often reminds his readers, is not only a nation-state but also a global superpower. To say that Said's work is informed by Adorno's thinking is to understand his analyses of Orientalism and culture and imperialism, his seemingly contradictory insistence on radically oppositional thought with a deeply humanist emphasis, and his nuanced distinction between nationality, nationalism, and nativism or between euphoric and enlightened nationalism as expressed in the perspicacious language of critical theory rather than the sinuous syntax of poststructuralism. It is not to claim that Said's work is somehow above theory or merely derivative of the Frankfurt School, for, as Said himself avers, one can be instructed and inspired by but cannot simply imitate as intransigent a thinker as Adorno (*Reflections on Exile* xxxii).

In his lectures on humanism Said at first stakes out a position that is adamantly antitheoretical, eschewing what he calls the "structuralist antihumanism" of thinkers such as Michel Foucault and Jean-François Lyotard (*Humanism and Democratic Criticism* 10). Yet Said's insistence on humanism is not of the classical sort that celebrates the triumph of the human subject as the center of all knowledge and experience. Instead, his project is a reconceptualization of humanism as the critical function of scholars who research and study literature and the humanities in our contemporary world, because "there can be no true humanism whose scope is limited to extolling patriotically the virtues of our culture, our language, our monuments. Humanism is the exertion of one's faculties in language in order to understand, reinterpret, and grapple with the products of language in history, other languages and other histories" (28). Said is keenly aware of his "dialectically fraught" position as an eminent professor of the humanities at Columbia University and considers it necessary to chastise the essentialist patriotism and global hegemony of the United States from within the American academy, and this he sees as "the crystallized role of the American humanist, the non-humanist humanist as it were" (77). One cannot miss the Adornian inflection of Said's thinking: he argues that American humanists must maintain their dialectically fraught position with "the consistent sense of nonidentity" (Adorno, *Negative Dialectics* 5) toward dominant political and sociocultural concepts without completely rejecting them, and the effort "to change this direction of conceptuality, to give it a turn toward nonidentity, is the hinge of negative dialectics" (Adorno, *Negative Dialectics* 12). The apparent contradiction of the term "non-humanist humanist" can be understood by Said's insistence on the negatively dialectical turn toward nonidentity rather than conceptual determination or resolution, because Said is arguing for a humanism understood as "critique [. . .] that gathers its force and relevance by its democratic, secular, and open character" (*Humanism and Democratic Criticism* 22) and for the role of the humanist in the American academy as that of "accept[ing] responsibility for maintaining rather than resolving the tension between the aesthetic and the national" (78). Said's emphasis on maintaining rather than resolving such tensions makes Adorno's thinking especially prominent in his text, as he refers to the dangers inherent in patriotic "nationalism, religious enthusiasm, and the exclusivism that derives from what Adorno refers to in his work as identitarian thought" (56). The non-humanist humanist and nonidentitarian intellectual must examine how "discreetly separated elements enter into a readable context" and how "through their own movement the elements crystallize into a configuration" (Adorno, "The Essay as Form" 102). Such configurations offer us "insight into the constitutive character of the nonconceptual in the concept [that] would end the compulsive identification which the concept brings unless halted by such reflection. Reflection upon its own meaning is the way out of the concept's seeming being-in-itself as a unit of meaning" (Adorno, *Negative Dialectics* 12), Said first reflects upon the history of humanism as a philosophical concept and then proceeds to reconfigure humanism out of its being-in-itself, or its "withdrawal and exclusion" (*Humanism and Democratic Criticism* 22), into a salient vocation for the American intellectual.

Understanding Said's later self-positioning as a non-humanist humanist who is inside and outside of dominant conceptual regimes clarifies his early writings about Orientalism, culture, and imperialism as a negatively dialectical critique of (on the one hand) Euro-American instrumentalized representations of the non-West as well as (on the other) essentialized and patriotic self-representations stemming from the "euphoric nationalism" (*Reflections on Exile* 530) that succeeds independence struggles in Europe's former colonies. Although Said invokes Michel Foucault's idea of discourse in *Orientalism*'s opening pages (*Orientalism* 3), his methodology actually consists of mapping a wide range of texts in the Orientalist force field in a constellation and bringing them into dialectical tension with one another: "Foucault believes that in general the individual text or author counts for very little; empirically, in the case of Orientalism (and perhaps nowhere else) I find this not to be so. Accordingly my analyses employ close textual readings whose goal is to reveal the dialectic between individual text or writer and the complex collective formation to which his work is a contribution" (*Orientalism* 23–24). Said's methodology, as that of "a critical historian of Orientalism" (148), takes Said both inside and outside of Orientalist studies: his detailed analyses of the life and writings of Silvestre de Sacy, Ernest Renan, and T. E. Lawrence, for example, not only recognize their immense contribution to European knowledge of the Arab world but also investigate their ideological construction of the Orient in the process of acquiring and disseminating such knowledge; critical rationality shades into instrumental rationality as "the Orient is overlaid with the Orientalist's rationality; its principles become his" (129). The instrumentalization of European Orientalist scholarship in the eighteenth and nineteenth centuries reaches its apotheosis in the twentieth century as the tensions between Europe and the Arab world are apparently resolved by "a new dialectic [that] emerges out of this project. What is required of the Oriental expert is no longer simply 'understanding': now the Orient must be made to perform, its power must be enlisted on the side of 'our' values, civilization, interests, goals" (238), which marks "the major shift in Orientalism [. . .] from an academic to an *instrumental* attitude" (246, original emphasis). Such instrumentalization of attitudes and knowledge not only affects Europeans but also gives rise to a primordially charged "patriotism" (333) as Arab communities in the late twentieth century respond to Orientalist representations and tropes without "going beyond the stifling hold on them of some version of the master-slave binary dialectic" that resolves into "extreme xenophobic nationalism" on both sides of the cultural divide (351, 333).

Extending Fanon's reconceptualizing of the Hegelian master-slave dialectic, Said uses the term "*reinscription*" to designate a process in which the colonized person is able "to rechart and then occupy the place in imperial cultural forms reserved for subordination, to occupy it self-consciously, fighting for it on the very same territory once ruled by a consciousness that assumed the subordination of a designated inferior Other" (*Culture and Imperialism* 210, original emphasis). But this subordinated and inferior Other can be neither valorized nor essentialized as a superior subject position as often occurs in both the former colonial metropolis and the newly independent postcolony. Said argues for a negatively dialectical understanding of a critical subject position that offers "not just the negative advantage of refuge in the émigré's eccentricity" but "also the positive benefit of challenging the system, describing it in language unavailable to those it has already subdued" (333). Adorno's importance for Said becomes clearer in *Culture and Imperialism* (intended as a sequel to *Orientalism*), because Adorno's work exemplifies "essayistic and algorithmic criticism" that is "oppositional and secular" rather than "systematic and doctrinal" (*Reflections on Exile* 168, 170). This forms the basis for Said's own conceptualization of "contrapuntal analysis" that can cultivate a "simultaneous awareness both of the metropolitan history that is narrated and of those other histories against which (and together with which) the dominating discourse acts" (*Culture and Imperialism* 18, 51).

A contrapuntal reading traces how a literary or cultural text "is shaped and perhaps even determined by the specific history of colonization, resistance, and finally native nationalism. At this point alternative or new narratives emerge, and they become institutionalized or discursively stable entities"; this in turn reminds us that that "we are dealing with the formation of cultural identities understood not as essentializations [. . .] but as contrapuntal ensembles, for it is the case that no identity can ever exist by itself and without an array of opposites, negatives, oppositions" (*Culture and Imperialism* 51, 52). Analyzing William Butler Yeats's poetry in relation to decolonization, Said observes that even though his early poems express a certain degree of nativism, they are points of departure rather than permanent scaffolding for erecting an insular identity, because "there is a good deal of promise in getting beyond them, not remaining trapped in the emotional self-indulgence of celebrating one's own identity" (229). As Adorno reminds us in his essay on lyric poetry, thinking once set in motion by the poem cannot be constrained and exhausted by the textual limits of the poem itself; so, too, for Said thinking and "moving beyond nativism does not mean abandoning nationality, but it does mean thinking of local identity as not exhaustive, and therefore not being anxious to confine oneself to one's own sphere" (229). Despite his own characterization as a cosmopolitan critic in both physical and intellectual exile from his Palestinian homeland and situated in an American academy where political quietism seemed the prevailing mood, Said is not "advocating a simple anti-nationalist position," because "nationalism—restoration of community, assertion of identity, emergence of new cultural practices—as a mobilized political force instigated and then advanced the struggle against Western domination everywhere in the non-European world" (218). Using terms recalling Fanon's distinction between various kinds of national thinking, Said argues that anticolonial national consciousness turns against those it is supposed to liberate when it shifts from "nationality" to "nationalism" and then into "nativism," a "progression" Adorno would construe as a shift from critical toward instrumental reason as the movement from nationalism into nativism becomes "more and more constraining" for postcolonial societies because their composition becomes increasingly exclusive and homogenized (*Culture and Imperialism* 229). Because the promise of liberation inherent in anticolonial struggles for nationality and nationalism has been "hijacked by a host of dictators and petty tyrants, enshrined in various state nationalisms," and hurriedly resolved into a patriotic national identity mapped onto nativist ideals, postcolonial literature and criticism in a global moment must proceed contrapuntally, for "in trying to connect experiences across the imperial divide, in re-examining the great canons, in producing what in effect is a critical literature," they "cannot be [. . .] co-opted by the resurgent nationalisms, despotisms, and ungenerous ideologies" (Said, *Culture and Imperialism* 54). Literature and the interpretation of literary and cultural texts play a key role in formulating a critical nationality, or contrapuntal "new and imaginative reconceptions of society and culture" that apprehend and "avoid the old orthodoxies and injustices" (Said, *Culture and Imperialism* 218) of instrumental nationality's insistence on nativism.

Gayatri Chakravorty Spivak:
National Identity, Native Informants, and New Immigrants

The hypostatization of national identity is also the target of Gayatri Chakravorty Spivak's critique of the diasporic longings of "New Immigrant[s]" ("Teaching for the Times" 177) who have moved to Euro-America. These new immigrants are called upon by the dominant powers there to serve as "Native Informant[s]" and to teach about their respective cultures and countries, thereby serving as avatars of their respective national identities (*A Critique of Postcolonial Reason* ix). While it is undeniable that Spivak's methodology explicitly draws on Jacques Derrida's deconstruction, I argue that her analyses of literary texts that eschew anticolonialism's ossification into patriotic identity and her strategic assumption of but refusal to identify with both subject positions of the native informant and new immigrant are consonant with Adorno's tracing of negative dialectics between subject and object and between the artwork and its social world. Spivak's thinking puts pressure on dominant binary oppositions and subject positions, for she not only makes an "attempt to undo the often unexamined opposition between colonizer and colonized implicit in much colonial discourse study" (*Critique* 46) but also reexamines postcolonial invectives relying on an unqualified nativist polemic, as "no perspective *critical* of imperialism can turn the other into a self, because the project of imperialism has always already historically refracted what might have been an incommensurable and discontinuous other into a domesticated other that consolidates the imperialist self" (*Critique* 130, original emphasis). In *A Critique of Postcolonial Reason,* Spivak's "strategy" is "to persuade through the discontinuity of odd connections or reconstellation" (65), to reveal how "truth, the constellation of subject and object in which both penetrate each other," cannot "be reduced to subjectivity" because "what is true in the subject unfolds in relation to that which it is not, by no means in a boastful affirmation of the way it is" (Adorno, *Nega-*

tive Dialectics 127). The unfolding of three subject positions sharing such a conceptual overlap that they have similar initials—native informant, new immigrant, national identity—within the larger field of globalization is performed through a literary cosmopolitics of "transnational literacy" (Spivak, "Teaching" 177) that requires the ability to "counterfocalize" from dominant discourses toward "the making of an alternative narrative" (Spivak, "Ethics and Politics in Tagore, Coetzee, and Certain Scenes of Teaching" 22), negating the determinate boundaries of these three subject-concepts and opening them up to the objective realities within which they are situated.

Although Spivak, in a recent interview, laments that "we cannot take national liberation as a model of anything any more," this comment must be placed within the context of another statement in the same interview that "in the name of anticolonialism you get the kind of national identity politics that can lead to fascism" ("Position without Identity" 248). We can see here that, like Said's distinguishing of nationality, nationalism, and national identity, Spivak too employs a graduated measure of nationalism, a spectrum of increasingly confining and constraining terms: anticolonialism, national identity politics, and, finally, fascism. On the other hand, Spivak has reservations about celebrating postnationalism and globalism, because "it is easy to cultivate 'postnationalism' in the interest of global financialization by way of the 'international civil society' of private businesses" and "powerful non-governmental organizations" (*Critique* 381), such that "the developing national states are not only linked by the common thread of profound ecological loss [. . .] but also plagued by the complicity, however apparently remote, of the power lines of local developers with the forces of global capital" (380). Nationalism seems, at first glance, to be a futile endeavor condemned either to run afoul of fascism or to fall into lasting impoverishment through global financialization. However, Spivak's insistence on transnational literacy and the parabasis (literally, "stepping aside") and counterfocalization of literary reading allows us to understand nationalism in terms less fatalistic. Spivak hints at this when she says that "we cannot think of sovereignty in terms of last century's nationalist struggles" because "*reinventing* the state" through national consciousness involves more than political and territorial sovereignty ("Position Without Identity" 246, original emphasis); such reinvention of the state aligned with critical rather than instrumental nationality involves literary reading and a keen sense of aesthetics.

It is to two key moments of reading and differentiation between national identity and national consciousness in *A Critique of Postcolonial Reason* that I now turn. My concern is less with the content of the literary texts themselves and more with Spivak's discussion of these texts in relation to nationalism and politics. In the first moment, Spivak offers a reading of the *Bhagavad Gita,* an important episode in the epic *Mahabharata,* to problematize both Hegel's interpretation of it as an example of India's ahistoricity and Hindu nationalist interpretations of the text as a timeless repository of cultural nationalism. Spivak performs "a crudely 'dialectical' reading" of the *Gita:* moving away from Hegel's reading that is invested with the "ideological motivation to prove a fantasmic India as the inhabitant of what we would today call the 'pre-conscious' of the Hegelian Symbolic" (*Critique* 47), and conjures a hypothetical reader of the *Gita* in order "to point out the moves in the *structure* and *texture* of the text [. . .] that will persuade the assenting reader or receiver of the epic to transform myth into scripture" (46, original emphasis). Spivak, taking up the position of her hypothetical reader, suggests that the dialogue between the mortal prince Arjuna and the god Krishna offers "a graphic and visible sublation (negation and preservation on another register) of the apparent phenomenality of lived time and affect" by an overarching, divinely sanctioned Time defined by a universal Law, "in the interest of the felicitous presentation of the *concrete* social order" (56, original emphasis), thereby confounding Hegel's use of the *Gita* "as proof of eons of a-historicity" (50) and temporal stasis in Indian culture and thought. Spivak occupies the standpoint of the native informant, but she does not allow her standpoint to be taken for a nativism that successfully recovers a true or authentic interpretation of the *Gita.* The reading Spivak offers is "'mistaken' because it attempts to engage the (im)possible perspective of the 'native informant,' a figure who, in ethnography, can only provide data, to be interpreted by the knowing subject for reading," but Spivak's project is to "transform into a reading-position the site of the 'native informant' in anthropology, a site that can only *be* read, by definition, for the production of definitive descriptions" (49, original emphasis). This dialectical reading of the *Gita* is not an act of recovery that definitively describes the classical text *contra* Hegel, but rather an act of reconfiguring the native informant as an active and critical epistemological position instead of a passive repository of information for the European inquirer. Spivak indeed employs an important Adornian term when she states that she is "refusing the centralized interpellation to be a native informant" and trying "to produce such a 'contemporary reader' [of the *Gita*] in the interest of active interception and reconstellation" (50). By reconstellating the native informant as a reading position, Spivak is also taking issue with another approach toward the *Gita,* this time by "the indigenous elite nationalists" coming after Hegel who insist that the text "is supra-historical" and can be a basis for Hindu cultural nationalism because of its "timeless core" (60, 61). Their "search for 'national identity'" defined as "a muscular fundamentalism or nativism" (63) instrumentalizes the negation and sublation of temporality in the *Gita* into a well-defined, well-muscled national body.

Similarly, in her analysis of J. M. Coetzee's novel *Foe,* Spivak attends "to the rhetorical conduct of the text" as it "stages writing and reading" rather than relying on "traditional historically contextualized interpretation" that "might produce closures that are as problematic as they are reasonable and satisfactory" (*Critique* 174), which explains why she interprets the *Gita* as a dialectical problem of temporality and social order staged through the dialogue between Arjuna and Krishna rather than as evidence of ahistorical thought or a historically embedded classic with a timeless core of Hindu cultural nationalism. Focusing on the failed efforts of *Foe's* Susan Barton to teach Friday the word "Africa," Spivak points out that "Africa is only a timebound naming; like all proper names it is a mark with an arbitrary connection to its referent, a catachresis. The earth as temporary dwelling has no foundational name. Nationalism can only ever be a crucial political agenda against oppression. All longings to the contrary, it cannot provide the absolute guarantee of identity" (188). Like the impossible yet necessary conjuring of a contemporary native informant who reads and reflects upon the *Bhagavad Gita,* Africa in Coetzee's novel is a catachresis, a sudden and unexpected yoking together of two terms or concepts that produces knowledge and insight unavailable to each concept as it exists singly. Here the catachrestic connection is between the signifier "Africa" and the national longing for a foundational name or an absolute guarantee of identity, and, to recall Adorno, "artworks would be powerless if they were no more than longing, though there is no valid artwork without longing. That by which they transcend longing, however, is the neediness inscribed as a figure in the historically existing. By retracing this figure, they not only are more than what simply exists but participate in objective truth to the extent that what is in need summons its fulfillment and exchange" (*Aesthetic Theory* 132). Spivak's reading of this episode of pedagogical failure in *Foe* suggests that the novel is inseparable from a longing for a renascent national identity, as no artwork can be completely free of longing. This identity is signified by the word "Africa" with its connotations of historical burdens of conquest, enslavement, anticolonial struggles, and self-determination, but the retracing of the figure of Africa in Friday's unsuccessful elocution transcends *what is longed for* and participates in the objective truth of *what is in need,* the former being what Spivak calls an absolute guarantee of national identity and the latter a crucial political agenda against oppression, or national consciousness. This explains Friday's inability to learn the word "Africa": the national identity that is longed for is figuratively retraced in *Foe* as a national consciousness whose fulfillment and exchange are deferred or yet to come, precisely because we are still in the thrall of an instrumental nationality. This catachrestic insight informs Spivak's final reflection on Coetzee's novel: "perhaps this is the novel's message: the impossible politics of overdetermination [. . .] should not be regularized into a blithe continuity, where the European redoes the primitive's project in herself. It can, however, lead to a scrupulously differentiated politics, depending on 'where you are'" (*Critique* 193). The politics of postcolonial nation-states are overdetermined by contrapuntal elements of colonialism's residual structures, anticolonial self-determination, and neocolonial struggles; the trajectory of sociocultural life in these nations thus cannot be regularized as a blithe and smooth continuous transition from colonial oppression to independence struggle to national identity. The vocation and position of the reader-critic—"where you are"—must be to scrupulously differentiate between the overlapping elements of colonialism, anticolonialism, and neocolonialism in the postcolonial lifeworld and also between the nation as a sociocultural formation and the state as an apparatus of power.

This differentiation between the nation and state is part of the transnational literacy Spivak advocates, although she does not explicitly name it as such. Distinguishing between what she calls the "nation thing" and national identity, Spivak explains the former as "collectivities bound by birth, that allowed in strangers gingerly" and as "in existence long before nationalism came around" (*Nation and Imagination* 13–14), whereas national identity—what Spivak calls "mere nationalism"—is marked by "possessiveness," "exclusiveness," and "isolationist expansionism" (32). But lest we construe the nation thing as a throwback to a primordial, natally determined social formation, Spivak, drawing on her own background as a child growing up in India, points out that "the love of my little corner of ground" is "more like comfort" than "the declared love of country, full-blown nationalism" in a patriotic fashion, and that "this rock bottom comfort, with which the nation thing conjures, is not a positive affect" (14, 15). The comforting relationship between the individual and the nation thing exists at the level of the personal and the private, and "this possibility of the private is not derived from a sense of the public" (15). As the nation thing does not conjure a positive affect, it should contain a negative or negating quality not reducible to the instrumentalization of nationalism under patriotic imperatives in which "this underived private has been recoded and reterritorialized as the antonym of the public" (16). The attachment and comfort one feels toward one's bit of ground can be expanded and reimagined in a broader, nonexclusionary manner into a national consciousness consisting of a cultural politics rather than a cultural identity, and this involves "the de-transcendentalizing of nationalism, the task of training the singular imagination, always in the interest of taking the 'nation' out of nation-state" (51). Taking the nation out of nation-state means interrogating nationalism as "a seamless identity" (53) and reconstellating the nation through a "comparative imagination" that can undo the "possessive spell" of the "collective imagination constructed through rememoration" (40) rather than rejecting nationalism and the nation thing outright. In the same way that postcolonial countries are situated within a cosmopolitical force field and imbricated with sociocultural formations that are both deterritorialized and attached to other territorial countries, so too the comparative imagination operates cosmopolitically, "keeping the civic structure of the state clear of nationalism and patriotism, altering the redistributive priorities of the state, creating regional alliances, rather than going the extra-state or non-government route" (55). Literature, and "the literary imagination," Spivak reminds us, "can continue to de-transcendentalize the nation and shore up the redistributive powers of the regionalist state in the face of global priorities" (58). This de-transcendentalization involves the negation of patriotic nationalism—"an affect that the abstract structure of a functioning state harnesses largely for defense" (54)—and a transnational literacy "trained in the play of language(s) [that] may undo the truth-claims of national identity" (48). The comparative imagination encourages us to understand literary texts in their relationship to nationalism as "nexuses of meaning [. . .] to the extent that they negate meaning" rather than consolidate meaning as rememoration (Adorno, *Aesthetic Theory* 153–54). Transnational literacy examines the relationship between national identity and national consciousness in terms of "identity and contradiction," where "contradiction is nonidentity under the rule of a law that affects the nonidentical" (Adorno, *Negative Dialectics* 6). The law Adorno speaks of here can be regarded as the principle of comparative imagination rather than collective imagination, and it affects the nonidentical—that which has not been instrumentalized under the spell of a declared love of country—by reconstellating it toward a critical nationality.

CHAPTER 2

"More English than English"

Kazuo Ishiguro's Negation of National Nostalgia

I F Kazuo Ishiguro did not exist, British literature would have had to invent him. His novels have been acclaimed as diasporic, international, or cosmopolitan, and Ishiguro's own Japanese-British cultural hybridity has often been lauded as the basis of his transnational perspectives. However, in this chapter my analysis of *The Remains of the Day*, *The Unconsoled*, and *When We Were Orphans* suggests that Ishiguro adopts a diasporic perspective toward an insular and patriotic British nationalism. However, this diasporic approach does not, as common wisdom would have it, distance him from a critical national consciousness; it instead enables his cogent analysis of late twentieth-century British identity and culture. Specifically, Ishiguro takes up two literary and cultural discourses in late twentieth-century Britain: first, the "condition-of-England" narrative and fiction's cultural-ethnographic turn, and second, the recovery of cultural authenticity embodied in romances of the archive. Ishiguro advocates what one critic in another context calls "critical nostalgia" (Brown-Rose 2009), taking issue with these two imaginative modes that, together with Britain's burgeoning heritage industry expressing a desire for bygone national glory, constitute a determinate and exclusive patriotic identity centered on an essentialist notion of what Britain was, is, and should be.

Ishiguro's Double Structure of Diaspora and National Consciousness

Born in Nagasaki, Japan, but living in Britain since the age of six, Kazuo Ishiguro is a prize-winning novelist who elicits curiosity among British and American critics about his background as an anglophone writer with a Japanese name and East Asian features. It is therefore necessary to consider Ishiguro's positioning and self-positioning as an ethnically marked anglophone British writer in terms of what Rey Chow calls "a coercive mimeticism—a process (identitarian, existential, cultural, or textual) in which those who are marginal to mainstream Western culture are expected [. . .] to resemble and replicate the very banal preoccupations that have been appended to them" (*Protestant Ethnic* 107). I will therefore spend some time discussing reviews of and commentary on Ishiguro's novels and his extensive interview with Japanese Nobel Laureate Kenzaburo Oe to illuminate the mimeticist expectations that Ishiguro is implicitly called upon to resemble and replicate and his own contestation of these ethnic appendages.

Several interviews with Ishiguro and commentaries on his work dwell on his "Japaneseness": his childhood in Nagasaki, his parents' relocation to Britain, his first visit to Japan as an adult after winning the Booker Prize, and the authenticity and artificiality of Japanese society and the Japanese characters in his first two novels, *A Pale View of Hills* and *An Artist of the Floating World*. Ishiguro's cultural Japaneseness is often highlighted and contrasted with his Britishness, and this fascination with Ishiguro's hybrid diasporic Japanese-*cum*-British nationality is sometimes expressed in bizarre ways: one interviewer is fascinated by the "startling juxtaposition" of Ishiguro's face, "with its broad Oriental planes and features," and his "clipped British accent," which makes his stature as an emerging young British writer all the more remarkable (Vorda and Herzinger 4). Such interest in Ishiguro's apparently Japanese name and appearance but lack of Japanese cultural familiarity together with corresponding affirmations of his British nationality suggest a cultural exoticism at work that makes Ishiguro's Anglo-Japanese hybridity a boon for British national identity. Japan and Japaneseness, embodied and represented by Ishiguro, are coercively mimeticized as a transnational cultural supplement that is incorporated into British national identity, "a process in which they are expected to objectify themselves in accordance with the already seen and thus to authenticate the familiar imaginings of them as ethnics" (Chow, *Protestant Ethnic* 107) and to make British literature more innovative and marketable.

Within the context of an instrumental nationality in which culture and ethnicity are used to authenticate the familiar imaginings of a national identity, Ishiguro comes across as a diasporic Japanese who crosses over Japanese national boundaries (he is not a Japanese citizen), but whose very lack of authentic Japaneseness (he neither reads nor speaks the Japanese language fluently) allows him to be incorporated into a British identity that celebrates itself as exuberantly multicultural such that Ishiguro can be included in a stable of young British writers of color who express "a new internationalism" (King, "The New Internationalism" 193). Ishiguro's Japaneseness is authenticated by artistic and cultural comparisons: his writing style is akin to "the deft brushwork of Japanese paintings" and "the way Japanese conversations move politely around the matter at issue" (207). Ishiguro's cultural but non-national Japaneseness enables him, along with others of this new generation, to "criticise the Third World both as insiders and as Westerners" (209) by showing "the contrast between older Japanese culture and the modern Westernised world" (206), with the implicit privileging of the latter, modernized world. However, Ishiguro himself is quite aware of this exotic fascination with his Japanese background; in both his interviews and his novels he contests the cultural and racial essentialism that undergirds this exoticism and reinforces a homogeneous white, British national identity.

Shortly after the prize-winning success of *The Remains of the Day* in 1989, Ishiguro was invited by the Japan Foundation to visit Japan for the first time since he moved to Britain as a child. During this visit, Ishiguro "spoke English all the time" as he knew Japanese well enough to be understood but not to observe the various social formalities in Japanese speech (Vorda and Herzinger 5). Ishiguro observes that he "touched a strange nerve" on "a live wire issue" in Japan; specifically, "this idea that somebody who is racially Japanese and looks very Japanese could go to England and have lost his Japaneseness in some ways is at the same time fascinating and [. . .] rather threatening" to people in Japan (Vorda and Herzinger 4). Ishiguro concludes that this anxiety over racial and national identity stems from Japanese people "spending more time abroad" on "business and international trade," and having "children who are growing up abroad"; this in turn leads to the "fear" that "their Japaneseness is going to become dissipated" (Vorda and Herzinger 5–6). In Japan, Ishiguro finds himself treated as a diasporic subject, as someone who looks Japanese with received but not intimate knowledge of the language and customs of his ancestral culture; who, having grown up in a European country, is suddenly expected to tell people in the homeland "what the West thought about Japan" (Vorda and Herzinger 4); who represents a threat and fear that Japanese cultural, racial, and national identity will be diluted or dissipated in diaspora. Although Ishiguro's remark (laced, perhaps, with a touch of resentment) that "just [his] very being is a kind of embodiment of the whole issue" (Vorda and Herzinger 4) may suggest that he ultimately rejects Japaneseness, his interview with the Japanese writer and Nobel Laureate Kenzaburo Oe (which occurred during his 1989 visit) points to some abiding personal and intellectual connections with Japan.

When Oe asks Ishiguro how he accurately described life in Japan in his first two novels, Ishiguro replies that he was fashioning his "own personal, imaginary Japan" as a writer in diaspora who remembers and reinscribes his homeland: "All the way through my childhood, I couldn't forget Japan, because I had to prepare myself for returning to it. [. . .] So I grew up with a very strong image in my head of this other country, a very important other country to which I had a strong emotional tie" (Ishiguro and Oe 164). Ishiguro admits that "one of the real reasons why [he] turned to writing novels was because [he] wished to recreate this Japan [. . .] to make it safe, preserve it in a book, before it faded away from [his] memory altogether" (164). We can infer from this that even though Ishiguro's later work neither is set in Japan nor features Japanese protagonists, this diasporic longing for an imagined Japan was crucial—even foundational—to his self-fashioning as a writer. Furthermore, even though Ishiguro stresses that he is not interested in recreating an authentic or historical Japan, Kenzaburo Oe observes that Ishiguro's novels—given his name and the publication of his work in English and in a Western country—will have some impact on the way Western readers perceive Japan. As Oe says, "the conception of Japanese people held by most Europeans has [the writer Yukio] Mishima at the one pole and people like Akio Morita, chairman of Sony, at the other pole. In my opinion, both poles are mistaken. [. . .] I think that your novel exerted a good influence on perceptions of Japan in Europe, a kind of antidote to the image of Mishima" (168). But Oe also argues that Ishiguro's representations of Japan cut both ways. Ishiguro's imagined Japaneseness challenges some of the myths the Japanese have of themselves in the late twentieth century, such as the desire "to be perceived as peaceful and gentle, like Japanese art [. . .] They don't want to be seen as economic imperialists or military invaders. They would like others to think of flower paintings, something quiet and beautiful, when they think of Japan" (168). While Ishiguro's reputation in Japan was at first that of "a very quiet author, and, therefore, a very Japanese author," Oe shrewdly detects in his writing "a tough intelligence" that "always involves a double structure, with two or more intertwined elements" and a "kind of strength [that] was not very Japanese" but "rather, from England" (169). Ishiguro, picking up on Oe's observation, elaborates on this double consciousness and twofold structure with appropriately twinned explanations: first, he reflects that his "very lack of authority and lack of knowledge about Japan" made him think of himself "as a kind of homeless writer" who "had no obvious social role" because he was neither "a very English Englishman" nor "a very Japanese Japanese either" (169). Second, he feels that his generation of British writers "have a kind of inferiority complex" because the important international issues of the late twentieth century seem to be occurring elsewhere in the world, whereas "that feeling doesn't exist in the United States or Japan, in that there is a strong sense that these two societies are now somehow at the center of the world, and the twenty-first century is going to be somehow dominated by these two powers" (173).

Of course, geopolitical events have not unfolded exactly according to Ishiguro's prediction, nor is his sense of frustrated provincialism necessarily widespread among other contemporary British writers. But what is significant here is that, taken together, Ishiguro's double consciousness, his ambivalent but abiding connections to Japan, his concern about Western stereotyping of both himself and Japanese society, and his sense of Britain's diminished international importance vis-à-vis Japan, point to a diasporic subjectivity simultaneously engaging with a national consciousness. Ishiguro's diasporic subjectivity is culturally productive and socially consequential as opposed to consummately deterritorialized and smugly cosmopolitan. Eschewing transnational mobility or hybrid exuberance, Ishiguro describes his situation as both peripheral and rooted; he is "stuck on the margins" and "looking for other ways in which to work" as a writer, ultimately deciding "to use the landscape" he knows about "in a metaphorical way" (Vorda and Herzinger 12). Ishiguro's employment of landscape as metaphor—the troping or turning of denotative meaning toward connotative associations—recalls Khachig Tölölyan's understanding of "diasporic existence as not necessarily involving a return but rather a re-turn, a repeated turning to the concept and/or the reality of the homeland and other diasporic kin through memory, written texts," and other "symbolic, ritual, religious" forms of expression ("Rethinking Diaspora(s)" 14–15). To make this connection is not to conflate cultural representations with social formations, because, as Kenzaburo Oe points out, whether Ishiguro intended to or not, his first two novels in which Japan appears as a metaphorical landscape have contributed to both the symbolic and the social discourse about Japan both in the West and in Japan itself. To wit: some are born in diaspora, some achieve diasporic consciousness, while some have diaspora thrust upon them by both countries of ancestry and countries of residence. Ishiguro belongs to this third category of diasporic subjects, and he makes a virtue of necessity by writing with what Oe calls a tough intelligence and double consciousness, exposing the essentialist stereotypes that nations use to fashion their self-identities. Ishiguro's literary cosmopolitics can be seen from his conversation with Oe and his reflections on the role that Japan—the country itself as well as his imagination and recollections of it—plays in his creative work. This cosmopolitics is connected to a critical national consciousness concerned with the social and cultural politics of late twentieth-century Britain as it contests two important discourses that construct national identity as cultural insiderism. First, there is the anthropological or ethnographic turn in late modernism described by Jed Esty (2004); second, the romance of the archive discussed by Suzanne Keen (2001). Both these tropes emphasize the recovery of an essential national identity out of (in the first case) the customs and cultures of whole ways of life as well as (in the second case) historical documents and literary archives.

At the social and cultural levels, Ishiguro is also responding to the British government's official heritage industry. The Department of National Heritage, established in 1992, is "responsible not only for the arts and for historic monuments, but also for tourism" (Stevenson 47). In other words, this Department identifies symbols and icons that embody national culture, and also makes these icons available for circulation and consumption within global capital. Furthermore, Ishiguro's rewriting of Englishness also interrogates the concept of "race relations" emerging in British politics and society since the 1970s. Race relations is a framework established for "the national accommodation of 'non-white' immigration" into Britain and sets up "a social equation in 'British' common sense between draconian, racialized immigration controls and good or harmonious 'race-relations'" (Hesse 7). This form of multiculturalism runs the danger of producing "showcases of culture" and leaving racism to be "perceived as merely resulting from ignorance, personal prejudice or mutual difficulties of cultural adjustment between majority and minority cultures" instead of a historical and political problem (Hesse 8). In short, the concept of race relations in Britain "incorporates yet disavows its indebtedness to a racist discourse, structured discursively around a racially unmarked (i.e. white) *British* perception of the problem of national identity induced by post-*1945 non-white immigration* from the New Commonwealth" (Hesse 11, original emphasis). Britishness as a national identity is perceived as under threat from nonwhite communities precisely because this idea of the nation is identified with one specific white ethnicity or race—specifically, the English—and that this Englishness is something the other "immigrant" or "diasporic" communities should aspire to. Stuart Hall further observes that throughout the twentieth century, "Britishness" has apparently served as "the empty signifier, the norm, against which 'difference' (ethnicity) is measured," but in fact, "as a category [it] has always been racialized through and through," connoting "whiteness" ("Multi-cultural Question" 221–22). With regard to race relations in Britain and British culture, Hall's critical attitude toward nationalism is more favorable than in his discussion of Caribbean cultural identity and diaspora. Hall argues for "a new multi-cultural political logic" (236) that can help in "the process of defining a more inclusive 'Britishness' with which, *only then,* might everyone be legitimately invited to identify. This constitutes *the democratic or cosmopolitan limit on both liberal and communitarian alternatives*" (237, original emphasis). The significance of Hesse's and Hall's examinations of the normative assumptions of Anglo-Saxon whiteness underlying British race relations for my analysis of Ishiguro's work is that the genre of the British archival romance, exemplified by A. S. Byatt's 1990 Booker-Prize-winning *Possession,* often features a heterosexual white scholarly couple whose affectionate sentiments develop in tandem with their literary quest for an authentic cultural tradition and national heritage. Ishiguro, on the other hand, departs from this essentially racialized and conservative vision of British national identity by inverting the assumptions that connect race with nation and literature.

Ishiguro's Landscapes of the Imagination and Adorno's Late Style

As Ishiguro states in an interview, he creates "a landscape of imagination" (Krider 151) rather than a fictional backdrop or cultural diorama determined by ethnic particularities or national heritage. His remarks suggest an affinity between his literary technique and thematic concerns and Theodor Adorno's formulation of the politics of late style and aesthetic form; they depart from a psychological realist or psychoanalytical reading of his novels that drives a substantial amount of criticism about his work. A fictional landscape that is primarily imaginary or imaginative undermines the tendency to treat Ishiguro's first-person narrators as realistically drawn or psychologically believable individuals and points toward the formal strategies Ishiguro employs in aesthetically framing and refiguring the historical and political realities his novels evoke. One important strategy—Ishiguro's use of nostalgia—has a strong connection with Adorno's ideas about late style in some of Beethoven's final musical pieces. In discussing Ishiguro's fiction in terms of late style, I am not implying that Ishiguro has reached a late or final stage in his career as a writer. Rather, I contend that the nostalgia exhibited by all of Ishiguro's narrators—a sense of belatedness and longing for a real or imagined past—animates his writing with the formal features Adorno discusses regarding late style in Beethoven. Nostalgia for Ishiguro is more than a simple longing to return to halcyon days; although he does acknowledge that in the British context nostalgia can glorify a history of imperial conquest, he also suggests rethinking the concept:

> nostalgia is a way of imagining the possibility of a world that is actually purer, one less flawed than the one we know we must inhabit. This is why I say that nostalgia is the emotional equivalent or intellectual cousin of idealism. It's something that anchors us emotionally to a sense that things should and can be repaired. We can feel our way towards a better world because we've had an experience of it. ("An Interview with Kazuo Ishiguro by Brian Shaffer" 7)

While it may be that "nostalgic dreams have become almost habitual, if not epidemic," such that "no better term expresses modern malaise" (Lowenthal 4), Ishiguro's comments are in line with recent scholarship on nostalgia and British literature revising the commonly held notion that nostalgia is a regressive sentiment expressing a misguided longing for a happier or more fulfilling past that never actually existed. Contrary to the claim that "a past nostalgically enjoyed does not need to be taken seriously" (Lowenthal 7), Ishiguro and revisionist accounts of nostalgia associate longing with an ethical turn in contemporary anglophone fiction, arguing that "fantasies of lost or imagined homelands do not serve to lament or restore through language a purported premodern purity; rather, they provide a means of establishing ethical ideals that can be shared by diverse groups who have in common only a longing for a past that never was" (Su 3). Such ethical ideals may be considered part of a national consciousness, a critical rather than redemptive understanding of nostalgia that interrogates and inverts instrumental nationality and the patriotic recovery of a glorious national past. Ishiguro distinguishes between nostalgia as "a bad political force" reinforcing a national identity "without actually taking into account all of the true costs and true evils of Empire," on the one hand, and nostalgia as a positive cognate to idealism, on the other ("An Interview with Kazuo Ishiguro by Brian Shaffer" 7). Whereas nostalgia as a bad political force involves "excursions" into the past that "are often brief, circumscribed, inconsequential" (Lowenthal 7), Ishiguro's extended journeys into a fictional landscape of memory and his literary attempts to imagine the possibility of a better world recall Theodor Adorno's reflections on nostalgia in two consecutive meditative pieces. Both pieces were written during

Adorno's period of exile from Germany in the United States, and in the first, bleakly titled "To them shall no thoughts be turned," Adorno issues a familiar lament of someone who has been estranged from his homeland: "The past life of émigrés is, as we know, annulled," and in the present time "anything that lives on merely as thought and recollection" is objectified and turned into information contained within "a special rubric [...] called 'background'" listed on official immigration and government documents (*Minima Moralia* 46, 47). This nullification of the past is nothing less than a "violation" for the émigré in which "life is dragged along on the triumphal automobile of the united statisticians, and even the past is no longer safe from the present, whose remembrance of it consigns it a second time to oblivion" (47). Picking up on the fatal encounter between an American present with a German past, in the next essay "#26. English spoken," Adorno summons a childhood memory, recalling how "some elderly English ladies with whom my parents kept up relations often gave me books as presents: richly illustrated works for the young, also a green bible bound in Morocco leather. All were in the language of the donors: whether I could read it none of them paused to reflect" (*Minima Moralia* 47). Adorno's recollection, however, does not offer the satisfaction of nostalgic enjoyment; as he dwells on the striking visual images of those incomprehensible English books of his childhood, he begins connecting those printed texts with both past and present industrial production and material culture:

> The peculiar inaccessibility of the books, with their glaring pictures, titles and vignettes, and their indecipherable text, filled me with the belief that in general objects of this kind were not books at all, but advertisements perhaps for machines like those my uncle produced in his London factory. Since I came to live in Anglo-Saxon countries and to understand English, this awareness has not been dispelled but strengthened. (*Minima Moralia* 47)

Adorno becomes aware that with the instrumentalization of culture and language in modern mass production, "culture displays its character as advertising" (*Minima Moralia* 47). Far from "alienating people from the present" (Lowenthal 13), Adorno's nostalgic remembrance of the English books and their powerful sensory impressions connects the past with the present, suggesting that "to 'indulge' in nostalgia need not imply an effort to escape present circumstances or to deceive oneself about the past; rather, it can represent the conscious decision to reject the logic of modernity" (Su 4). Adorno's nostalgia inverts the halcyon logic of selective remembrance and recovery in order to illustrate and reject the commodification of culture inherent in the logic of modernity. His childhood memories strengthen his awareness of this commodification, recalling what Kenzaburo Oe detects in Ishiguro's writing: "a tough intelligence" that "always involves a double structure, with two or more intertwined elements" ("The Novelist in Today's World" 169), the intertwined elements in Adorno's case being his childhood in Germany and his exile in America. Adorno reverses nostalgia's backward gaze by following the grain of its longing for the past and then turning that longing around toward the present, a move he explains elsewhere: "nothing past is proof, through its translation into mere imagination, against the curse of the empirical present. The most blissful memory of a person can be revoked in its very substance by later experience" (*Minima Moralia* 166). This chiasmus, or reversal, of nostalgia through the nostalgic's imagination in the face of the empirical present does not, however, result in an accursed or odious predicament, because "no other hope is left to the past than that, exposed defencelessly to disaster, it shall emerge from it as something different" (167). The difference that emerges from the reversal of a nostalgic imagination of the past in the face of a disastrous present is akin to the difference between a national identity that emphasizes the continuity and traditions of a homogeneous community extending backward through time, and a critical national consciousness that engages with such a determinate national identity through negative dialectics.

Ishiguro makes a similar move by revising nostalgia chiasmatically, reversing its conventional associations of halcyon recovery and historical evasion. His novels exceed their narrators' attempts to reconcile their present disillusionment with past optimism and engage with the cultural politics of the heritage industry and national identity in late twentieth-century Britain. This explains why Ishiguro characterizes the narrative voice of Stevens (the butler in *The Remains of the Day*) as "an exaggerated version of this buttoned-up stuff" about English decorum and diction, a "stylized version, almost a caricature" of English demeanor (Jaggi 162); Stevens inhabits "a mythical England," a world "which at first resembles that of those writers such as P. G. Wodehouse" that Ishiguro "undermine[s] [. . .] in a slightly twisted and different way" (Vorda and Herzinger 14, 15). Ishiguro foregrounds his own reception (in Britain) as a diasporic Japanese subject in order to question the exclusionary construction of an insular British national identity. Hence his comment that *The Remains of the Day* "has the tone of a very English book, but actually I'm using that as a kind of shock tactic: this relatively young person with a Japanese name and a Japanese face who produces this extra-English novel or [. . .] a super-English novel. *It's more English than English*" (Vorda and Herzinger 14, original emphasis). Ishiguro combines his diasporic perspective and his recasting of nostalgia to advance a literary cosmopolitics paired with a critical nationalism, taking issue with "an enormous nostalgia industry" that "is used as a political tool" by "the political right who say England was this beautiful place before the trade unions tried to make it more egalitarian or before the immigrants started to come" (Vorda and Herzinger 14, 15). By writing a super-English novel, Ishiguro works in the mode of what Mark Stein calls "posed-ethnicity," where the prose is "*self-consciously* post-colonial" such that "the expectations of the field are neither rejected wholesale nor noiselessly imbibed. Instead, these expectations are embraced, parodied, and tampered with" (115, original emphasis). I suggest that not only *The Remains of the Day* but all of Ishiguro's novels work along these lines: they at first seem to embrace but subsequently parody and tamper with literary and cultural conventions of patriotic and nostalgic British national identity.

To put Stein's observation about posed ethnicity in different terms, the self-consciousness at work in the fiction of black British writers who share thematic and formal concerns with Ishiguro reflects upon and refigures literary and cultural expectations and conventions rather than establishing a coherent and vivid portrait of a character as a lifelike individual. This formal refiguring is similar to the role that the subject and subjectivity play in Adorno's essay on late style and Beethoven's final musical compositions. The subject—the conscious mind that is aware of itself and capable of action and change—is for Adorno never autotelic or self-enclosed even in moments when it appears to be wholly independent or completely dominant, because "the mind will then usurp the place of something absolutely independent—which it is not; its claim of independence heralds the claim of dominance. Once radically parted from the object, the subject reduces it to its own measure; the subject swallows the object, forgetting how much it is an object itself" ("Subject and Object" 499). I have already discussed in chapter 1 how for Adorno the concept-subject is mutually imbricated with the object and the other; what is important here is how Adorno's explanation of late style can illuminate the stylistic representation of objects (figures and conventions associated with Britishness) in Ishiguro's fiction as a turn away from the subject of a British literary and liberal humanist tradition toward a critical nationalism and literary cosmopolitics.

An artist's late or mature works, Adorno argues, "often lack sweetness, and their bristly, austere husk resists straightforward tasting," and critics often explain this "by declaring them to be the products of a subjectivity, or rather a 'personality,' ruthlessly expressing itself," that "scorns sensuous charm in favor of the autocratic gestures of the liberated spirit," hence the willful disregard of a pleasing or harmonious form and content in the work ("Beethoven's Late Style" 295). That Ishiguro's novels all have first-person narrators offering their personal perceptions and interpretations of events gives his writing an appearance of such subjective and psychological analysis. Adorno, however, begs to differ by focusing instead on the formal evocations of earlier artistic conventions and tropes as a way of understanding how subjectivity is represented and at the same time problematized within the work of art. In late work, "formulae and phrases drawn from convention are scattered throughout. [. . .] the conventions become visible in a quite open, undisguised, and unmodified way" ("Late Style" 296). But these conventions are not guarantees of subjectivity, because "the power of subjectivity in late works of art is the sudden flaring up with which it abandons the work of art" (297). In the wake of subjectivity's departure, the artistic conventions become "splinters, fragmented and abandoned," an "expression no longer of the isolated self but of the mythical nature of the living creature and its demise" (297). Because "subjectivity communicates itself [. . .] only through the hollowed-out forms from which it escapes" (297), the work of art dialectically transforms subjectivity into a negative presence within an objective structure of conventional elements and tropes; subjectivity is therefore not a controlling or determining consciousness that subordinates these objective conventions. As Adorno remarks, in his late work "Beethoven no longer gathers up the landscape, assembling it [. . .] into a picture," but "irradiates it with the fire that subjectivity ignites by bursting out and colliding with the walls of the work" (298), or, as one commentator observes, "late works are characterized by the disappearance of the work from the work as such; by the dematerialization of the work, its liberation from the inadequacy of its material form [. . .] this eventuality represents the highest fulfilment of the work itself" (Bewes 173). In his novels, Ishiguro attempts to "purify the clichés" of instrumental nationality "of control by subjective spirit" and to subject the determinate identity between the nation and essentialized culture "to a series of shocks" (Adorno, "Late Style" 298). The flaring up and abandonment of subjectivity—to wit, the artwork's emphasis on and subsequent negation of subjectivity—is the formal process enacted by Ishiguro's employment of nostalgia within his fictional landscapes. Nostalgia for Ishiguro means more than a longing to reassemble the emotional landscape of a novel into a halcyon picture of the past; it has a radical impulse similar to what Adorno describes as the irradiating fire that bursts out and collides with the walls of the artwork and gives us "a way of imagining the possibility of a world that is actually purer, one less flawed than the one we know we must inhabit" ("An Interview with Kazuo Ishiguro by Brian Shaffer" 7), even though Ishiguro's narrators themselves may not be aware of these other possibilities. Ishiguro's landscapes of the imagination perform a chiasmatic literary maneuver that pushes subjectivity to its limits in order to negate it and to draw our attention to the objective conventions and tropes of literary and cultural Britishness that both constitute and frame this narrating subjectivity.

Ishiguro's chiasmatic negation of instrumental nationality as a controlling subjectivity contests the patriotic sentiment of late twentieth-century Britain embodied in literary romances of the archive and the heritage industry, which can be described as a culture industry that plays on nostalgia in its reactionary or escapist sense to create a national identity. To paraphrase Adorno, neither the concept of nationalism nor that of culture in the subjective position exhausts the other term in the objective position; complete subordination of the object by the subject does not occur. Instead, through the force of the encounter, the connections between the constitutive parts that make up the apparent wholes of both terms are illuminated across the subject-object relationship, negating the initial semblance of wholeness in both subject and object. Ishiguro's novels also reveal the terms on which a normative, white Anglo-Saxon ethnicity is constructed, interrogating the apparent naturalness of this ethnicity as the basis of British national identity. Ishiguro's novels confound readerly expectations that formal genres should correspond to certain cultural and national communities, thereby challenging his "commodification as a supplier of English and Japanese *authenticity*" and the idea that literary texts and their narrators should be native informants of a culture and nation (Sim 103, original emphasis). This refusal to fulfill conventional expectations has also been read as "the treason of representation" that Ishiguro commits by showing "how cultural stereotypes work by constructing his novels as national allegories, allowing the characteristics of his texts to stand for the characteristics of the cultures they seem to describe," but then disrupting these allegories by foregrounding how his novels are "fictionalization[s] of cultural truths" (Walkowitz, "Ishiguro's Floating Worlds" 1052). Understood in terms of a negative dialectic, the critical cosmopolitanism Sim and Walkowitz detect in Ishiguro may be understood as the failure or interruption of an enforced identification between nationalism and cultural insiderism or ethnic particularity. In Ishiguro's fiction, the relationship between national consciousness and culture is not a subordination of culture to nationalism or vice versa, but a constellation that reveals the discursive suturing inherent in the apparently seamless identification and one-to-one correspondence between the two terms. As Jed Esty persuasively argues, "culturalism" and "the anthropological turn" in late modernist and post-imperial British fiction is "the discursive process by which English intellectuals translated the end of empire into a resurgent concept of national culture," and this process took shape as "an ethnographic and anti-elitist approach to symbolic practices" and as "the rise of an Anglocentric culture paradigm" (2). As my readings of *The Unconsoled, The Remains of the Day,* and *When We Were Orphans* will show, Ishiguro's late style and his vivid evocations of cultural and social landscapes (whether Japanese or English) contest and invert this resurgent concept of the nation as patriotic subject by working through the ethnocentric expectations and conventions of the heritage culture industry itself.

The Unconsoled and the Reversal of the Archival Romance

Even though *The Unconsoled* was published after *The Remains of the Day,* I examine this text first as an articulation of Ishiguro's aesthetic theory that provides a hermeneutic for comprehending the literary strategies he employs in his other novels. *The Unconsoled* evokes and inverts contemporary romances of the archive, a genre in which the discovery and recovery of art and culture through literary scholarship and investigation play key roles in consolidating a homogeneous British national identity. Romances of the archive are extremely popular and critically acclaimed—A. S. Byatt's *Possession,* often considered an exemplary text of this particular genre, won the Booker Prize in 1990 (the year after Ishiguro's *Remains of the Day*), and was adapted into a film featuring Hollywood stars Gwyneth Paltrow and Aaron Eckhart. This particular genre details "the emergence of the library and the archive as privileged cultural sites, and the elevation of research questers to popular protagonists" and is "not only redemptive, but escapist, defensive, nostalgic, and revisionist in both traditional historical and postmodern senses" (Keen 215, 34). Romances of the archive often "contribute to nostalgic fantasies about the uses of the past," as "the endogamous Englishness of the past discovered within romances of the archive can add to a celebratory narrative of homogeneity, continuity, native virtues, and cultural survival" (Keen 215). They play up an evasive and escapist patriotic nostalgia because of Britain's apparent lack of purpose and impotence on the global stage of a post-imperial world where cultural survival and the reinforcement of a national identity become paramount through the work of scholars who become paramours. Culture, in the form of a recoverable literary archive, recuperates national identity as heritage or hidden essence tucked away in dusty documents waiting to be discovered by the right person rather than as a historically inflected and shifting discursive formation. It should come as no surprise that the rise of the heritage industry in Britain coincides with the increasing prominence of the romance of the archive in fiction during the late twentieth century. Literature and art become key elements in a national identity expressed as an essentially cultural possession through the conventions of the romance: heterosexual love, genealogical inheritance, foreign adversaries, heroic expertise, and affectionate consummation of the central pair of protagonists.

The Unconsoled is an anti-romance that takes issue with the instrumental use of literature and art by official or state nationalism for the suturing of a national identity, and it does so by inverting and exaggerating the manner in which literature is often employed as a corporeal embodiment and expression of such an identity. I am reading *The Unconsoled* as Ishiguro's fictional equivalent of Adorno's formulations of negative dialectics in his aesthetic theory: a recasting of the relationship of equivalence and identity (in which the subject or concept dominates the object) into one of mutuality and reciprocity. The identification of literature with nation and its function as collective *Bildung* is paralleled in *The Unconsoled* by the importance that the inhabitants of an unnamed, possibly Eastern European city ascribe to music as the basis of their social and cultural identity. The first-person narrator, Ryder, is a world-renowned music expert and "the finest pianist in the world" (507), invited by the city to resolve a terrible crisis. The citizens want to choose a new direction for the city by removing the incumbent musical doyen, Mr Christoff, whose style is too formal and functional, and replacing him with an inspiring but temperamental conductor, Mr Brodsky. They invite Ryder to give a piano recital and a speech on Thursday night to champion Mr Brodsky as the city's new artistic luminary. Ryder also meets various people who ask him for many favors and requests—his estranged wife and son, his aging father-in-law, old schoolmates from England, the hotel manager and his wife and son—and he realizes that he needs to make arrangements for his parents' arrival and attendance at his recital. In the end, both Christoff and Brodsky fall from grace, Ryder's attempts at reconciliation with his wife and child fail, his parents never arrive, he is unable to deliver his speech or perform his piece, and he fails to fulfill any request made by the citizens except one.

The citizens' obsession with music as the guiding force for their community and the absurdly comic downfall of both Christoff and Brodsky suggest that Ishiguro is satirizing a deeply held humanist belief in British letters, namely that art and literature can serve as a cultural bulwark against the social alienation and potential anarchy caused by the increasingly industrialized and economically based relations among people. This view is most firmly expressed in the late nineteenth century by Matthew Arnold, whose argument for culture as "sweetness and light" (78) providing "a *national* glow of life and thought" (79, original emphasis) has close connections to the corporeal theories of literary nationalism proposed by Herder and Fichte I discussed in chapter 1. Picking up where Arnold left off, F. R. Leavis argues that the critic also contributes to the luminescence of British literature as a cultural tradition by showing that "it is alive in so far as it is alive for us" as "a kind of ideal and impersonal living memory" (*Living Principle* 2)—in other words, a cultural heritage that, in the romance of the archive, can be recovered by deserving individuals who are the true heirs of British national identity. *The Unconsoled* undermines this romanticized and corporeal conjunction of literature and nationalism by showing Ryder's inability to resolve the cultural crisis plaguing the city and denigrating Christoff and Brodsky, the two resident maestros. The idea of a great tradition of culture and literature passed down as a living memory to future generations and embodying a vital national identity is further contested by the twists and turns of *The Unconsoled*'s plot, its dreamlike displacement and condensation of people and places, and a writing style that one critic calls "oneiric realism" (François 79). Because of its Kafkaesque style, many commentators interpret the book as a psychoanalytical treatment of Ryder's personality, while others offer a humanist and cosmopolitan perspective suggesting that Ryder's harried professionalism advocates "a broader and more inclusive civility" as a way of "cohabit[ing] with less indecency in a world of immigrants, refugees, and strangers" (Robbins 439–40). However, such readings conflate literary psyche for psychological being and do not pay adequate attention to the ways in which *The Unconsoled* itself turns away from a psychoanalytical framing of Ryder's personality toward a discussion of aesthetics, cultural politics, and national identity. While *The Unconsoled* seems to lend itself to or temptingly invite "psychological interpretation" of Ryder's thoughts and feelings, in treating fiction as if it were "the expression of subjectivity" that can be correlated or reconciled with a human psyche, these interpretations do not consider how "the power of subjectivity in late works of art is the sudden flaring up with which it abandons the work of art" rather than its expression through the voice or thoughts of a character or narrator (Adorno, "Beethoven's Late Style" 297). *The Unconsoled*'s flaring up of subjectivity is most evident in the exaggerated, almost absurd, emphasis on music as the moral compass for the city and on musicians as messianic figures who can both cause and resolve a social and cultural crisis and subsequently restore the community to its original state of happiness. Instead of assuming that the dominant subjectivity in the novel is Ryder's and examining his flawed personality through psychoanalysis, we should direct our attention to the treatment and function of music in order to better understand *The Unconsoled*'s negation of Ryder's subjectivity and interrogation of literature's instrumentalization within a collective, national identity.

Music takes the place of literature in the eyes of the city's inhabitants in providing a way back to a prelapsarian past, expressing a nostalgia that Ishiguro would call both evasive and escapist. Mr Pedersen, a member of the city council, is achingly nostalgic for a time when "this was a very happy community" with "large happy families here" and "real lasting friendships" where "people treated one another with warmth and affection" (*Unconsoled* 97). The current unhappy state of the city is due to Mr Christoff, the incumbent artistic leader, whose approach is rigorously formalist. As Mr Pedersen explains the problem to Ryder, it becomes evident that he and the rest of the citizens conflate art, culture, and identity when he acknowledges with "profound shame" that the people of the city "must look to an outsider, to someone like [Ryder]" in order to "rectify" the mistake of following Mr Christoff's artistic and cultural leadership "for so long" (100). Speaking in his own defense, Christoff argues that what "he has come to represent" is a much-needed hermeneutic for art and, by extension, culture and nationalism:

> They say my approach celebrates the mechanical, that I stifle natural emotion. [. . .] I merely introduced an approach, a system that would allow people like this some way into the likes of Kazan and Mullery. Some way of discovering meaning and value in the works. I tell you, sir, when I first came here, they were crying out for precisely this. For some ordering, for a system they could comprehend. The people here, they were out of their depth, things were breaking down. People were afraid, they felt things slipping out of control. (*Unconsoled* 190)

Christoff advocates a tightly systematic form of analysis and performance, "a system" that clarifies the nuances of art so that most people "could comprehend" it, rather than an intuitive mode that depends on or appeals to "natural emotion." However, the "widespread misery" in the city comes from his artistic style, described as "functional," "cold," with a "dryness" (*Unconsoled* 101, 102) that "celebrates the mechanical" and "stifle[s] natural emotion" (190). Ryder himself denounces Christoff at a public gathering originally meant to garner support for the embattled luminary. In response to a question about the "circular dynamic in Kazan," Ryder condemns the schematic approach that Christoff represents: "My own view is that Kazan never benefits from formalised restraints. [. . .] There are simply too many layers, too many emotions, especially in the later works" (201). With this denunciation, "an angry circle" (203) of audience members surrounds and physically assaults Christoff, which is ironic since Christoff himself adheres to a strict dynamic of circularity.

A similar fate befalls Mr Brodsky, whose musical approach is the antithesis of Christoff's. Brodsky's emotional depth is matched by his legendary moodiness: he becomes a loud, abusive drunk because of a failed romance; he has an amputated leg that will not heal properly, and both his romance and his music are just "a wonderful consolation" for his festering and fascinating wound (*Unconsoled* 313). But when the city's leaders listen to a recording of Brodsky's music, they are lulled into tranquility and moved to tears by what they praise as "true music," something that "shared [their] values" and that they had "so sorely missed over the years" under Christoff (113). However, during his performance at the end of the novel, Brodsky reveals that his passionate approach produces results equally unwelcome and discordant as Christoff's artistic direction. If Christoff's mechanical approach seems to be too functional and "cold" by its focus on formal details, then Brodsky's approach represents the other extreme that stresses the artist's subjectivity over the artwork. Brodsky's conducting excavates "the peculiar life-forms hiding just under the shell," but, because it is "something close to exhibitionism," whatever "life-forms" are hiding there come not from the music itself but from Brodsky's own tortured and ecstatic mental state while he conducts, a state in which he loses volition and cannot "resist the compulsion to go yet further," exposing himself to the audience (492). Indeed, Brodsky's conducting becomes progressively "unnerving" as the performance unfolds: "that tentativeness of technique that so often signals a disaffinity between a conductor and his musicians had entered the orchestra's sound. The musicians [. . .] were wearing expressions of incredulity, distress, even disgust" as Brodsky's "conducting now took on a manic quality and the music veered dangerously towards the realms of perversity" (494). The audience members also begin expressing a "disaffinity" between Brodsky and the civic and cultural values they originally thought he shared: they "were now exchanging worried looks, coughing uneasily, shaking their heads," while "one woman stood up to leave" (494). Brodsky finally collapses before he can finish his performance, and his former lover, Miss Collins, rebukes him on stage in a way that parallels Ryder's earlier denunciation of Christoff. Miss Collins prophesies that Brodsky is destined for someplace "dark and lonely" because his music is "only ever about that silly wound"—his amputated leg—and for that reason Brodsky will "never be able to serve the people of this city," because "[he] care[s] nothing for their lives" (499). If Christoff is condemned by the city council to "some dark corner of [the city's] history" (100) because his music is only ever about formal constraints, then Brodsky is condemned to somewhere dark and lonely because his music is only ever about the turbulent emotion of his own pain and suffering, which, when translated into artistic performance, is at first compelling but becomes unnerving and perverse. Like Christoff, who is assaulted by an angry circle of former fans of his circular dynamic, Brodsky is also hoisted by his own musical petard. His methodology uses music to manifest and assuage his own aggrieved emotions, and as a result a serious disaffinity emerges between him, his orchestra, and his originally sympathetic audience through his resolutely subjective artistic expression. As a symbolic parallel, the ironing board Brodsky uses as a crutch during his final performance also collapses under him, signaling the breakdown of both the artist and his artistic composition. If the city were to "build something all over again" based on Brodsky's music, it would only magnify the wonderful consolation for Brodsky's leg wound, "the one true love of [his] life," and "destroy everything" in the end because it is so subjectively focused on the musician's natural emotions (498).

Within the formal logic of a romance of the archive, Christoff and Brodsky would be scholarly antagonists caught up in the central struggle of cultural survival through artistic recuperation. But *The Unconsoled*, as an anti-archival romance, negates such projects that attempt to justify a national identity based on the instrumentalization and corporatization of art as an embodiment of cultural tradition. Mr Pedersen and the city council are a miniature national community desiring a cultural framework, and the corresponding national culture is narrow and exclusive: it must be either Christoff's formalism or Brodsky's romanticism, nothing in between. At the very moment in which Christoff and Brodsky appear to be at the height of their powers in the novel—Christoff at his public address about the circular dynamic, Brodsky conducting the orchestra to mark his ascendency—they fall from grace in a darkly comic way, marking the initial flaring up and subsequent failure of their subjectivity as a guiding force for the community. What *The Unconsoled* shows us, however, is the potential of the work of art as framework that negates instrumental rationality and reveals the reciprocal relationship between concept and object, nation and culture. The relationship between concept-subject and object outlined by the artwork is "strictly negative. Artworks say what is more than the existing, and they do this exclusively by making a constellation of how it is" (Adorno, *Aesthetic Theory* 133). The focal point—rather than the dominant subjectivity—of this constellation is Ryder and the manner in which he performs his music. *The Unconsoled* presents the failures of Christoff's and Brodsky's music as the basis for the city's insular national culture in a darkly comic and satirical manner to foreground Ryder's own artistic style, which combines both Christoff's formal restraint and Brodsky's natural emotion. Ryder's music functions as the negative dialectic between nationalism and culture that disrupts the objectifying power of instrumental rationality. The only time Ryder succeeds in playing the piano is when he thinks he is alone in a hut near a graveyard, but it turns out he is unwittingly providing musical accompaniment for Mr Brodsky as the older musician buries his dog. I focus on this seemingly minor episode in the novel because, although its context may sound ludicrous, it is the only instance of Ryder performing as a musician rather than acting like a beleaguered artistic consultant; it also serves as an excellent example with which to elucidate how the negative dialectic works in the novel through the formal framing of the participants and their actions.

Ryder, anxious to rehearse before his scheduled concert later that evening, finds a small hut on a hillside with a piano and begins playing. On hearing the noise of someone digging a grave outside the hut, Ryder suddenly remembers that he had earlier agreed to play the piano while Brodsky buries his pet dog Bruno, and he obliges by continuing his musical accompaniment. The significance of this is that Ryder's incidental elegy for Brodsky's dog is the only request that Ryder agrees to and successfully completes in the entire book. There are three diegetic frames nested within the overall action of Ryder's piano-playing: Ryder remembering his childhood in England, Brodsky burying his dog, Brodsky remembering his failed romance with his ex-lover Miss Collins. While Ryder plays, his reactions evince his combination of Christoff's "tight control of dynamics" (*Unconsoled* 136) and Brodsky's penchant for "natural emotion" (190): "I was in absolute control of every dimension of the composition" and "enjoying the ease with which the tangled knots of emotion rose languidly to the surface and separated" (357). This unique piano performance is also the moment where Ryder is most at home and at ease with himself, and the "sublime melancholy of the third movement" of *Asbestos and Fibre* evokes a specific impression tied to a national geography that forms the first nested frame in this scene:

> before long [I] began to picture the faces of my parents, sitting side by side, listening with looks of solemn concentration. Oddly I did not picture them sitting in a concert hall—as I knew I would see them later in the evening—but in the living room of a neighbour in Worcestershire, a certain Mrs Clarkson, a widow with whom my mother had for a time been friendly. (*Unconsoled* 357)

The novel drops numerous hints that Ryder is English and grew up in Worcestershire, but unlike a romance of the archive in which ethnicity and place of birth would be crucial to recovering a national identity, in *The Unconsoled* such references to England's West Midlands have another function. Ryder's music evokes a past grounded in one national milieu, but instead of nostalgically emphasizing a British national identity, it moves toward a connection with "none other than Brodsky in the process of burying his dog" (*Unconsoled* 358)—the second nested frame of this episode. Brodsky's grave-digging quickly gives way to the third nested frame, in which Ryder empathetically recalls Brodsky's tragic romance with Miss Collins through free indirect style:

> At first, naturally enough, Brodsky would have turned over memories of his late companion [his dog Bruno]. But as the minutes had ticked by and there continued to be no sign of me, his thoughts had turned to Miss Collins and their forthcoming rendez-vous at the cemetery. Before long, Brodsky had found himself remembering again a particular spring morning of many years ago, when he had carried two wicker chairs out into the field behind their cottage. That had been no more than a fortnight after their arrival in the city, and despite their depleted funds Miss Collins had been going about furnishing their new home with considerable energy. (*Unconsoled* 359)

Just as the reference to Worcestershire in the earlier passage is a marker of national geography, the cottage beside the field inhabited by a poor but genteel couple is a pastoral image that *The Unconsoled* invokes but undermines. This scene of pastoral tranquility quickly sours as Miss Collins inadvertently refers to Brodsky's "recent failures" (*Unconsoled* 359) and he in turn is offended by "her perfectionism" and "high-mindedness" (360); as a result "something cold had remained in their lives" (361). Despite this bucolic image of an affectionate couple living in foreign seclusion, Ishiguro's free indirect discourse pulls us away from the certainty of ethnographic detail and the resolution of personal difficulties that are staples of an archival romance. Instead, *The Unconsoled* matches Brodsky's thoughts and actions with Ryder's music and moves outward from the innermost frame of Brodsky's memories back to the diegetic present of Ryder's piano-playing:

> It was while he had been lost in such memories [of Miss Collins] that I had finally arrived at the hut and begun to play. For the first several bars, Brodsky had gone on staring emptily into the distance. Then, with a sigh, he had brought his mind back to the task in hand and picked up his spade. [. . .] He had actually started to shovel some earth back when something, perhaps the sadness of the music, had finally made him pause.

As I concluded the third movement, I could hear Brodsky still hard at work and decided to forget the final movement—it was hardly suitable for the proceedings—and simply recommence the third once more. This, I felt, was the least I could do for Brodsky after having kept him waiting. [. . .] (*Unconsoled* 361)

As Ryder plays the third movement of *Asbestos and Fibre* again, he finds himself "lending a greater emphasis to the elegiac nuances than [he] had previously" (*Unconsoled* 362). When he concludes his playing, Ryder finds himself in a state of peace and tranquility, a rarity in this novel whose dominant tone is one of harried, dreamlike—almost nightmarish—bustling and busyness: "When I had come once more to the end of the movement, I remained sitting quietly at the piano for several minutes before rising to stretch my limbs in the combined space. The afternoon sun was now filling the hut, and I could hear crickets in the grass nearby" (362). When Ryder steps out of the hut, Brodsky, also in a rare moment of lucidity and sincerity, thanks the younger musician profusely: "That was very beautiful. I'm grateful, very grateful" (362).

What is important in this episode is how Ryder combines both Christoff's formal constraints and Brodsky's emotional expressiveness without turning either artistic methodology into an instrument or scaffolding for a determinate cultural or national identity. *The Unconsoled* asks us to consider how the symbols and structures of feeling commonly associated with such identities are literary figures and clichés rather than the foundations of cultural tradition or national heritage. *The Unconsoled* focuses on the manner in which these national and cultural figures are worked over and connected through the formal frames in this episode instead of identifying them with a national subject or cultural tradition. When Ryder repeats the third movement of *Asbestos and Fibre,* the passage of music moves him and the reader into and out of the narrative frames, thereby using Christoff's circular dynamic, not as a formal constraint, but as a means of coalescing his own memories, and then leaving them behind as he enters Brodsky's point of view and emotional recollections. Ryder's music fulfills, but not through his own volition, the unspoken expectations raised in the first and third frames: Ryder's parents watching him with "solemn concentration" as he plays, and Miss Collins's "perfectionism" and "high-mindedness" toward Brodsky's failures. By playing the third movement over again, giving Brodsky "a little more time to stand over the grave with his thoughts" and playing "the very best music" he is capable of (*Unconsoled* 361, 362), Ryder belatedly fulfills these unspoken expectations by providing musical accompaniment for the burial of Brodsky's dog—the only request he is able to complete in the entire novel. Brodsky fails to live up to Miss Collins's and the city council's expectations later in the novel during his own musical performance because his music is centered on his own wounded subjectivity. But Ryder's fulfillment comes precisely when his subjectivity is emptied out through music, when conventional markers of nationalism and culture "are no longer permeated and overwhelmed by subjectivity but simply allowed to stand" and "end up transforming themselves into expressions" ("Late Style" 297). Ryder's music offers a negatively dialectical alternative to the corporeal theory of literary nationalism, as the artwork is no longer an embodiment of cultural tradition. Instead, the artwork moves toward a sense of community by relating one subjectivity to another (Ryder to Brodsky, in this case) without subordinating one to the other or objectifying one at the expense of the other. It is in this reconfigured constellation of subject and object that a sincere compassion and peaceful, mutual recognition—evoked in the tranquil scene at the end of Ryder's piano-playing—may come about. Ryder's music in *The Unconsoled* works through conventions and clichés of nationalism and culture in order to throw into sharp relief their objectification, reconfiguring them as constellations rather than absolutes to help us glimpse the connections that are possible between both terms.

Professional Landscaping:
The Remains of the Day and National Identity

The objectification of the landscape into an embodiment of national identity is a crucial part of the posed-ethnic representation Ishiguro undertakes in *The Remains of the Day*. Ishiguro reveals what seems to be a readily apparent landscape of *identification* as a landscape of the *imagination* through the negation of that identity's grounding assumptions. *The Remains of the Day* appears at first glance to be a condition-of-England novel, with Stevens, the aging butler of Darlington Hall, deeply concerned with the general loss of prestige and dignity in his profession as well as in his personal life. His journey in the countryside and his reflections on the greatness of the English landscape echo the sentiments of works that sound an elegiac note about Britain's national identity and its natural environs such as Margaret Drabble's *A Writer's Britain*, published in 1979, the same year Conservative prime minister Margaret Thatcher assumed office. Drabble's book combines numerous photographs of the British landscape with summaries of important literary works set in these geographical regions, illustrating how "English writers have persisted in seeing and praising the distinctive beauties of their own country" due to their "passionate attachment to the places of childhood, and an almost mystic devotion to the land itself" (7). Yet this photographic-*cum*-literary tour of Britain is also an elegy for its fading pastoral heritage, as Drabble concludes that the conflict between town and country "today is deeper, perhaps, than it has ever been" in modern Britain, but what keeps this heritage alive is literature itself, "a tradition unbroken from the days of Marvell and Vaughan" linking twentieth-century poets such as Ted Hughes and Geoffrey Hill (277). Drabble's detailed description of the British landscape and its literary incarnations is, ultimately, laced with an escapist and evasive nostalgia, as she concludes that "The Golden Age [of pastoral bliss] never existed, but by the same token it will never die, while there is a writer left to embody our desire" (277). This notion of writers and their literature embodying a collective desire to retrieve a Golden Age of pastoral simplicity is an extension of the corporeal idea of literature as an embodiment of a collective *Bildung* espoused by eighteenth-century philosophers of nationalism, and, as Drabble avers, it is British writers who must profess this mystic devotion to and desire for the natural landscape and its corresponding national heritage. Rather than affirm this profession of the landscape as a key characteristic of national identity, Ishiguro in *The Remains of the Day* negates its identification with the nation as well as two other cultural and literary tropes closely identified with being British: the figures of the butler and the aristocratic great house. The novel gestures toward a different kind of professionalism linked with a critical national consciousness that is beyond the narrator's ken but which we, as readers, can recognize. Furthermore, Stevens's continued reference to his national and cultural identity as essentially English brings to mind white, Anglo-Saxon Englishness as the normative model in British race relations. It is this unspoken norm that Ishiguro interrogates because it is linked with the instrumentalization of nationalism, even though Stevens is blithely unaware of its racist and essentialist implications.

Set in 1956, *The Remains of the Day* is a first-person narrative by Stevens, an aging butler who formerly served Lord Darlington, an English aristocrat and diplomat, in the 1930s. The international context of the novel emerges on two levels: 1956 marked Britain's involvement in the Suez Crisis; Stevens's flashbacks show us Lord Darlington's gentleman diplomacy in the 1930s to prevent World War II. However, Lord Darlington unwittingly becomes a Nazi sympathizer, is publicly disgraced, and dies soon after the war. Stevens now works for an American employer, John Farraday, who has recently bought Darlington Hall. On Mr Farraday's advice, Stevens takes a trip into the country to visit a former housekeeper, Miss Kenton, with whom he once shared some romantic affection. Miss Kenton is now unhappily married, and Stevens concludes the novel wondering whether his professionalism and loyalty to Lord Darlington were misplaced.

The Remains of the Day reveals the instrumentalization of nationalism through the antagonism between Britishness and Americanness as seen in the exchanges between Stevens the butler, his former employer Lord Darlington, and the new owner of Darlington Hall, Mr Farraday. The opposition is apparently simple: for Stevens, Englishness and its representative figures appear to be grounded in an essential heritage and dignity that smugly confounds the craftiness and crass mercantilism of the Americans. Early in the novel, Mr Farraday suggests that Stevens should take a vacation and "see around this beautiful country of [his]" (*Remains* 4). Stevens's both unspoken and spoken responses suggest a depth of Englishness that his new American employer can never fathom, but in ways that highlight the clichés of the country house and aristocrat–servant relationship. Stevens reflects that "those of our profession, although we did not see a great deal of the country in the sense of touring the countryside and visiting the picturesque sites, did actually 'see' more of England than most, placed as we were in houses where the greatest ladies and gentlemen of the land gathered," and that "it has been [Stevens's] privilege to see the best of England over the years [. . .] within these very walls" of Darlington Hall (4). Stevens emphasizes his own national identity by appealing to the idea of the landed aristocracy as embodiments of the nation's nobility and greatness. Seeing one's country involves not touring the countryside but being in the immediate presence of "the greatest ladies and gentlemen of the land" who themselves experience the state of the nation firsthand. For example, Lord Darlington witnessed "with [his] own eyes" how "ordinary, decent working people are suffering terribly" when he "went north" to look at the state of Britain in the 1930s, but his admiration for the German and Italian fascist regimes' "strong leadership" in "set[ting] their houses in order" (198) tragically leads him to support Nazi Germany during the buildup to World War II. Yet Darlington represents a typically English sense of fair play and dignity, lamenting that his country's complicity with the harsh French and American treatment of a defeated Germany after World War I is "deeply disturbing" and "a complete break with the traditions of this country" (71). Second, Stevens reckons national greatness in very formal terms: it lies embodied within physical structures such as "these very walls" of Darlington Hall as well as the social hierarchy with its "ladies and gentlemen of the land" and those who serve them, such as Stevens himself. Moreover, this formal greatness must be earned through hard work, for Stevens stresses that it is "those of [his] profession" who serve and wait upon ladies and gentlemen that earn the "privilege" to share in that greatness. Lord

Darlington, whose title comes through aristocratic birthright, makes a committed effort at gentleman diplomacy and "close personal contact" (91) with the other foreign dignitaries gathered at the 1923 conference he organizes to defuse the growing international tensions in Europe. For Stevens, Darlington earns and performs his nationally derived greatness as an aristocrat by opposing the "cheating and manipulating" Americans in the sphere of international relations, challenging Senator Lewis's idea of "professionalism" with his commitment to a sense of "honour" and "the desire to see justice prevail in the world" (103). Even if those efforts prove to be "misguided," as Stevens remarks at the end of the novel, "at least he had the privilege of being able to say at the end of his life that he had made his own mistakes. His lordship was a courageous man" (243). Such courage and commitment to either a principle or an employer that "embodies all that [one] finds noble and admirable" (200), even if the principle or employer eventually causes harm, seems to bestow the privilege of dignity to its adherents, and this quality is glossed by Stevens as an essential feature of being English.

In contrast, Stevens implicitly finds his new employer Mr Farraday and the other Americans lacking the sterling qualities found in Lord Darlington and himself. The Americans' shallowness is emphasized by their amateurish desire for an authentic Englishness and their unwillingness to dedicate any labor and effort to achieving it. Mr Farraday is neither an aristocrat nor a peer; he belongs to a new class of rich Americans who enjoy travelling and owning properties in Europe. As Stevens reflects with more than a touch of regret, Mr Farraday's purchase of Darlington Hall has taken "this house out of the hands of the Darlington family after two centuries" (*Remains* 6) and broken the distinguished lineage that ties this aristocratic family with its eponymous abode. The grand social functions that Lord Darlington enjoyed are also to disappear, for Mr Farraday "made it clear that he planned to hold only very rarely the sort of large social occasions Darlington Hall had seen frequently in the past" (7). With the passing of the hereditary residence of an English peer into a bourgeois American's hands, both the greatness of the house and Stevens's occasions for basking in that greatness are diminished. Moreover, Mr Farraday's calculating and miserly streak comes across when he asks Stevens to run the large estate with a staff of only four members (as opposed to seventeen in Lord Darlington's day), and, while admitting that "this might [. . .] mean putting sections of the house 'under wraps,'" instructs Stevens to "bring all [his] experience and expertise to bear to ensure such losses were kept to a minimum" (7). The degradation of Darlington Hall and the loss of its symbolic Englishness are palpable in Stevens's restrained reflections on Mr Farraday's instructions. Although the butler does not directly accuse Mr Farraday, "something of [his] scepticism" toward his new American employer's fitness to own and occupy a great English house is indeed "betrayed" (7) by his constant comparison of how things were under Lord Darlington and how things will be under Mr Farraday. Without the social occasions to serve "the greatest ladies and gentlemen of the land," and bereft of his impressively large household staff to manage Darlington Hall, Stevens can neither enter the presence of those who embody great Englishness nor perform the expert butlering that also marks his essential Englishness.

Within America's global compass, Englishness as symbolized by Darlington Hall and Stevens himself becomes a commodity to be consumed and enjoyed, a leisurely pastime to be indulged in rather than a consciousness of national purpose and greatness. "At a time when his enthusiasm for his acquisition was at a height," Mr Farraday shows some visiting American friends, the Wakefields, around Darlington Hall like a child showing off a new toy, and their "various American exclamations of delight" (*Remains* 122) as they tour the Hall earn Stevens's silent disapproval. Mr Farraday, with his "deep enthusiasm for English ways," and the Wakefields, who themselves "were owners of an English house of some splendour" (122, 123), are depicted as connoisseurs of Englishness, hobbyists purchasing and collecting relics of English national culture for fun. As Mr Farraday says to Stevens with typical American frankness, "This is a genuine grand old English house, isn't it? That's what I paid for. And you're a genuine old-fashioned English butler, not just some waiter pretending to be one. You're the real thing, aren't you? That's what I wanted, isn't that what I have?" (124). Within the novel's internal logic defined by Stevens's inherent sense of Englishness, Mr Farraday and the Wakefields can never be truly English, because their pursuit of "the real thing" is something they have "paid for" financially rather than a professional dedication to an ideal or committed effort to serve a dignified personage.

At first glance, Stevens, through the fate of the once-glorious Darlington Hall, seems to express a sense of national decline in the face of American economic power and commodity culture akin to what Margaret Drabble observes in her lament that Britain's pastoral heritage is going gently into the good night of the twentieth century. But Ishiguro takes issue with this essentialist identification of the nation with its landscape and landed aristocracy by stressing how Stevens constructs nationalism as "cultural insiderism" and "ethnic absolutism" (Gilroy 3, 2). On his journey to see Miss Kenton, Stevens takes a break in Salisbury and marvels at the countryside as he pontificates on what makes up the "greatness" of "*Great* Britain": "it is the very lack of obvious drama or spectacle that sets the beauty of our land apart. What is pertinent is the calmness of that beauty, its sense of restraint. It is as though the land knows of its own beauty, of its own greatness, and feels no need to shout it" (*Remains* 28, original emphasis). For Stevens, national identity, or Great Britain's "greatness," is defined by a "lack of obvious drama or spectacle" that cannot be explained. It can be intuited only by someone truly in the know, with an innate connection to the landscape and its unsurpassed restraint and calmness, such as Stevens himself. Here, national greatness is embodied in a landscape that itself embodies the conventional idea of British reserve or the dignified "stiff upper lip." Furthermore, Ishiguro shows us the colonial discourse underlying Stevens's appreciation of national greatness: Great Britain is defined by a *relative* lack; it is superior only in relation to "such places as Africa and America," which are "inferior" due to their "unseemly demonstrativeness" (29). This colonialist vocabulary becomes more pronounced when Stevens discusses butlering as an essentially English profession. After opining how truly great butlers "wear their professionalism as a decent gentleman will wear his suit" and "will not let ruffians or circumstance tear it off him in the public gaze," Stevens emphasizes that "butlers only truly exist in England," defining butlers as paragons of national identity, of an Englishness formed through the vocabulary of class, colonialism, and race (43). The class hierarchy can be seen from the way Stevens compares his professionalism to a gentleman's attire that no ruffians will tear off him in public. The butler becomes a class all to himself, slightly below the "decent gentleman" whom he serves, but far and above the crowd of "ruffians" and "manservants" (43). Stevens further explains his idea of dignity in decidedly colonialist and racist terms: the "Continentals" are likened to savages, "a breed incapable of emotional restraint," who will rip off their clothes and "run about screaming"; dignity is "beyond such persons," simply because they are not part of the "English race" (43). Stevens's circular logic at the end of this passage—"it is for this reason that when you think of a great butler, he is bound, almost by definition, to be an Englishman"—echoes his earlier idea of Britain's greatness embodied in a landscape that always already "knows of its own beauty, of its own greatness" (43). Ishiguro critiques an exclusionary and homogeneous national identity by evoking symbols and icons we would readily associate with Englishness—the butler, the decent gentleman, the pastoral countryside, unflappable dignity. Ishiguro pushes the internal logic of these symbols to the extreme in order to show the underlying discourses of class, colonialism, and race. Even though Stevens's narration is sincere, Ishiguro's narrative is ironic: as readers, we do not necessarily agree with Stevens's equation of greatness and dignity with a self-evident and holistic national identity of "Great Britain." In other words, Ishiguro critiques the idea of nationalism as nativism, as an essential cultural or racial identity existing outside of time and space, and this critique occurs within a transnational context because Ishiguro connects Stevens's insular national identity with the larger framework of American global ascendancy and the post-imperial world situation.

Stevens's nostalgia for a time when Lord Darlington and Darlington Hall's fortunes were at their height and when Stevens himself enjoyed the privilege of waiting on the aristocracy who personify Britain's greatness is essentially conservative and regressive. Ishiguro and the novel, however, evince a different kind of nostalgia of the sort that Ishiguro himself explains in his interview, which involves a "feeli[ng] our way towards a better world because we've had an experience of it" ("An Interview with Kazuo Ishiguro by Brian Shaffer" 7). This more idealistic form of nostalgia that points toward the possibility of change can be seen in two minor characters in *The Remains of the Day*: Doctor Carlisle and Mr Cardinal. Dr Carlisle is the local physician in the village of Moscombe where Stevens spends the night after his car runs out of fuel, and as he tells Stevens, "when I first came out here, I was a committed socialist. Believed in the best services for all the people and all the rest of it. First came here in 'forty-nine. Socialism would allow people to live with dignity" (*Remains* 210). However, Dr Carlisle comes to the bitter conclusion that while the people of Moscombe "do have a political conscience of sorts," in the end "no one in the village wants upheaval even if it might benefit them. People here want to be left alone to lead their quiet little lives" (209–10). Dr Carlisle represents a residual form of critical national consciousness that works toward equality and liberation through a thorough transformation of political and economic structures. However, the ideal of "dignity" as social justice and an equitable distribution of services and resources is marginalized by the more patriotic strand of nationalism espoused by a character such as Harry Smith, another Moscombe villager. Smith argues that what the British "fought Hitler for" was dignity: "dignity's something every man and woman in this country can strive for and get," and what it means for Smith is that "you're born free, and you're born so that you can express your opinion freely, and vote in your member of parliament or vote him out" (186). Harry Smith's idea of dignity becomes simply a matter of freedom of speech and expression, but this freedom is limited only to people who are British, as Smith also opposes Dr Carlisle's view that Britain's former colonies should be allowed to attain independence (192). Therefore, Harry Smith's notions of dignity and freedom match Stevens's own nostalgia for the halcyon days of dignity and freedom in his profession and at Darlington Hall, and both forms of nationalism appear to marginalize the critical nationalism represented by Dr Carlisle. However, Dr Carlisle marks the presence of a nostalgia pointing toward the novel's abiding attachment to the possibility of a critical nationalism, or, as Ishiguro says, "the possibility of a world that is actually purer, one less flawed than the one we know we must inhabit" ("An Interview with Kazuo Ishiguro by Brian Shaffer" 7). That Dr Carlisle is the only person in the entire village of Moscombe who can see through Stevens's charade as a gentleman from Darlington Hall emphasizes his perspicacity and does not allow us to dismiss his socialist ideals. Instead, the doctor's own nostalgia for a time when socialism was meaningful both as a personal goal and as a social vision represents a national consciousness that has not yet been achieved or attained within the contemporary climate of patriotic exhortation and a burgeoning heritage industry.

This critical national consciousness is also exemplified in less socialist but more personal tones through the character of Mr Cardinal, who is Lord Darlington's godson and a journalist for a left-wing newspaper, and who is later killed in action in World War II as an indirect consequence of Lord Darlington's actions. Toward the end of the novel, Lord Darlington arranges secret meetings at Darlington Hall with the German foreign minister, and Mr Cardinal tries to get hold of the details. Mr Cardinal employs his professional skills as a journalist to the fullest, doing "a lot of investigating" in order to "know the situation in Germany [. . .] as well as anyone" in England, and realizes that Lord Darlington is being manipulated by the Nazis "like a pawn" (*Remains* 222). He confronts Stevens, arguing that Darlington is being manipulated by the Nazis, but the butler will not be moved. Stevens's conflation of dignity, greatness, and national identity creates a professional devotion that places "every trust" in Lord Darlington, an unshakeable belief that his lord and master is doing "that which is highest and noblest" (225). Although his appeals to Stevens to use his own judgment fall on deaf ears, Mr Cardinal represents a salutary professionalism. Mr Cardinal belongs to the same social class as Lord Darlington, for his father Sir David Cardinal was "his lordship's closest friend and colleague" (212). But the novel highlights Mr Cardinal's journalistic skills and critical thinking—his professional acumen—rather than his national and cultural heritage as an English peer. Mr Cardinal's critical nationalism is motivated by his professionalism as a journalist and an active social and political consciousness, a skepticism about "that which is highest and noblest," and the "good judgement" that is not afraid to criticize a prominent national figure when he is "out of his depth" (225). That Stevens's recollections of Mr Cardinal in the present time of the novel are tinged with nostalgia is especially telling, as it suggests he finally recognizes the importance of Mr Cardinal's salutary professionalism: "We had been enjoying some recollection or other concerning the young Mr Cardinal, so that I was then obliged to inform Miss Kenton of the gentleman's being killed in Belgium during the war. And I had gone on to say: 'Of course, his lordship was very fond of Mr Cardinal and took it very badly'" (234). Stevens feels obliged to recount Mr Cardinal's death as a war casualty, a death that is the indirect result of Lord Darlington's appeasement efforts toward Nazi Germany. Furthermore, because Stevens hastily adds that Lord Darlington was "very fond" of Mr Cardinal, we may infer that Stevens himself too held some affection for the young journalist and feels remorse and regret over his death. What Stevens feels or senses but cannot articulate directly is that Mr Cardinal's pointed words to him during the night of the fateful meeting between Lord Darlington, the German ambassador, and the British Prime Minister are an accurate critique of Stevens's blind faith in and patriotic loyalty toward his master's actions. It is therefore no surprise that when, toward the end of the novel, Stevens finally admits that Mr Cardinal was correct, that he had "trusted" Lord Darlington so completely such that "[he] can't even say [he] made [his] own mistakes," he takes this realization very badly, as badly as Lord Darlington took Mr Cardinal's death (243). The feelings invoked by Dr Carlisle and Mr Cardinal are a chiasmatic inversion of the sentimental ideals held by Lord Darlington and the younger Stevens who believed in professional dignity and greatness. The sense of loss and nostalgia associated with both these seemingly minor characters is, to use Ishiguro's words, "the emotional equivalent or intellectual cousin of idealism" that "anchors us emotionally to a sense that things should and can be repaired" ("An Interview with Kazuo Ishiguro by Brian Shaffer" 7). Just as Mr Cardinal points out that "no one with good judgement could persist in believing anything Herr Hitler says after the Rhineland" (*Remains* 225), in the same way, no reader with good judgment can believe Stevens's ideas of a "great" national identity, defined by an inherent cultural and racial dignity, after the history of colonialism. *The Remains of the Day* is a study of the clichés and stereotypes resulting from the hypostasized identification of particular cultural objects and figures with a dominant national identity. In Stevens's case, a sense of professionalism has become conflated with an essential Englishness based on dignity and hierarchy, whereas Mr Cardinal's professionalism is a critical negation that points out the hypostatization of Darlington's and Stevens's authoritarian nationalism behind a cultural mask of English fair play. To return to the interview between Ishiguro and Kenzaburo Oe, Ishiguro's writing does not affirm such an essentialist national identity, just as he is not "a very English Englishman" nor "a very Japanese Japanese" (169). Instead, Ishiguro rethinks nationalism as a sustained political and cultural critique, as a literary and discursive counterpoint to the symbolic objectification of nationalism by a heritage industry and its corresponding fictional counterpart in the romance of the archive. This critical national consciousness is closely linked and not opposed to Ishiguro's diasporic subjectivity, a subjectivity that—far from valorizing dispersal and mobility—offers an intertwined literary-symbolic and sociopolitical intervention in both national and transnational representations of Britain and Japan.

The Empire Within:
WHEN WE WERE ORPHANS AND COSMOPOLITICAL CRITIQUE

While *The Remains of the Day* offers a critique of a patriotic national identity through its representations of essentialist ideas of dignity and greatness embodied in the English landscape and aristocracy and narrated by a butler, *When We Were Orphans* presents a similar critique-*cum*-inversion of a nostalgic and patriotic sense of nationalism through another conventional literary figure—the private detective. The feeling of British diminishment on the world stage after World War II, evidenced by Stevens's carefully veiled resentment toward Mr Farraday and the other Americans in *The Remains of the Day*, seemed to be assuaged by the military victory over Argentina in 1982 in the Falklands War, and then compounded by the handover of Hong Kong, Britain's last colonial possession, to China in 1997. Ishiguro uses Christopher Banks, the detective narrator of *When We Were Orphans*, as a figure who represents this nostalgic desire for recuperating national greatness on an international level and, at the same time, through his (mis)adventures and self-discoveries, destabilizes the insularity and homogeneity upon which such greatness is predicated, revealing what is domestic and national to be always already intermingled with and interdependent upon what is foreign and international. In other words, to invert a famous phrase in postcolonial criticism coined by Salman Rushdie, *When We Were Orphans* shows us that the Empire does not simply write back to Britain; rather, it is always standing back-to-back with modern British self-fashioning.

When We Were Orphans is an amalgam of domestic detective story and colonial adventure tale, with its protagonist Christopher Banks born in the International Settlement in Shanghai at the turn of the century and losing both his parents, who, he believes, were zealous anti-opium crusaders kidnapped by the Chinese. Dedicating his life to his parents' rescue, and believing that accomplishing this rescue will strike a blow for justice in the grand global scheme of things, Banks comes of age in Britain and becomes a celebrated detective, eventually returning to Shanghai in 1937 as the Japanese military invades the city and reduces most of it to rubble. Banks reaches the house where he believes his parents are being held, but he does not find them. Instead, both his investigation and his heroic sense of self are gravely undermined when he learns the truth about his parents from Uncle Philip, an old family friend who now works for the Chinese military: his father abandoned Banks and his mother for another woman and died overseas; his mother was kidnapped by Wang Ku, a Chinese warlord in the opium trade, and acquiesced to a life of sexual slavery in return for Wang providing financial support for Banks's upbringing and education in Britain. In an epilogue set twenty years later, Banks reunites with his aged and senile mother in a nursing home in Hong Kong, and muses on the prospects of spending his remaining years with his adopted daughter Jennifer. Both the British detective story and the tale of colonial espionage became popular in the late nineteenth and early twentieth centuries, and the literary and scholarly gulf between the two genres helped maintain the demarcation between "the nation as a domestic core that was purely English and a colonial periphery that was foreign and racially marked," and this distinction "prevented the reader from acknowledging the manifold interdependencies between the two domains" (Reitz xvii). Detectives, it would seem, are concerned with criminals at home, while spies are engaged with enemies abroad. This generic boundary, however, obscures the ways in which "detective fiction [. . .] refashioned Englishness as an imperial instead of an insular identity" (Reitz xxv), such that the detective and the imperial explorer "collaborated to make understanding the interpenetration of core and periphery essential to the integrity of the nation" and need to be considered "*together* in their proper global context [. . .] in which the detective is brought to life amidst anxieties about increasing imperial power and the imperial explorer is shaped by domestic ideas about power" (Reitz 65, 80, original emphasis). In light of Britain's global situation in the late twentieth century, Christopher Banks, as a detective implicated in Britain's imperial adventure, offers a more recent incarnation of the desires and anxieties of a nation trying to retain a key role in international affairs.

Throughout the novel, Ishiguro foregrounds the extremely studied efforts Banks undertakes to fashion himself as a typically British subject through the figures and tropes of nineteenth- and twentieth-century literature and culture, even though these details seem to elude Banks and appear to be second nature in his own character formation. As an adult, he lives in a London flat furnished "in a tasteful manner that evoked an unhurried Victorian past" (*Orphans* 3), and he remembers his mother, Diana, as "a beauty in an older, Victorian tradition" who "is certainly elegant, stiff-backed, perhaps even haughty, but not without the gentleness around her eyes that [he] remember[s] well" (58). Banks's mother's physical beauty, coupled with her ardent opposition to the British opium trade with China, makes her a paragon of Victorian feminine virtue and therefore an object to be protected and rescued from the clutches of the Chinese. Banks's father, on the other hand, does not appear in any descriptive detail in Banks's childhood recollections, and Banks's belief, up till Uncle Philip's revelation at the end of the novel, that his "father made a stand, a courageous stand against his own employers concerning the profits from the opium trade [. . .] and was thus removed" (306) actually projects his mother's principles onto his father's character and covers up the sordid truth of his father's elopement. The central role played by an idealized image of British culture and history in Banks's self-fashioning is further evinced by his memories of young men from Britain who visited his parents and "brought with them the air of the English lanes and meadows [he] knew from *The Wind in the Willows,* or else the foggy streets of the Conan Doyle mysteries," young men whom Banks felt "were all of them figures to study closely and emulate" (54). Not only does Banks read the adventures of Conan Doyle's most famous detective, Sherlock Holmes, who serves as the template for Banks's own detective persona; his imagined geography of English lanes, meadows, and the streets of London are also formed through literary texts. Banks's observation, thrown in as an afterthought, that the visitors were figures to study and emulate for their inherent national identity belies Banks's own protestations as an adult that he "blended perfectly into English school life" and had no trouble "grasping the deeper mores and etiquettes" of life in Britain (7). The adult Banks, like Stevens gazing upon the plain features of the English countryside, believes that national identity can be readily grasped and attained if—and *only* if—one has an innate connection with the landscape and country, but this confidence in a rooted national identity is continually questioned in Banks's own childhood memories, where he is often beset by doubts about being (in the words of his Japanese friend Akira) "not enough Englishman" (76). Uncle Philip, to whom the young Banks turns in an effort to "become more English," readily admits that, being raised in the International Settlement "with a lot of different sorts around [him]," Banks is "a bit of a mongrel" (79), but Philip also recognizes that "people need to feel they belong. To a nation, to a race"; otherwise "this civilisation of ours, perhaps it'll just collapse" (80). Uncle Philip's words are important here for two reasons: first, his observation that Banks is a bit of a mongrel is forgotten or repressed by the adult Banks, who rejects any hint that he is not English enough and maintains he can fit seamlessly into an idealized version of his national identity back in London; second, his equation of national identity and racial belonging with civilizational survival is taken up by Banks as an adult as the key principle in his crime-solving methodology.

Banks cannot admit that he does not have an Antaeus-like relationship with Britain and its culture and history; therefore, he must construct a national identity out of an idealized and imagined detective persona gleaned from the pages of Conan Doyle's mysteries he read as a child and then endow this persona with a sense of national destiny and purpose on par with that of Sherlock Holmes. Banks states with adamant determination that "[his] intention was to combat evil—in particular, evil of the insidious, furtive kind" (*Orphans* 22), and "that the task of rooting out evil in its most devious forms, often just when it is about to go unchecked, is a crucial and solemn undertaking" (31). Banks finds his sentiments mirrored by other characters in Britain who remind him that evil is "conspiring to put civilisation to the torch" (45) and that "the eye of the storm" that is building up into World War II "is to be found not in Europe at all, but in the Far East" (146). The sheer absurdity of the idea that a world war can be caused by the abduction of Banks's parents and that their rescue can avert the impending global catastrophe shows us that Banks is absolutely caught up in playing the role of a detective to the extent that the role itself has taken over—Banks views the world through the lens of a Conan Doyle mystery that pits himself, the heroic detective, against innumerable and implacable forces of evil. But, as one commentator points out, "despite his gumshoe appellation, Banks never gets to exhibit ratiocinative brilliance or to engage in intricate spadework" (Sim 108). Our only knowledge of Banks's acumen as a detective is hearsay from other characters who describe him as "the most brilliant investigative mind in England" (*Orphans* 34) and "a greater man" than run-of-the-mill police inspectors (144). Unlike in a typical Conan Doyle mystery, we only see Banks wearing the persona of a detective—just as Stevens the butler dons his professionalism like a gentleman puts on his suit—without any evidence of the perspicacity or deductive powers possessed by a literary antecedent such as Sherlock Holmes. Ishiguro shows us that Banks must *first* construct the persona of a detective to create the fiction of national identity rather than allow his professional self to be an emanation or outgrowth of a preexisting and determinate nationalism. In *The Remains of the Day,* butlering is Stevens's way of participating in a national greatness he feels is innate but that he never actually possesses; in *When We Were Orphans,* detecting crime is Banks's mode of maintaining a national identity through a civilizational struggle that divides the world into two clear camps of good and evil, domestic and foreign.

Ishiguro's literary cosmopolitics extends beyond its interrogation of Banks's self-deluding detective role-playing and points out that the same cultural discourses of national identity and civilizational greatness are at work in other societies besides Britain. Banks, having concluded a fruitless search for his parents in Shanghai's war zone, is escorted back to the British Consulate by a Japanese officer, Colonel Hasegawa, who spent some time in Britain before the war. Hasegawa fondly recalls the "calm, dignified" and "beautiful green fields" and—more important—English literature: "Dickens, Thackeray. Wuthering Heights. I am especially fond of your Dickens" (*Orphans* 296). When Banks questions how such a cultured man such as Hasegawa could participate in the brutal invasion of China, the colonel chillingly echoes Stevens's earlier remarks about greatness when he replies that "if Japan is to become a great nation" then the violence is "necessary. Just as it once was for England" (297). Although there are, of course, myriad historical and geopolitical reasons for Japan's militarism during World War II, what Ishiguro points out here is the continuity between Eastern and Western discourses of national identity, imperial expansion, and military conquest, since Hasegawa's replies juxtapose the apparent tranquility of the English countryside and the domestic context of English literature with Japanese national aggrandizement linked to an earlier period of British imperialism. It is this continuity between and interpenetration of the domestic and the foreign that Banks, in his Manichean ordering of the world into good and evil through a fictional detective's eyes, cannot possibly comprehend.

This interpenetration of the nation and what lies outside of it destabilizes any attempt to forge a national identity premised on cultural characteristics that are supposedly innate or inherent, and it comes to a climax when Banks learns from his old family friend, Uncle Philip (now a shadowy, ex-Communist informer for the Chinese Kuomintang military regime), that his mother's agreed to be Wang Ku's concubine in return for the Chinese warlord's provision of opium money for Bank's education and life in Britain: "Your schooling. Your place in London society. The fact that you made of yourself what you have. You owe it to Wang Ku. Or rather, to your mother's sacrifice" (*Orphans* 313). Uncle Philip's revelation is an inversion of the usual climactic scene of a detective story, in which the indefatigable investigator unveils the truth of the crime before an assembled cast of characters and suspects. Uncle Philip's anguished disclosure is the final demonstration of Banks's investigative ineptitude and acts as the final blow to the fictional persona Banks has built up over the years:

> You see what made possible your comfortable life in England? How you were able to become a celebrated detective? A detective! What good is that to anyone? Stolen jewels, aristocrats murdered for their inheritance. Do you suppose that's all there is to contend with? Your mother, she wanted you to

live in your enchanted world for ever. But it's impossible. In the end it has to shatter. (*Orphans* 315)

The point Ishiguro drives home in this final confrontation between Banks and Uncle Philip is similar to what Edward Said calls contrapuntal reading, "a simultaneous awareness both of the metropolitan history that is narrated and of those other histories against which (and together with which) the dominating discourse acts" (*Culture and Imperialism* 51). The enchanted world of the celebrated detective fighting a shadowy worldwide conspiracy of evil that Banks has been living in is premised on the obscuring and denial of the simultaneous awareness of Britain's imperial enterprise and the opium trade that was actively encouraged by the British government and trading companies, as well as certain Chinese authorities such as Wang Ku. Just as Colonel Hasegawa argues that Japan's military ambitions are a counterpoint to an earlier era of British imperial expansion, so too Uncle Philip's revelation points out that the suturing of Banks's apparently seamless national identity is possible only with the threads of empire and exploitation, and that "we are dealing with the formation of cultural identities understood not as essentializations [. . .] but as contrapuntal ensembles, for it is the case that no identity can ever exist by itself and without an array of opposites, negatives, oppositions" (Said, *Culture and Imperialism* 52). The contemporary relevance of Said's and Ishiguro's contrapuntal and cosmopolitical critique of a determinate and instrumental national identity can be seen from British reactions to the handover of Hong Kong to the People's Republic of China on July 1, 1997, during which "Britain stressed its own contribution to Hong Kong's prosperity while China barely acknowledged Britain's presence" and the outgoing governor of Hong Kong, Chris Patten, opined that "this is a Chinese city, a very Chinese city with British characteristics" (Higgins para 11). While the British authorities and Governor Patten were trying to protect Hong Kong's democratic and capitalist political and economic systems from rapid dismantling by the new Chinese government, read contrapuntally their emphases on British contributions to Hong Kong and the city's very Chinese-but-also-British character cuts both ways—Hong Kong has contributed significantly to Britain's prosperity, and Britain is a country that has also taken on Chinese characteristics. In the context of black British literature and culture, Ashley Dawson argues that since the influx of immigrants from the Caribbean, Africa, and South Asia after World War II—if not earlier—Britain has undergone what Jamaican poet Louise Bennet calls a colonization in reverse and is now undeniably a mongrel nation (Dawson 2007). Christopher Banks, if we recall, is also "a bit of mongrel," having grown up in Shanghai's International

Settlement surrounded by various people from different Asian and European cultures; hence Ishiguro's literary cosmopolitics insists that a critical national consciousness must acknowledge and affirm these international and "mongrel" elements in the nation's social body and cultural community.

Moreover, just as Mr Cardinal the journalist offers a note of critical nationalism in a narrative that is dominated by Stevens's professional voice, so too *When We Were Orphans* gestures toward cosmopolitical connections that cannot be actualized or realized because of Banks's steadfast identification with his heroic mission. Returning to the International Settlement in Shanghai in 1937, Banks is "shocked" by "the refusal of everyone here to acknowledge their drastic culpability" in the brutal violence of the Sino-Japanese War; he is appalled by "a denial of responsibility which has turned in on itself and gone sour, manifesting itself in the sort of pompous defensiveness" among "the so-called elite of Shanghai" who are "treating with such contempt the suffering of their Chinese neighbours across the canal" (*Orphans* 173). At the beginning of the next chapter following this acerbic observation, Banks appears to be doing his part to alleviate the suffering of the Chinese as he helps the local police investigate a boathouse where "three bodies had been discovered," but he quickly leaves the crime scene and winds up in a "small club" where "a lone French pianist will give melancholy renditions of Bizet or Gershwin" (175). Nothing more is ever heard about this case of the three boathouse bodies once Banks is further drawn into the improbable attempt to rescue his parents. Banks's retreat into the melancholic comfort of the International Settlement's entertainment marks his complicity with the indifference he chastises in his fellow Europeans, but his initial response to this contempt for the Chinese is Ishiguro's way of gesturing toward a more active and engaged cosmopolitical consciousness that echoes Mr Cardinal's willingness to challenge the noble but misguided instincts of Lord Darlington in *The Remains of the Day*. Just as Banks's British national identity is constituted in no small part by Chinese culture and coin, so too the Sino-Japanese conflict is, as Colonel Hasegawa reminds the crestfallen detective, connected to a history of British imperial exploits against China during the Opium Wars and, as such, cannot be disowned with a flourish as simply a foreign affair.

Read in this contrapuntal fashion, Banks's sense of belatedness and nostalgia for a childhood in which his parents seemed to be virtuous and heroic figures should be thought of as affective expressions of what Raymond Williams calls a "structure of feeling," made up of "characteristic elements of impulse, restraints, and tone" (132). Williams's explication of a structure of feeling as "affective elements of consciousness and relationships: not feeling against thought, but thought as felt and feeling as thought" (132), reminds us of Ishiguro's own description of nostalgia's critical and idealistic aspects as opposed to its more conventionally accepted conservative and imperialistic forms. Williams's characterization of a structure of feeling in the sense of "thought as felt and feeling as thought" is itself a chiasmatic formulation that inverts the commonly held assumption that feelings are opposed or subordinate to rational and critical thinking. The difference here lies in a state of belonging as opposed to a condition of longing: in the former, as Uncle Philip says, "people need to feel they belong. To a nation, to a race," and thus, to a determinate form of national identity that offers a secure sense of subjectivity; in the latter, one feels that something is out of joint in the present and works toward setting things aright, and this structure of feeling highlights the "specific internal relations, at once interlocking and in tension" within British culture and society and between Britain and its former empire as "a social experience which is still *in process*" (Williams 132, original emphasis) rather than institutionalized or determined. Banks's persistent need to maintain and perform his British identity through the figure of the fictional detective and Uncle Philip's final shattering of this persona are a critique of the British heritage industry and its attempts to recover an authentic cultural and national identity through the commodification and preservation of landscapes, landmarks, and monuments. But Banks's persistent efforts to overcome his predicament of being "not enough Englishman" also points to a constitutive lack or absence in any determinate national identity and, beyond that, to the always already hybrid and mongrelized conditions of British culture and society thanks to the nation's history of colonialism, slavery, and immigration.

In *The Remains of the Day*, Ishiguro inverts the condition-of-England narrative and signature figures of Englishness such as the country house and the impeccable butler to interrogate the pretensions of a national identity premised on an essentialized greatness and dignity; in *When We Were Orphans*, his diasporic perspective enables a chiasmic maneuver that inverts the Victorian detective story and colonial adventure precisely by combining them in the dissatisfying figure of Christopher Banks, the flawed detective and inept explorer. Ishiguro accomplishes in fiction what Caroline Reitz and other recent studies of detective stories have done in criticism: "the detective [. . .] shows us how national identity is at once a part you play and a thing you become," and that we need to contextualize this identity by placing it "back into the vast, interconnected world that produced it" (87). The contextualization of national identity in Ishiguro's novels not only offers a specific cultural and historical framework for its construction but also interrogates the regressive form of nostalgia inherent in late twentieth-century British invocations of national symbols and heritage. If "nostalgia is often for past thoughts rather than past things" and "less the memory of what actually was than of what was once thought possible" (Lowenthal 9), then Ishiguro's novels underscore Adorno's observation that "just as no experience is real that has not been loosed by involuntary remembrance from the deathly fixity of its isolated existence, so conversely, no memory is guaranteed, existent in itself, indifferent to the future of him who harbours it" (*Minima Moralia* 166). Ishiguro's negation of nostalgia follows the grain of a contemporary yearning for past thoughts and experiences without hypostasizing these thoughts and experiences within their isolated existences or recreating the present as a pristine, unaltered version of the past. His novels do not maintain indifference to the possibilities of the future, as they offer "a sense that things should and can be repaired" ("An Interview with Kazuo Ishiguro by Brian Shaffer" 7) even though his characters may not be aware of it. It is this revised understanding of nostalgia, combined with posed-ethnic style, tacking between cosmopolitical structures of feeling and national symbols of heritage, that characterizes Ishiguro's tough intelligence.

CHAPTER 3

"The Possibilities of the New Country We Are Making"

Transnational Fragments and National Consciousness in Derek Walcott's Writing

MIDWAY through *The Prodigal* (2004), Derek Walcott, whose speaker in this book-length poem is almost a direct expression of Walcott himself as both an aging writer and a frequent transatlantic traveler, catches sight of the Caribbean islands as he moves through the coastal region of Colombia and responds with qualified joy, calling "the Caribbean, owned and exultant grinning and comforting," a place that is "not a new coast, but home" (Chapter 7, Canto II, lines 28, 30). Walcott's use of the adjective "owned" expresses not only his claim that the islands are his and he theirs but also the impoverishment and dependency of many Caribbean countries that are "owned" economically by European and American companies despite being sovereign nation-states. Walcott does not shy away from this grim reality, and it is not a stretch to say that a recurring concern in the Nobel laureate's poetic vision is the marshaling of aesthetic and cultural resources to exult and comfort those who call the Caribbean "home" despite its obvious shortcomings, himself included. In this chapter, I argue that Derek Walcott reconfigures tropes of racial identity and hybridity dominant in discussions of literature and culture in the Caribbean to foreground a cosmopolitics that is not only rooted in the national consciousness of his home country of St. Lucia but also intertwined with sociocultural formations beyond its shores. Instead of thinking of the nation in terms of a determinate and homogeneous identity tied to a notion of civilizational or racial purity and progress, Walcott envisions it as a social, political, and cultural formation wrought out of lateral connections both within and without the Caribbean, as can be seen from his remarks in a 1983 interview: "the Caribbean is both a new and an old society. Old in history, new in the experiment of multi-national concentration in small spaces. To look backwards is to think linearly, the fate of any concept of progress" ("An Interview with Derek Walcott by Leif Sjöberg" 79). When scholars of Caribbean literature and culture privilege its transnational and hybrid characteristics, they contend either implicitly or explicitly that Caribbean literature cannot be thought of in national terms. They habitually subsume the nation within a regional Caribbean consciousness that, by virtue of its heterogeneous mix of cultural and linguistic traditions, transcends the nation's premises of purity and homogeneity. In short, because Caribbean subjectivity is considered to be historically, culturally, and linguistically heterogeneous, the literature produced by such subjects is correspondingly multifarious and trans- or postnational in form and content. Thus Caribbean literature can be thought of as an idealized model of the complex interweaving and crosshatching of histories, cultures, and languages in a world where nation-states are increasingly obsolete, resulting in such valorizing statements as James Clifford's "we are all Caribbeans now in our urban archipelagos" (*Predicament* 173). Certainly Walcott himself has been celebrated as a Caribbean writer whose winning of the 1992 Nobel Prize for literature has, according to some critics, "demonstrated the ongoing vitality and growing global prominence of Anglophone Caribbean fiction" (Booker and Juraga 22).

However, Walcott's meditations about culture and nationalism in his interviews and essays, together with his treatment of these topics in his poetry, point to a literary cosmopolitics redefining the idea of nationalism in the context of the anglophone Caribbean. Walcott shows us that a national consciousness committed to social justice and political liberation is still alive and well in the Caribbean, and he expresses this national consciousness through his cultural interventions as an artist and poet. Walcott departs from the dominant view of Caribbean cultural hybridity as exemplifying the opposition of nationalism and culture or the transcendence of cultural forms over national borders in current discourses of globalism, where culture—as lived experience, artistic expression, and intellectual production—opposes and transcends the limitations of the nation as a determining political institution. These conceptualizations of culture versus nation may have started out as local concerns, but they have taken on a global scale with the recent turn from postcolonial to globalizing paradigms of reading literature. But what is elided in this move from national and postcolonial frameworks to transnational and global hermeneutics is a consideration of how Caribbean literature and discourse need to be appreciated as a form of literary cosmopolitics in which the dynamic connections between national consciousness and transnational cultural flows continue to be salient and visible. At one level, Walcott's national consciousness accords with the aspirations of political independence and economic development advocated by political leaders such as the historian and statesman Eric Williams. Not long before he became prime minister of Trinidad in 1962, Williams, ever the skilled rhetorician, declared in a political address that "Massa Day Done." Williams is certainly condemning the British colonial master who was "owner of a West Indian sugar plantation, frequently an absentee, deliberately stunting all the economic potential of the society, dominating his defenceless workers by the threat of punishment or imprisonment," and at the same time he intends to chastise anyone in Trinidad who is "using his political power for the most selfish private ends" and who conducts himself as "an uncultured man with an illiberal outlook" ("Massa Day Done" 245–46). Williams stresses that "Massa is not a racial term" but is "the symbol of a bygone age," and if "Massa Day is a social phenomenon," then "Massa Day Done connotes a political awakening and a social revolution" (239). Like Walcott, Williams exhorts his audience to look beyond the racial *ressentiment* of white versus black and think about the nation's future and its economic challenges along political and social lines. Yet despite his rhetorical flourishes against the masters of British colonialism and their neocolonial counterparts, Williams holds on to an important and hierarchical symbol of British imperial power by inviting Queen Elizabeth II of Britain to "inaugurate the first Parliament of the Independent West Indies" of which he is prime minister (263). Massa Day might be done, but hard on his heels comes Her Majesty the Queen. Furthermore, Williams's anticolonial and nation-building rhetoric is steadily focused on the problem of economic development and productivity, such that the national "slogan" he bestows on Trinidad in his first Independence Day Address in 1962 is "Discipline, Production, Tolerance" ("Independence Day Address" 267). As Trinidad's chief executive, Williams is primarily concerned with the economic stability and viability of his fledgling nation-state, but for someone who earlier berated "uncultured [men] with an illiberal outlook," Williams seems to lack a cultural vision for his new nation. Where Williams stops short, Walcott steps in and contends that a revision—literally, a seeing-again—of Caribbean history and culture through poetry and aesthetics must be simultaneous with the struggle for economic and political freedom.

Both Walcott's emphasis on the relative autonomy of art in relation to society and its power to negate and reconfigure the relationships between society, culture, and politics through its own formal complexity are crucial to understanding his rethinking of nationalism in the Caribbean. His understanding of the relationship between art and lived reality recalls Theodor Adorno's own accounts of the artwork as a monad, formed through its conditions of possibility but also exerting a force field that negates and reconnects these conditions into a different arrangement or constellation that has yet to be imagined. As Walcott, referring to Auden's famous elegy to W. B. Yeats, avers in high modernist tones, "you want something to happen with poetry, but it doesn't make anything happen"; yet at the same time, although poetry does not have any grand designs to make anything happen, things are changed or altered when they are touched and drawn into poetry's formal design: "As a matter of fact, poetry *does* make something happen because in the flow of the river which [Auden] talks about, the river touches many things as it passes by" ("An Interview with Derek Walcott by William Baer" 202, 203, original emphasis). This double sense of poetry as a negation of the logic of cause and effect as well as a powerful current that rushes past or through and connects many things without determining their identity or nature accords with Adorno's discussion of the artwork as both a negating and a (re)connecting force. In light of this conjunction between poetry and aesthetic theory, I examine Walcott's literary cosmopolitics as expressed in his essays, lyric poetry, and three of his longer poems, tracing his critical engagement with both European and Caribbean literatures and theories of modernity and nationalism. This critical framework illuminates the literary cosmopolitics within Walcott's apparently migrant and cosmopolitan texts as well as the interrelations between nationalism and culture against the backdrop of globalization's administered world. Walcott rethinks, but does not reject, the legacy of the European Enlightenment by playing on the symbolic power and luminous connotations of his home country's name—St. Lucia—as a new way of illuminating the possibilities of national consciousness in a geographical region historically marked by colonial violence and postcolonial exploitation.

"The Care and Pain of the Antilles":
National Consciousness and the Reassembling of Fragments

As I discussed earlier in this book, Stuart Hall's metaphorization of Caribbean hybridity into a cultural identity that exemplifies our globalized world both assumes that the diasporic condition is an already accomplished fact and elides the national consciousness present in the diasporas he cites to support his argument. Hall's field-defining idea of the Caribbean diaspora as a metaphor for global cultural identity has informed both postcolonial and Caribbean literary studies. Various critics have claimed that because "cultural clash and miscegenation formed the brutal texture of Caribbean life," "those theories developed in the polydialectical communities of the Caribbean have been amongst the most complex and have displayed the greatest potential for abrogating Eurocentric concepts" (Ashcroft, Griffiths, and Tiffin 146, 117); others have argued for the global significance of Caribbean writing as "a major canon of world literature" that "has contributed enormously to the strength of Caribbean culture against oppression and foreign appropriation" (Savory 746). Hall's view, however, has not gone unchallenged. Shalini Puri is among those who argue that hybridity in the region does not always possess the postnational qualities Hall ascribes to it. Because "invocations of cultural hybridity have been crucial to Caribbean nationalisms," Puri claims, they "undo the generalized claim that hybridity and the nation-state are opposed to one another and enable a broader questioning of invocations of a 'global village' and the death of the nation-state" (6). Puri counters such thinking by attending to historically specific instances of hybridity in Caribbean literary texts and social practices, showing their importance in political discourse and economic and cultural production. However, Puri enacts an unwarranted split between literary form and radical politics in her reading of Derek Walcott. In her view, lyrical and affective representations of people or groups that do not explicitly delineate social and political conflicts weaken these subjects' historical and political import and gloss over the community's social problems. In particular, Puri focuses on Derek Walcott's 1992 Nobel lecture "The Antilles: Fragments of Epic Memory" and interrogates a moment where the poet describes the fragments of a broken vase being lovingly reassembled. She considers this piecing together "an act of love" that is problematic because of "the way that the sentiment becomes a ruse for silence on inequitable relations of power" (69). Puri concludes that "Walcott's treatment of hybridity [in *The Antilles*] within Caribbean nation-states thus appears to be an aesthetically accomplished reinscription of official Caribbean national mottoes" and that therefore his lecture "attempts to forge a unity without attending to the unequal terms of inclusion in the national imaginary or the unequal access to the resources of the state; it posits in advance a unity and equality that has yet to be achieved" (69). Puri contrasts this aesthetic reinscription with Walcott's earlier play, *Pantomime,* which seems to be a more successful and pointed interrogation of hybridity discourse. As a play within a play, *Pantomime* literally and metaphorically stages the tensions between Harry (an

Englishman) and Jackson (his Trinidadian employee) and becomes "a dramatization of a hybridity that deconstructs essential oppositions" based on race and skin color while emphasizing a more salient "opposition understood as arising out of one's social location and relationship to material privilege" (Puri 135). From this perspective, Walcott's art is complicit with national ideology unless it uses symbolic language to clearly mark the oppositions that arise out of social and material struggles. Moreover, such a critical perspective that prizes political resistance equates nationalism with authoritarian state ideology that must be opposed and transcended by deterritorialized and decentered culture. It passes over "the thinking through of a work of art [that] justly requires a concrete inquiry into social content" demanded by the aesthetics of Walcott's own writing and reads "vague feelings of universality and inclusiveness" (Adorno, "Lyric Poetry" 156) as the sum and purpose of his meditations on poetry and history.

Rather than focus on the dramatization of political and social tensions, Walcott articulates a set of dynamic relations between culture and nationalism, language and history, and politics and literary form in a series of essays that shuttle between the particular national contexts of St. Lucia, Jamaica, and Trinidad and a larger transnational Caribbean framework. Although born in St. Lucia in 1930, Walcott is very familiar with the two other anglophone Caribbean countries as he obtained his university degree in Jamaica and founded a theater company in Trinidad. In a 1957 essay about Jamaica, "Society and the Artist," Walcott argues that history in the Caribbean lies "not in the quick political achievements [. . .] but in the deepening stream of the way we are now learning to think. To see ourselves, not as others see us, but with all the possibilities of the new country we are making" (15). Walcott further elaborates that "the people of all these islands know that they must share their countries. [. . .] They are now a people who possess the land in thought and share it" (15). What is important here is that, even in this early theorization of nationalism and culture, Walcott locates the specific national consciousness of "the new country we are making"—namely Jamaica—within a larger transnational framework of the Caribbean, or "the people of all these islands [who] know that they must share their countries." The national and the transnational are not opposed; in fact, what ties them together is a shared sense of the "new possibilities" of each country expressed through creative language and "possess[ing] the land in thought." This is national consciousness expressed in cultural and artistic creativity more so than institutionalized political activity. Walcott develops this double sense of political consciousness and cultural politics in a later essay: "We have broken up the archipelago into nations, and in each nation we attempt to assert characteristics of the national identity. Everyone knows that these are pretexts of power if such power is seen as political" ("The Caribbean: Culture or Mimicry?" 3). Instead of thinking about nations as homogeneous identities created by state *fiat*, Walcott emphasizes the social and cultural work necessary for a politically engaged nationalism: "what energizes our society is the spiritual force of a culture shaping itself, and it can do this without the formula of politics" (4). The energizing, shaping force of a national consciousness is neither tied to "the formula of politics" with a definite ideology nor driven by a grand historical narrative that Walcott calls "the Muse of History" ("Muse" 36). The Muse of History is Walcott's figure for a Eurocentric version of historical events in which Enlightenment Europe conquers, enslaves, and indentures the peoples of the New World, thereby portraying the diverse peoples of the Caribbean as perpetual victims of colonial and postcolonial violence and exploitation. Without downplaying the trauma of physical and symbolic violence suffered by those in the Caribbean, Walcott castigates the politicians and poets who are inspired by the Muse of History and who yearn for an authentic cultural identity expressed through "an oceanic nostalgia for the older culture" of Europe, Africa, or South Asia while simultaneously issuing "a rejection of the untamed landscape" of the Caribbean islands (42). The alternative Walcott proposes lies in seeing how "history is fiction, subject to a fitful muse, memory," and to be inspired by the muse of fitful memory as opposed to the muse of temporal continuity and world historical time is to become a "revolutionary" poet with a vision of Caribbean humanity as "a being inhabited by presences, not a creature chained to his past" (37). The presences that Walcott describes here are the cultural and historical memories both indigenous to the Caribbean and brought to the region from Africa, South and East Asia, and Europe. The figure of the writer inhabited by these presences recalls Walcott's earlier discussion of national consciousness, described as "a people who possess the land in thought and share it"—a possession of the land not only in a physical form but also as a form of knowledge and culture. Not only do the people of Jamaica possess the land with their contemporaries, they also share it with their forebears: they are not "chained" to the ancestral "past" but are responsible for reworking the memories of dislocation and suffering into a promise of a better future, "in the deepening stream of the way we are now learning to think" ("Society and the Artist" 15).

By distinguishing memory from history, Walcott distances himself from those who believe in the myth of "elemental man" ("Muse" 37). Those "New World poets" who consider the traditions and forms of European literature as "historical degradation, rejecting it as the language of the [colonial] master" (39) are those who also see in the Caribbean only the ruin and "the shipwreck" of colonialism, such that "the New World offers not elation but cynicism" (42). For Walcott, the veneration of elemental, mythic man and the fixation on the repetition of colonialism's mistakes prevents a clear understanding of the past as the lived experience of time and the corresponding symbolic expression of this experience as memory. This lived experience and symbolic expression is what Walter Benjamin, in another context, calls ruin and rune, out of which the historical relations of the postcolonial situation crystallize into poetry (176). In order to grasp these historical relations and their poetic crystallization, Walcott examines how poetic language "combines the natural and the marmoreal" and "conjugates both tenses [of past and present] simultaneously," bringing together the vital rhythms of Caribbean vernaculars with the stentorian syntax of official speech in a way that does justice to them both ("Antilles" 70). The deeper one delves into the poetic form and history of the local, the larger one's historical and geographical consciousness must become, a paradox Walcott captures when he observes that "yet the older and more assured I grew, the stronger my isolation as a poet, the more I needed to become omnivorous about the art and literature of Europe to understand my own world" ("Muse" 63). But it is in his Nobel lecture "The Antilles: Fragments of Epic Memory," which Shalini Puri considers an apology for state multiculturalism, that Walcott offers his most thought-provoking elaboration of poetic thought in terms of the fragmented histories and cultures that make up the Caribbean. In this essay Walcott talks about watching a village in Trinidad prepare for a performance of the Indian epic *The Ramayana*. As he witnesses the excited and festive spirit of the performers, he begins "filtering the afternoon with evocations of a lost India" ("Antilles" 68). But then he checks himself and asks—"Why should India be 'lost' when none of these villagers ever really knew it" (68)? He then reflects that he is "entitled like any Trinidadian to the ecstasies of their claim," this claim being the villagers' performance of *The Ramayana* that brings their community together, but the performance is not limited to those of Indian descent, for Walcott himself is of mixed parentage. In fact, Walcott realizes that though he is an accomplished poet, he is "only one-eighth the writer [he] might have been had [he] contained all the fragmented languages of Trinidad," but even so, he is still "entitled to the mirrors and crepe-paper temples of the Muslim epic, to the Chinese Dragon Dance, to the rites of the Sephardic Jewish synagogue" (69). The various fragments, languages, cultures, and histories in Trinidad are distinct but cannot be sealed off from one another. They do not disseminate or dissolve the nation into diaspora. On the contrary, these aspects and fragments of several diasporic cultures come together to form the critical national consciousness of the Caribbean artist:

> Break a vase, and the love that reassembles the fragments is stronger than that love which took its symmetry for granted when it was whole. The glue that fits the pieces is the sealing of its original shape. It is such love that reassembles our African and Asiatic fragments, the cracked heirlooms whose restoration shows its white scars. This gathering of broken pieces is the care and pain of the Antilles, and if the pieces are disparate, ill-fitting, they contain more pain than their original sculpture, those icons and sacred vessels taken for granted in their ancestral places. ("Antilles" 69)

For Walcott, Trinidad's national consciousness and culture cannot be deduced from a set formula of politics; they are not a pretext of power, but rather a loving labor of "care and pain" that reassembles a fitful past into a livable present. Walcott sees nationalism not as a native identity but as a crystallization of "broken pieces" into "cracked heirlooms," and this is (to use his earlier term) "revolutionary." The cultural politics of nationalism in Trinidad become evident when we recall that Walcott is rebutting another Trinidadian Nobel laureate, V. S. Naipaul. Naipaul claims that "nothing has ever been made in the Caribbean" because there is no originality in its culture, only imitation ("Culture or Mimicry?" 8–9). But we can see from this passage about the broken vase that Walcott is making a political claim in a cultural register, turning Naipaul's own "nothingness" against him—as Walcott says: "Nothing will always be created in the West Indies, [. . .] because what will come out of there is like nothing [any]one has ever seen before" ("Culture or Mimicry?" 8–9). The idea of "nothing," for Walcott, does not mean an emptiness or a vacuum. Instead, it is, at one level, the negation of a discourse of civilizational backwardness and inferiority propagated both by Caribbean intellectuals such as Naipaul and Caribbean political leaders who continuously emphasize the trauma and victimization of their people under Europe's colonial regimes in order to make them compliant. At another level, this nothingness is also the condition of possibility out of which a cultural politics and a political consciousness of nationalism can emerge within a larger cosmopolitical framework. The solitary work undertaken by Walcott paradoxically requires a relational understanding of the historical forces that make up his "own world." Furthermore, in the context of the passage from "The Antilles," the poetic function of being a "filter and purifier" becomes the "glue that fits the pieces" of the broken vase, the "love that reassembles our African and Asiatic fragments." This "care and pain" of Caribbean poetry connects the African and Asiatic fragments, the Caribbean present and its colonial and postcolonial past, and out of this connection crystallizes the living element of poetry. While the reassembling of broken fragments into a coherent whole might seem to recall liberal multiculturalism as it is promoted by the United States or other European countries to deal with ethnic and racial differences, it is significant that Walcott stresses how the fragments are "disparate, ill-fitting," and therefore not homogeneous like the smoothly contoured pieces of a jigsaw puzzle that can be assembled and reconciled into a neat whole. Furthermore, while Euro-American liberal multiculturalism is often promoted by state governments, it is unclear in the passage from Walcott's speech who is the actual agent or active subject reassembling these fragments. By eschewing a direct subject, Walcott focuses our attention on the process—"the gathering of broken pieces"—and the indelible "white scars" of the imperfectly reassembled sculpture, rather than the "ancestral places" where the different peoples of the Caribbean originally came from. In this arresting analogy, Walcott envisions national culture in the Caribbean as predicated upon a critical national consciousness that takes "care and pain" to reassemble "African and Asiatic fragments" rather than affirming an already accomplished "symmetry" or "whole."

Walcott's poetic representations of a critical national consciousness is a literary rejoinder both to the British colonial imagination of the Caribbean as a backward and primitive region and to the contemporary image of the Caribbean as a primarily tourist-driven economy marginalized by and dependent on the First World. My reading of Walcott's literary cosmopolitics places him alongside scholars who argue that Caribbean literature both is modernist and makes aesthetic and political claims to modernity—that is, it employs stylistic techniques associated with European modernist writing to claim a contemporaneous rather than belated historical and epistemological position in the world-system along with Europe and America. Simon Gikandi, for instance, discusses anglophone Caribbean literature within the literary problematic of modernism because "Caribbean writing is not so much motivated by the desire to recover an 'original' model [...] as by the need to inscribe Caribbean selves and voices within an economy of representation whose institutional and symbolic structures have been established since the 'discovery'" of the region by Christopher Columbus (*Limbo* 10). For Gikandi, Caribbean writing is more than an expression or manifestation of an already existing historical and cultural hybridity. The aesthetic register—inscription and production of "selves and voices" through writing—becomes an important intervention into the "economy of representation" of the "Caribbean imagination" that has set up "institutional and symbolic structures" made up of "its imposed metropolitan identity [Europe] and its desired ancestral image [Africa]," neither of which can be wholly realized or rejected (10). Gikandi tracks in "Caribbean fiction" a "shift from a dramatization of the power of the self and the uniqueness of its utterance" all the way to "a moment of a closure [in texts such as Michelle Cliff's *Abeng*] marked by silence and emptiness" (251). Thus, the images of lyrical polyvocality or representations of mythopoetic figures in Caribbean writing do not necessarily denote or refer to a fullness of hybrid histories and irrepressible identities that already exist or are coming into existence. Nor do the closures and reconciliations of the literary text "marked by silence and emptiness" point to a tidy summation or an ineffable void. Instead, in Gikandi's formulation, writing becomes one of "the contending discourses" in which "the existence of a gap in language affirms the continuing need for a narrative form that will take into account the contradictory impulses of Caribbean culture" and where "the underprivileged Caribbean subject will find and affirm its voice" (251). For Maria Cristina Fumagalli, a search for a suitable narrative form for Caribbean subjectivity is already moot, because "the Caribbean 'non-modern others' whom North Atlantic modernity creates and then petrifies, objectifies, abjectifies, and subalternizes do not desire to exist in its gaze but actually have and always have had a character and a purpose of their own as well as their own views on what it means to be modern" (9). Fumagalli implicitly revises Gikandi's argument about Caribbean literature by reading the modernist strategies of Caribbean writers not as a search *for* modernity but as an articulation *of* a modernity that already exists and is actively negotiating with local and Euro-American culture. If Caribbean writers such as Derek Walcott "foreground the mutual permeability between cultures" as part of a larger artistic project of "exchanging glances and unstitching the fixed viewpoints at the basis of North Atlantic narratives of modernity, which depend on the exploitation of non-modern 'others'" (Fumagalli 11), then we can apprehend Caribbean heterogeneity and hybridity valorized by critics such as Stuart Hall as part of a literary cosmopolitics rather than as an expression of postnational cultural subjectivity.

In fact, a cosmopolitical register is already present in the heterogeneous and polyvocal texture of Caribbean writing and interwoven with a critical national consciousness, because "since their inception, anglophone Caribbean literature and literary criticism have been the products of nationalist discourses designed to extend the political rights of Caribbeans," and that "after independence, the ability to produce national literature became a basis for claiming the right to determine national culture" (Rosenberg 3). Even critics who take a multilinguistic view of Caribbean literary production across the region as a whole concur that there has been a "recurrence of ideological propositions of national identity in the region from as far back as the nineteenth century" (Torres-Saillant 65). If, as Silvio Torres-Saillant argues, "European languages [. . .] are rendered new in the Caribbean, particularly in the hands of Caribbean writers who are in touch with the sociocultural specificity of their world" (82), the same can be said for European conceptualizations of the nation as a sociopolitical formation and of literature's imbrication with nationalism. For Derek Walcott, there is "no nation now but the imagination" ("The Schooner *Flight*," Canto 3, line 1), which suggests that European concepts of the nation must undergo a sea change; nationalism must be reconfigured anew in the Caribbean imagination rather than dismissed as an outdated legacy of European colonialism.

A Crystallization of Fragments:
Walcott's Lyric Poems

European colonialism and the neocolonial state of the nation immediately after decolonization must be interrogated by a negating and critical national consciousness to prevent a slide into nativist identity, as Frantz Fanon reminds us. With a Caribbean context, Walcott examines the relationship between colonialism's aftermath and critical nationality in a poetic idiom similar to what Theodor Adorno elsewhere describes as the characteristics of the modern artwork: a carefully crafted artifact that is always in a productive tension with its historical and political conditions of possibility. Consider this passage from *Minima Moralia,* in which Adorno likens literary texts to "spiders' webs" that are "tight, concentric, transparent, well-spun and firm":

> They draw into themselves all the creatures of the air. Metaphors flitting hastily through them become their nourishing prey. Subject matter comes winging toward them. The soundness of a conception can be judged by whether it causes one quotation to summon another. Where thought has opened up one cell of reality, it should, without violence by the subject, penetrate the next. It proves its relation to the object as soon as other objects crystallize around it. In the light that it casts on its chosen substance, others begin to glow. (*Minima Moralia* 87)

Here, the emphasis is on the tautness and yet openness of the form and structure of the artwork, like a spider's web; the artworks' capacity to "draw into themselves all the creatures of air" depends upon their "tight, concentric," and "firm" construction. For Adorno, productive artwork does two things: first, it negates the apparent wholeness and identity of those historical and political forces within which it finds itself. This explains the violent, predatory image of the artwork trapping "metaphors" (literary devices that rely upon the *identification* of a vehicle with a tenor) as "nourishing prey" for its own meaning-making. This recalls moments of similar negation and violence in *Aesthetic Theory*, where Adorno treats a work of art as "a thing that negates the world of things" (119); artworks are "a priori negative" because "they kill what they objectify by tearing it away from the immediacy of its life. Their own life preys on death" (133). But this symbolic violence neither abjures nor obliterates the represented objects (whether they are individuals, collectives, or political and historical events) because of the second important aspect of the artwork. Negation for Adorno means displacing or tearing objects from their contextual "immediacy" through representation and foregrounding the text's own status as a form of mediation. This framing medium is what catalyzes and motivates critical thought, and (looking back at the passage from *Minima Moralia*) it is not the artwork or the literary text itself that executes the penetration or the crystallization. Rather, it is "thought" that is activated once the immediacy of the object is torn away and put to death (i.e., once it becomes represented by the artwork), and thought that forms the nexus around which other objects (things that are represented in art) crystallize. Adorno develops this idea further in *Aesthetic Theory*, where the artwork is understood as a monad that is "both the result of the [dialectical] process and the process itself at a standstill," or, more concisely, "at once a force field and a thing" (179). In this way, "the monadological constitution of artworks in themselves points beyond itself" (*Aesthetic Theory* 180) and does not leave the artwork as a hermetic or self-enclosed, self-referential entity. Using the analogy of a spider's web, within the context of the Caribbean, Walcott's artwork draws the "subject matters" of national consciousness, historical events, cultural particularities, and radical politics into relational and penetrative articulation.

By arguing for a critical nationalist approach and connecting his aesthetics with modernist theories about art, my reading of Walcott's poetry takes issue with biographical interpretations of his work that focus on their transnational significance by tracing the poet's own transatlantic peregrinations from the 1970s to the 1990s. Bruce King, for example, suggests that Walcott traveled extensively in the United States and Europe because of marital problems and extramarital affairs.[1] Paul Breslin argues that the 1981 publication of *The Fortunate Traveller* marks "a restless decade of shuttling between the Caribbean and North America, with increasingly frequent trips to Europe as well" (216), and that the increase in poetic self-reflexiveness in Walcott's

---

1. See Bruce King, *Derek Walcott: A Caribbean Life*, chapters 19–23, for an exhaustive account of Walcott's personal life and career during this time period.

poetry from this period can be understood in terms of his "increased contact with U.S. writing and its intellectual ambience" as well as his "attenuated relation to the Caribbean, which deprived him of the naturalizing trope of an Antaeus-like power derived from place" (217). While such studies of Walcott's life history and career trajectory are informative, my own reading of his work focuses on the elaborations and reconfigurations of literary figures that are both naturalizing and exilic. In his shorter lyric poems, Walcott develops an understanding of the artwork as a physical and a temporal moment in which historical and political forces are crystallized and initiated as forceful thought by what he calls "the toil that is balance" (43). Using Walcott's conceptualization of artwork in the two shorter poems "Sea Grapes" and "To Return to Trees" as a key to reading his longer works *Another Life,* "The Schooner *Flight*," and *Omeros,* I argue that these two poems illuminate the interrelationship of art and life within the context of the postcolonial Caribbean, recasting nationalism as a critical consciousness against the authority of the neocolonial state and of global capital.

In the title poem of *Sea Grapes,* Walcott's speaker identifies the Caribbean with the Aegean of classical Greek literature and mythology. The first two stanzas of the poem take up the familiar, wandering figure of Odysseus on his journey back to Ithaca:

> That sail which leans on light,
> tired of islands,
> a schooner beating up the Caribbean
>
> for home, could be Odysseus,
> home-bound on the Aegean;
> that father and husband's
>
> longing, under gnarled sour grapes, is
> like the adulterer hearing Nausicaa's name
> in every gull's outcry ("Sea Grapes" 1–9)

The alliteration of "L" sounds in the first line gives us an impression of movement that is "light" in the physical sense of fleet-footedness. But the opening image qualifies that movement as "tired" and leaning, unable to stand upright or lacking strength; furthermore, the schooner's tiredness robs it of fleetness and becomes ominous when we are told that the schooner is "beating up the Caribbean." This phrase might suggest a plodding trudge, the pulsing of a heart strained with tension and worry, but could also mean physical assault and violence on the numerous "islands" of which it has grown weary. A further tension is introduced in the next two stanzas with the explicit evocation of Odysseus—the schooner, which began the poem as a vessel bearing the poetic force of the Caribbean, now becomes coded with the ambivalence associated with the famous Greek hero. The purposiveness of the schooner's homeward journey is now undermined by an Odyssean "longing" which is not "for home" but rather for "Nausicaa's name" and the detour of infidelity and illicit liaison. The formal breaks in the stanzas also disrupt the smooth flow of the sense of two important lines, namely "a schooner beating up the Caribbean // for home" (3–4) and "that father and husband's // longing" (6–7), heightening the uneasiness and disconnection of the initial identification between the Caribbean and the Aegean. The second half of the poem expands on the tension and violence implied in line 3 by evoking the Trojan War as a framework to discuss the purpose of literature and art:

> This brings nobody peace. The ancient war
> between obsession and responsibility
> will never finish and has been the same
>
> for the sea-wanderer or the one on shore
> now wriggling on his sandals to walk home,
> since Troy sighed its last flame,
>
> and the blind giant's boulder heaved the trough
> from whose groundswell the great hexameters come
> to the conclusions of exhausted surf.
>
> The classics can console. But not enough. ("Sea Grapes" 10–19)

Here Walcott's speaker argues that the evocation of a classical frame (that of the Trojan War) to discuss the Caribbean and its poetics is inadequate. "This brings nobody peace," he asserts, because the "age-old" question of art for art's sake (the "obsession" of the "adulterer") and that of social purpose and "responsibility" (the "father and husband's" duty) cannot be resolved. This irresolvable situation stems from the sheer enervation and loss of vitality in the form and content of the classical references themselves, or what the poem calls "the conclusions of exhausted surf." But the last line, made up of two short declarative sentences, stands as both a statement and a challenge: "The classics can console. But not enough" (18). If the classics offer "not enough" consolation regarding the purpose and meaningfulness of art because of their sheer enervation, then Walcott's poem suggests two possibilities: first, rephrase the question in a way other than the "ancient war / between obsession and responsibility"; second, find a different framework for conceptualizing a Caribbean poetics besides the identification with the Aegean and classical Greek verse evoked in this poem.

Both possibilities are illuminated and elaborated in another poem in this collection, "To Return to the Trees." Here, Walcott's speaker begins his conceptualization of the work of art by observing "not only the sea" (marking a departure from the maritime milieu of "Sea Grapes") but also "the changes on Morne Coco Mountain" (18) in Trinidad: "from flagrant sunrise / to its ashen end; / grey has grown strong to me, // it's no longer neutral, / no longer the dirty flag / of courage going under" ("To Return to the Trees" 19–24). On the one hand, the "flagrant sunrise" and the "ashen end" of Morne Coco Mountain parallel the rise and fall of Troy and classical Greek verse with their "last flame" and "exhausted surf," but in this poem, the "ashen end" of the twilight mountainscape becomes an inspiration: "grey has grown strong to me." Walcott's speaker's affirmation of this newfound sense of "grey" rejects the ambivalence of the "ancient war" between art for art's sake and art as responsibility that "brings nobody peace" in "Sea Grapes." Here, the artistic impulse is not rendered in terms of a "war" at all, as it "no longer" involves acts of martial valor or "courage going under." Instead, Walcott's poem envisions the "grey"ness of the work of art as "an immanent, crystallized process at a standstill" or "both the result of the process and the process itself at a standstill" (Adorno, *Aesthetic Theory* 180, 179). By process, Adorno refers to "the relation of [the artwork's] whole and parts" but "without [the whole and parts] being reducible to one side or the other" (178), and this is borne out in Walcott's lyric:

>   it is speckled with hues
>   like quartz, it's as
>   various as boredom,
>
>   grey now is a crystal
>   haze, a dull diamond,
>   stone-dusted and stoic,
>
>   grey is the heart at peace,
>   tougher than the warrior
>   as it bestrides factions ("To Return to the Trees" 25–33)

Formally speaking, the tercets of this poem contrast with those of "Sea Grapes" in that the sense of each unit is not broken or confounded by the stanza breaks. Moreover, each tercet bears an aphoristic quality that builds on the associations offered by the previous one: for example, "grey now is a crystal / haze, a dull diamond, / stone-dusted and stoic" draws on the description of "speckled" quartz in the previous stanza, and the adjective "stoic" in the last line prepares us for a shift in register from minerals to emotions in the next stanza, where grey becomes "the heart at peace." In other words, it is as if each stanza illustrates the crystalline quality both Walcott and Adorno ascribe to the work of art: for the poet, art is "a crystal / haze, a dull diamond," and for the philosopher, it is a "crystallized process at a standstill."

This sense of the work of art as a process at a delicate standstill is complemented by the poem's deft rendering of the enormous forces immanent to such a crystalline framework. An emphasis on the "crystalline" aspect of the artwork risks falling into an autotelic concept of art as self-sufficient and self-referential. But "To Return to the Trees" does not stop there, for it describes the "force field" aspect of the artwork just as well in the next three stanzas:

> it is the great pause
> when the pillars of the temple
> rest on Samson's palms
>
> and are held, held,
> that moment
> when the heavy rock of the world
>
> like a child sleeps
> on the trembling shoulders of Atlas
> and his own eyes close,
>
> the toil that is balance. ("To Return to the Trees" 34–43)

Here, Walcott's poem draws on biblical as well as Greek mythological references, but unlike the story of Odysseus in "Sea Grapes," these references are incorporated into the poem's relational scheme rather than forming a larger interpretive framework for the lyric. The biblical allusion to how "the pillars of the temple / rest on Samson's palms" recalls the crystalline structure of the artwork in the image of a man standing with his palms supporting two pillars, but our thoughts, set in motion by the Old Testament allusion, cannot miss the cataclysmic force of Samson's strength that is deferred and yet heightened by "the great pause" of the poem. Similarly, the childlike sleep of the "the heavy rock of the world" upon "the trembling shoulders of Atlas" belies the mythical giant's own impending slumber and possible release of his burden. The "grey"ness of art, which has grown strong in both Walcott's mind and verse, becomes that moment where such a catastrophic release can be figured and comprehended in thought, deferred but also precipitous. To put it another way, Walcott's speaker expounds on the color grey—by this point in his lyric standing both for the crafting of poetry and for the form of poetry itself—to give us a breathtaking analogy of how historical, political, and social forces (represented by the pillars in Samson's palms and the world on Atlas's shoulders) are immanent to the artwork. Thought itself is catalyzed once we recognize in the apparent harmony and fullness of the whole artwork the laborious relations and telling gaps between the work's constitutive parts, or, "the toil that is balance."

"The Fervour and Intelligence of a Whole Country": ANOTHER LIFE

The balance between nationalism and cosmopolitics that Walcott strives to achieve is expressed in autobiographical and aesthetic terms in his first long narrative poem, *Another Life* (1972). Walcott focuses on his home country of St. Lucia and emphasizes the important role that artists and writers play in forming a national consciousness vis-à-vis the island nation's colonial history, its neocolonial state, and global capital. This can be seen from the metaphors he uses to describe both his artistic mission and his vision of St. Lucia at the opening of the poem: "Verandahs, where the pages of the sea / are a book left open by an absent master / in the middle of another life— / I begin here again" (*AL* 1–4). The physical space of the "verandahs," which are threshold spaces between the inside and outside areas of houses in tropical regions, and the rustling waves sounding like open "pages of the sea" that surround St. Lucia become metaphors for the writing of poetry, and this writing will offer "another life" that Walcott must "begin here again." By "here" Walcott refers not only to the beginning of the poem itself but also to his home country of St. Lucia with its colonial history and postcolonial present. This double significance is borne out in the next stanza, where Walcott's gaze moves from the sea onto the landscape of the island marked by British colonialism: "as a sun, tired of empire, declined. / It mesmerized like fire without wind, / and as its amber climbed / the beer-stein ovals of the British fort / above the promontory, the sky / grew drunk with light"

(*AL* 11–16). Walcott plays on the common saying that "the sun never sets on the British empire" by personifying the sun itself as growing "tired" of British colonialism. Instead of being a symbol associated with colonialism, the sun's "amber" light becomes part of the elemental forces of the island, "mesmeriz[ing]" and inspiring Walcott the poet "like fire," and it finally makes the sky itself "drunk with light." The reference to light here is not only a visual image but a reminder of the luminous connotations of the island's name, St. Lucia. Walcott portrays St. Lucia's natural landscape as a fiery and illuminating inspiration for his poetry that will rise above European colonialism, with "the British fort" and its rotund, "beer-stein ovals" suggesting a colonial lifestyle of military conquest and excessive luxury. The economic exploitation of St. Lucia is compared to a physical dismemberment of the land itself, as Walcott observes later in the poem: "the island quartered / into baronial estates, gone, gone, / their golden bugled epoch. / Aubrey Smith characters in khaki helmets, / Victorian flourish of oratorical moustaches" (*AL* 902–6). The repetition and alliteration of "gone, gone" and "their golden bugled epoch" emphasizes the swift demise of the British colonial aristocracy with their "baronial" land and monetary holdings. Walcott also mocks this aristocracy with his reference to Charles Aubrey Smith, a British actor famous for playing military and aristocratic characters in early twentieth-century films. He makes the British colonizers seem larger than life, out of time and place with their "Victorian flourish[es]," and ridiculously pompous and self-important, such that it is their bristling "moustaches" rather than their voices that are "oratorical." However, Walcott also depicts how colonialism has imprinted itself onto the patriotic identity of St. Lucia sponsored by the postcolonial state in a classroom exchange between a schoolmaster and his students:

> "Boy! Name the great harbours of the world!"
> "Sydney! Sir."
> "San Franceesco!"
> "Naples, sah!"
> "And what about Castries?"
> "Sah, Castries ees a coaling station and
> der twenty-seventh best harba in der worl'!
> In eet the entire Breetesh Navy can be heeden!"
> "What is the motto of St. Lucia, boy?"
> "*Statio haud malefida carinis.*"
> "Sir!"

"Sir!"
"And what does that mean?"
"Sir, a safe anchorage for sheeps!" (690–703)

Walcott's satirical humor is evident in the contrast between the schoolmaster's stentorian questions and the students' answers, rendered in vernacular speech. Furthermore, national and colonial authority are ironically undermined by the students' sincere and enthusiastic responses. Not only is Castries, the port capital of St. Lucia, a "coaling station," but it can hide "the entire Breetesh Navy," which, rendered in a student's voice, becomes a cowardly herd of "sheeps" instead of a mighty fleet of ships. Walcott satirizes the idea of a national identity expressed as a motto given by colonial authority, or what he calls in an earlier essay the formula of politics.

But the most pernicious effect of colonialism for Walcott is the creation of an instrumental nationality in the hands of Caribbean politicians and intellectuals. They become enamored with the Muse of History and instill in the people they govern a sense of constant suffering and victimization as perpetually colonized subjects, while at the same time lining their own pockets with the power and wealth of political office. In *Another Life,* Walcott expands on the criticism of the Muse of History he advanced in his earlier essay of the same name, arguing that in St. Lucia art itself has become an excuse for a collective fixation on colonialism and slavery, because there are "Too many penitential histories passing / for poems" (*AL* 3444–45). Walcott warily observes "the process of history machined through fact / for the poet's cheap alcohol, / lines like the sugarcane factory's mechanization of myth / ground into rubbish" (*AL* 3447–50), a sentiment that reminds us of Theodor Adorno's cautions regarding the instrumentalization of culture and the transformation of Enlightenment thought into a myth that it was supposed to overcome. Walcott provides a specific Caribbean context for the instrumental rationalization of thought and culture Adorno was concerned about by using an analogy of one of the primary industries associated with the colonial and neocolonial economy in St. Lucia, namely the "sugarcane factory" and its "mechanization of" not only sugarcane but "myth" itself. St. Lucia's postindependence government, like Trinidad's under Eric Williams and his national slogan of "Discipline, Production, Tolerance," becomes a highly efficient economic apparatus that manufactures sugar, alcohol, and—on a cultural register—a persistent myth of social and national marginalization. This stands in contrast to the efforts of Walcott's teacher and friend, Harry Simmons, a local painter who tries to portray the everyday life, struggles, and survival of ordinary St. Lucians. Toward the end of *Another Life,* however, Walcott learns that Simmons committed suicide out of despair, and the poet criticizes the St. Lucian state's economic opportunism as opposed to his mentor's artistic attempts to create a national consciousness among the St. Lucian people.

> all o'dem big boys, so, dem ministers,
> ministers of culture, ministers of development,
> the green blacks, and their old toms,
> and all the syntactical apologists of the Third World
> explaining why their artists die,
> by their own hands, Magicians of the New Vision.
> Screaming the same shit.
> Those who peel, from their own leprous flesh, their names,
> who chafe and nurture the scars of rusted chains,
> like primates favouring scabs, those who charge tickets
> for another free ride on the middle-passage,
> those who explain to the peasant why he is African (*AL* 2946–57)

Walcott sees "dem ministers" of St. Lucia as "syntactical apologists" who rhetorically and economically position his country into the category of the "Third World," thus turning St. Lucia into a marginalized Third World country dependent on Europe and America for its economic sustenance. Walcott emphasizes that these politicians are cunning persuaders or "Magicians," who try to "explain to the peasant why he is African" rather than St. Lucian by deciding to "chafe and nurture the scars of rusted chains" that metaphorically recall the physical and psychic violence of slavery and colonialism, thus binding the people of St. Lucia to historical bondage even after independence. This emphasis on a specific identity of African abjection in the form of perpetually recalled slavery is part of the state's economic exploitation of its people, such that the state "charge[s] tickets for another free ride on the middle-passage." In short, instead of promoting "development" and "culture," St. Lucia's state ministers regress the island and its people back into colonial enslavement while they line their own pockets, as seen from the phrase "green blacks" that plays off the slang term for U.S. currency "greenback." Moreover, these ministers wish to create a "New Vision" for St. Lucia, "a new art" that will result in their local "artists" such as Harry Simmons "dying in the old way" (*AL* 2966–67) through official rejection and dismissal. The "new art" these ministers demand transforms St. Lucian national culture into commodities to be readily consumed and circulated in the culture industry of globalization:

> They had not changed, they knew only
> the autumnal hint of hotel rooms
> the sea's engine of air-conditioners,
> and the waitress in national costume
> and the horsemen galloping past the single wave
> across the line of Martinique, the horse or *la mer*
> out of Gauguin by the Tourist Board.
> Hotel, hotel, hotel, hotel, hotel, and a club: The Bitter End. (3572–79)

Here, St. Lucia's national culture is reduced to "the waitress in national costume," an object of a thriving tourist industry in St. Lucia, an industry whose proliferation is signified by the monotonous repetition of "hotel, hotel, hotel, hotel, hotel" as well as the objectification of St. Lucia's neighboring country Martinique as a replica of Gauguin's painting, possibly commissioned by St. Lucia's own "Tourist Board." In the hands of neocolonial politicians, gripped by instrumental nationality, Walcott's home country of St. Lucia is threatened with the "Bitter End" of becoming a series of hotels and a club for foreign tourists instead of building a progressive and liberating society with the goal of improving the lot of its people.

Faced with such instrumental nationality expressed through the state's formula of politics, artists such as Harry Simmons, and his students Derek Walcott and Dunstan St. Omer, offer an aesthetic counterpoint of national consciousness that is always intimately connected with the lives of the St. Lucians whom they live among and represent in their paintings and poetry. Yet given the marginalization of local art in favor of the beautification of St. Lucia for the tourist economy, this artistic practice is fraught and fragile, as Walcott reveals in his description of Simmons's predicament:

> Now, where he had beheld
> a community of graceful spirits
> irradiating from his own control and centre,
> through botany, history, lepidoptery, stamps,
> his mind was cracking like the friable earth,
> and in each chasm,
> sprung nettles like the hands of certain friendships. (*AL* 2771–77)

Walcott describes Simmons's artistic methods in terms that recall the luminous symbolism of St. Lucia's name. Like the sun that grew tired of the British Empire at the beginning of the poem, Simmons's paintings conjure the people around him as "a community of graceful spirits / irradiating" or emanating from and inspired by his artwork. Simmons's paintings represent St. Lucians through his meticulous observation of their lives and their surroundings, as can be seen from his studies in "botany, history, lepidoptery, stamps," rather than being compelled by the edicts of economic and cultural development issued by the state ministers and the Tourist Board. But, despite the illumination of his paintings, Simmons and the radiating national consciousness he represents are infected by the "leprous flesh" and "scabs" of the ministers of culture and development, false friends whose handshakes are as stinging as "nettles," such that Simmons's mind begins "cracking like the friable earth," unable to nurture the spirit of his people as it crumbles. The simile Walcott uses here to compare Simmons's despair to crumbling earth is significant, as it serves as a contrast to the vivifying and inclusive national consciousness that Simmons represents in his paintings, expressed here through the metaphor of a commonplace earthenware bowl or jug:

> People entered his understanding
> like a wayside country church,
> they had built him themselves.
> It was they who had smoothed the wall
> of his clay-coloured forehead,
> who made of his rotundity an earthy
> useful object
> holding the clear water of their simple troubles, (*AL* 3135–42)

But Harry Simmons's death is not in vain; it paradoxically allows him to live on in the hearts and minds of St. Lucians, for Walcott avers that "he is a man no more / but the fervour and intelligence / of a whole country" (*AL* 3150–52). Walcott elaborates what he learned from Harry Simmons, namely an "understanding" that artists bear a responsibility to the "people" of their community, and that this responsibility can be understood in national terms: "They had built him themselves," Walcott says, and Simmons's life and work becomes "the fervour and intelligence of a whole country." Harry Simmons's art does not resolve the "simple troubles" of the people, unlike the ministers of culture and development who want to resolve social and cultural issues by enforcing a St. Lucian national identity centered on Africa. Instead, the metaphor of Simmons himself as a "clay-coloured" and "earthy useful object" that nonetheless embodies the "fervour and intelligence" of St. Lucia itself reminds us of the broken vase that is lovingly reassembled in Walcott's Nobel Prize speech, itself an analogy of the care and pain of national consciousness taking shape in each Caribbean country. Walcott's comparison of the people's troubles as clear water carried by the earthenware vessel of Simmons's art, and of broken fragments reassembled into a scarred and battered vase, suggests the artists' belief in the power of poetry to reconfigure or form a constellation of culture, politics, and history that make up the nation of St. Lucia.

Although Harry Simmons might be dead, his two students inherit his mantle of a critical national consciousness that is represented through painting and poetry and that draws on the vibrant and vivid particularities of St. Lucia's landscape and society. Dunstan St. Omer, Walcott's fellow student and friend whom he christens Gregorias in *Another Life*, "possessed / aboriginal force and it came / as the carver comes out of the wood. / Now, every landscape we entered / was already signed with his name" (1380–84). St. Omer's art is at once "aboriginal" and autochthonous in his robust renditions of St. Lucia's landscapes, and, "as the carver comes out of the wood," these landscapes also shape St. Omer himself in a fashion similar to the ordinary people who had built Harry Simmons's artistic vision like a wayside church. Walcott, who "lived in a different gift, / its element metaphor" (*AL* 1355–56), describes his gift in terms that recall the idea of poetry as a crystallization of different elements in his own lyric poem "To Return to the Trees" as well as in Theodor Adorno's aesthetic musings: "in every surface I sought / the paradoxical flash of an instant / in which every facet was caught / in a crystal of ambiguities" (*AL* 1348–51). If St. Omer's paintings express the muscular and aboriginal power of St. Lucia's natural landscape, Walcott's poetry evinces the crystallizing and relational constellation of St. Lucia's society, history, and culture in which precolonial, colonial, and postindependence St. Lucia are drawn together and crafted anew through Walcott's poetic vision. As he avers in a passage that combines Christian belief that is prevalent in present-day St. Lucia and the memory of an older, pre-Columbus native culture: "The Church upheld the Word, but this new Word / was here, attainable / to my own hand, / in the deep country it found the natural man, / generous, rooted" (*AL* 979–83). The "new Word" Walcott has attained by his own hand is not a divine command from the mouth of the Christian God but a poetic language that can challenge the "New Vision" foisted on St. Lucians by their ministers of culture and development by seeking out and finding a "generous, rooted" past obscured by colonialism, slavery, and now neocolonialism. The "natural man" refers, on the one hand, to the original Arawak and Carib inhabitants of St. Lucia, but, on the other, it also recalls the generous and rooted nature of Harry Simmons's art and his dedication to the people living in present-day St. Lucia. Certainly, Walcott is not replacing the Afrocentric identity promoted by the state ministers in favor of one centered on resurrecting an authentic Arawak or Carib past, as we see here:

> here was a life older than geography,
> as the leaves of edible roots opened their pages
> at the child's last lesson, Africa, heart-shaped,
>
> and the lost Arawak hieroglyphs and signs
> were razed from slates by sponges of the rain,
> their symbols mixed with lichen,
>
> the archipelago like a broken root
> divided among tribes, while trees and men
> laboured assiduously, silently to become
>
> whatever their given sounds resembled, (1233–42)

Walcott's image of Africa as an "edible root" and a "heart-shaped" lesson for the St. Lucian child may at first glance suggest a diasporic longing for Africa. Similarly, the evocation of "lost Arawak hieroglyphs and signs" could be read as a recovery of a native identity before colonialism, "a life older than geography." But Walcott reminds us that the "symbols" of Arawak culture have been "razed from slates by sponges of rain," while the memory of Africa is "like a broken root / divided among tribes." Neither image suggests the possibility of recovering or reestablishing either an African or an Arawak identity for the nation, although both remain, like "opened pages" and "mixed" patches of "lichen," as part of St. Lucia's collective history and cultural dispensation. What is more important for Walcott in this passage is the idea of "trees and men" who "laboured assiduously" to create a new life and identity from the given conditions on the ground, or "whatever their given sounds resembled." The visual, static images of leaves, pages, and hieroglyphs early in the passage are no longer "silently" suffering, but, through Walcott's assiduous poetic and cultural labor, become "given sounds" as they are given a voice and an utterance. Finally, without forgetting the aboriginal inhabitants or the history of slavery and indentured servitude, Walcott brings the renewal of St. Lucia's natural landscape and its culture and society to an apotheosis: "Gregorias, listen, lit, / we were the light of the world! / We were blest with a virginal, unpainted world / with Adam's task of giving things their names" (*AL* 3624–27). In this concluding passage Walcott plays again on the name of his nation—St. Lucia—and its symbolic associations with brightness and illumination as well as the spiritual task of the Caribbean artist to rejuvenate the world around him by naming things afresh. The island's appellation connotes both the European Enlightenment and the divine light of European Christianity, which Walcott acknowledges when he exclaims that he and Gregorias

/ St. Omer "were the light of the world." But this gesture toward Europe is qualified by the next two lines, in which Walcott reminds himself and his readers that the figure of Adam he invokes is a "new" figure entirely, not simply the first man of biblical provenance. Walcott's is not a religious or evangelical but an aesthetic and epistemological "task of giving things their names," of redefining through painting and poetry the objective reality of the Caribbean nature and culture that was hypostasized through colonialism's instrumental rationality and neocolonialism's determinative identity. In *Another Life* Walcott reenvisions the island as a nation not determined by an Afrocentric racial identity or social and economic marginalization promoted by the state for the benefit of the tourist industry. Walcott draws inspiration for his national consciousness from the poetic craft of local artists such as his mentor Harry Simmons instead of the political vision of state ministers such as Trinidad's Eric Williams. In so doing he is able to recognize how St. Lucia is a community made up of multiple peoples, histories, and cultures that are indigenous and hail from other lands, and to reveal the unevenness and the problems facing the nation as a social formation and a political collective.

Walcott does not resolve these difficulties by dissolving or deterritorializing the nation into diaspora; instead, he sounds a cautiously optimistic note, or what he calls "teetering and tough in unabashed unhope" (*AL* 3594), similar to that raised in his earlier essay "Society and the Artist": nationalism does not revolve around "quick political achievements" but involves "the deepening stream of the way we are now learning to think," to think about "the possibilities of the new country we are making" (15). In *Another Life*, Walcott works out a poetic practice drawn explicitly from his mentor Harry Simmons's and implicitly from Theodor Adorno's ideas about the modernist artwork. In so doing, he articulates a critical St. Lucian national consciousness, laying the ground for a literary cosmopolitics in his later work that moves beyond the shores of St. Lucia onto the regional space of the Caribbean in "The Schooner *Flight*," and the black Atlantic as a historical and a cultural expanse connecting Europe and the Caribbean in both *Omeros* and *The Prodigal*.

"Either I'm Nobody, or I'm a Nation":
Caribbean Literary Cosmopolitics in "The Schooner *Flight*"

The national and historical significance of these figures is further elaborated in Walcott's long poem "The Schooner *Flight*," which begins his collection *The Star-Apple Kingdom* (1979). The poem tracks its speaker, Shabine, a sailor of mixed European and African ancestry, as he journeys on the schooner *Flight* from various islands and places in the Caribbean, and marks Shabine's encounters and engagements with the history of colonial conquest, slavery, and revolutionary independence throughout these islands. The poem ends with the *Flight* engulfed in a sudden storm, and a transfigured Shabine delivering his benediction to the islands "from the depths of the sea" (Canto 11, line 51). Paul Breslin connects the poem's genesis closely with the poet's personal difficulties with his marriage as well as the Trinidad Theatre Company, such that "knowing the circumstances, one can hardly help reading the poem as grounded in autobiography, preoccupied as it is with the sundering of ties to marriage and nation and with a quest for self-transformation" (11.189). While "The Schooner *Flight*" does distance itself from any explicit national identification, nonetheless the self-transformation that Breslin suggests may be thought of as a rearticulation of nationalism, or the relationships between self, culture, and politics within a transnational framework, rather than a complete sundering of the self through poetic disavowal. I suggest "The Schooner *Flight*" illustrates a literary cosmopolitics, first, by reiterating the aesthetic ideas that I inferred from in Walcott's earlier poems, and second, by invoking figures who represent the dominant concepts of diasporic hybridity and then reconfiguring them to reveal the continued salience of nationalism as political consciousness and cultural critique rather than as a determinate ethnic or racial identity.

In formal terms, the poem begins with an image of the departing Shabine standing in the yard of his lover's house that recalls Walcott's elaboration of "grey" as a simultaneously crystalline and motive structure in "To Return to the Trees":

> Out in the yard turning grey in the dawn,
> I stood like a stone and nothing else move
> but the cold sea rippling like galvanize
> and the nail holes of stars in the sky roof,
> till the wind start to interfere with the trees. (1.6–10)

Shabine and his surroundings are caught in a frozen instant, poised on the verge of portentous movement. Even the sea and stars have their apparent motions described in ways that reinforce their solidity and stillness in physical terms: the sea is "rippling" like "galvanize[d]" metal, while the stars are like "nail holes" pierced in "the sky roof." This description of Shabine standing "like a stone" in the yard "turning grey in the dawn" immediately signals to us that we are not in the presence of an autobiographical self; in other words, Shabine is a figure who is part of the poem's aesthetic force, "stone-dusted and stoic" (to use a phrase from "To Return to the Trees") rather than a stand-in for Walcott himself. Furthermore, the "wind" that snaps the stillness of this passage and sets the poem in motion is the same wind that will have an important part to play in Shabine's role as both a sailor and a poet, as he says at the end of canto 1: "my common language go be the wind" (75). For Shabine, poetry is an act of imagination and articulation immanently associated with his own vocation as a sailor rather than a transcendental vision that lifts him out of the lifeworld of the poem. Toward the end of the first canto of the poem Shabine adopts the register of shipboard labor to describe his own poetic craft:

> [. . .] Well, when I write
> each phrase go be soaked in salt;
> I go draw and knot every line as tight
> as ropes in this rigging; in simple speech
> my common language go be the wind,
> my pages the sails of the schooner *Flight*. (1.71–76)

The image or conceptual metaphor of the ship has become important in postcolonial and cultural studies ever since Paul Gilroy introduced it as a Bakhtinian chronotope in his groundbreaking transnational project *The Black Atlantic*. However, the eponymous schooner in Walcott's text does not serve as such a chronotope, and in fact challenges some of Gilroy's premises. Although Gilroy offers an important transnational perspective that challenges what he calls the "cultural insiderism" of nationalizing narratives (3), Walcott's poem questions the claim that "the image of ships in motion across the spaces between Europe, America, Africa, and the Caribbean" forms "a central organising principle for this enterprise" which is "the rhizomorphic, fractal structure of the transcultural, international formation" Gilroy terms "the black Atlantic" (4). "The Schooner *Flight*" does not "focus attention on the middle passage, on the various projects for redemptive return to an African homeland" (Gilroy 4). As we shall see later in the poem, Shabine's own encounter with the Middle Passage in canto 5 is not one of remembrance or commemoration. For now, what is important in the lines from canto 1 cited earlier is the artistic conjunction of two figures—sailor and ship—through the deceptively "simple speech" of poetic structure. This conjunction, however, stops short of identifying or reducing the craft of the poet to the work of a sailor, because it does not reduce the poem as artwork to life or the circumstances that allow the creation of art. In other words, while sailing becomes an analogy for elaborating the work of poetic art (seen, for example, in the simile "draw and knot every line as tight / as ropes in this rigging") Shabine does not employ the ship as an overarching metaphor for the poem; thus there is no identification between the tenor of the poem and the vehicle of the ship. Instead, the comparison of Shabine's working out of a poem to his working onboard a ship recalls the descriptions of Samson and Atlas in "To Return to the Trees": all three figures are intimately connected with physical objects, and the conjunction of the figure with the object generates a motive force. For Shabine, unlike Samson and Atlas, this force is more explicit in its purpose, for it is Shabine's "common language" that will propel the *Flight* and the poem along, for this language will be the "wind" that blows "the sails of the schooner."

Thematically, canto 1 also challenges the focus on Caribbean identity as hybrid or creolized. In a well-known passage from the middle of canto 1, Shabine narrates the origin of his name and his background:

> a rusty head sailor with sea-green eyes
> that they nickname Shabine, the patois
> for any red nigger, and I, Shabine, saw
> when these slums of empire was paradise.
> I'm just a red nigger who love the sea,
> I had a sound colonial education,
> I have Dutch, nigger, and English in me,
> and either I'm nobody, or I'm a nation. (1.36–43)

Shabine turns out to be a local appellation for "any red nigger," and this description may suggest that he stands for the mixed-race inhabitants of the Caribbean. But this can be refuted on two counts. First, the poem emphasizes that Shabine is a figure of *poiesis* (like Samson and Atlas in "The Return to Trees") rather than an identity position who corresponds to Walcott himself or to any actually existing individual or collective subjects. Second, a formal analysis of lines 39 through 43 challenges the claim that the sea-loving Shabine is representative of Caribbean hybridity because he has "Dutch, nigger, and English" in him and that this makes him, if not a "nobody," then someone who stands for "a nation" of racial and cultural heterogeneity. Rhetorically, the first three lines are marked by asyndeton: no conjunctions join them in a causal or subordinating relationship, thus the fourth line "and either I'm nobody, or I'm a nation," does not necessarily follow as a result of the mixing of "Dutch, nigger, and English" in the preceding line. Moreover, the ABAB rhyme scheme points us to the feminine rhyme of "education" with "I'm a nation" that suggests Shabine's national consciousness emerges not because of the mixing of European and African ancestry, but rather from the "sound colonial education" he received. From this perspective, national consciousness becomes more a matter of knowledge, learning, and art rather than ancestry and race, and this point is emphasized later in the canto where Shabine avers that "I loved them, my children, my wife, my home; / I loved them as poets love the poetry / that kills them, as drowned sailors the sea" (1.67–69). Shabine's love and affection for his family and home are expressed not in patriotic sentiments, but instead in artistic terms of death and violence that recall Theodor Adorno's discussion of how the "life" of artworks "preys on death" and how "they kill what they objectify by tearing it away from the immediacy of its life" (*Aesthetic Theory* 133). The schooner *Flight* (with its name suggesting the release or "flight" of thought), together with Shabine (himself a figurative poet participating in the elaborative process of Walcott's poem), eventually succumbs to this predatory aspect of the artwork that objectifies aspects of reality and sets in motion a process of thought that "opens up one cell of reality" and then "penetrate[s] the next" (Adorno, *Minima Moralia* 87). Moreover, Walcott's poem does not espouse a transnational identification or subject position premised on the history of transatlantic slavery. This is illustrated most clearly in Shabine's refusal to sympathize with or lament the suffering of the multitudes of slaves he and the *Flight* encounter in canto 5.

Contrary to Paul Gilroy's use of the chronotope of ships in *The Black Atlantic,* Walcott's Shabine's identification with the African slaves brought across the Middle Passage is not as strong or pronounced as his affinity for the sailors working on board the ships commanded by famous historical admirals. In this canto the *Flight* encounters two fleets of ghostly ships, the first being "a rustling forest of ships / with sails dry like paper" (5.9–10), setting up an auditory as well as thematic resonance with the schooner *Flight,* which has as its sails the pages of Shabine's own poetry. Shabine sees "great admirals" on the deck such as "Rodney, Nelson, de Grasse," but more importantly focuses on "the hoarse orders / they gave those Shabines" (5.16–18) under their command. But when Shabine sees the next fleet of "slave ships" flying "flags of all nations" with "our fathers below deck too deep [. . .] / to hear us shouting" (5.29–30), his response is muted, pensive, even noncommittal. Shabine supposes that their ancestral fathers cannot hear the shouting of their present-day descendants since they are physically and temporally "too deep," and his response is to "stop shouting" entirely (5.31). The poet-sailor then shrugs off the entire encounter with a dismissive question: "Who knows / who his grandfather is, much less his name?" (5.31–32). Here, Shabine cuts off any nostalgia or diasporic longing for a real or imagined Africa as the land of "our fathers" with his refusal to search for or ponder his genealogical roots. More important is the poem's questioning of the routed form of transnationalism implicit in Gilroy's concept of the black Atlantic with its "flags of all nations." In other words, Shabine is part of the poem's literary cosmopolitics that takes up and extends Gilroy's chronotope of being "rooted in and routed through the special stress that grows with the effort involved in trying to face (at least) two ways at once" (3). This may become clearer when we remember that Shabine focuses on "those Shabines," his predecessors who work on board naval vessels rather than the slaves held captive in the holds of slaving vessels. At one level, Shabine may represent the actual, hybrid peoples of the Caribbean and the actual descendants of these slaves from Africa. But what is important here is that his "memory revolve[s] / on all sailors before [him]" (5.26–27). The poem foregrounds, through Shabine's memory, the vocational expertise of those sailors "before" or preceding Shabine, extending a diasporic identity into a professional camaraderie and also (given the structural intertwining of Shabine's poetic craft and his maritime skills) emphasizing the importance of such craft and skills over any rooting in or routing through the Middle Passage.

"The Schooner *Flight*" thus offers an artistic rendering of Shabine and the schooner as figures of poetic thought rather than representational subjects, and it is the movement of these two figures in the time and space of the poem that enacts the work's intertwining of national consciousness and cosmopolitics. The poem expresses a clear disappointment with and disapproval of the authority figures who govern the various Caribbean nation-states by linking oppressive nationalism and corrupt government with the only explicitly hybrid figure: Shabine's former employer O'Hara. O'Hara is a "big government man" (2.1) and is described as a "minister-monster who smuggled the booze" (2.24) and "a half-Syrian saurian" (2.25). The alliteration of "minister" and "monster" and the sibilance of "half-Syrian saurian" emphasize how O'Hara's hybridity becomes a savage and bestial bastardization rather than a liberating or emancipative mixing of races and roles. Furthermore, in canto 9, as the *Flight* approaches Dominica, Shabine and his shipmate Vince have a conversation about modernization and "Progress," in which Vince delightfully exclaims that "One day go be planes only, no more boat" (9.5), to which Shabine retorts that "Progress leaving all we small islands behind" (9.8) and that if they were to ask the original Carib inhabitants of the Dominica they would find that Progress had "kill[ed] them by millions, some in war, / some by forced labour dying in the mines" (9.12–13). "Progress" does not lead to any tangible improvement, but becomes "history's dirty joke"

(9.16): it becomes a euphemism for the history of conquest, massacre, and subjugation of the Caribbean peoples, and an obscene and "dirty" reminder of the regression (as opposed to progression) of neocolonial regimes where ministers such as O'Hara have not been "guardians of the poor" (2.21) but instead "smuggled the booze" for their own pleasure. Despite this express hostility toward the governments of these Caribbean countries, the poem nonetheless cherishes national consciousness and the liberating promise of nationalism, and this critical consciousness and political promise are presented in artistically evocative language rather than rousing political speech. Canto 3, "Shabine Leaves the Republic," seems to suggest a departure from the political and national community of Trinidad, identified earlier as "The Limer's Republic" (2.34). The canto begins with Shabine's famous declaration that "I had no nation now but the imagination" (3.1), which may be read not as a refutation of nationalism but rather as a reconfiguring of nationalism as a problematic in aesthetic and imaginative terms. In other words, Walcott's poem critiques the either-or dilemma in which progress and neocolonial regimes have trapped popular nationalism "between / the Police Marine Branch and Hotel Venezuela" (3.23–24), and therefore no political solution presents itself unless the terms of the dilemma are recast. Although Walcott's poem does not explicitly schematize such a revision, the poetic and visionary rendering of both Maria Concepcion and the young men in canto 3 might point to certain pertinent aspects. Even though Shabine declares "I no longer believed in the revolution" (3.20), his lack of political conviction is immediately linked with another, personal loss in the next line: "I was losing faith in the love of my woman" (3.21). The political inflection of love and romance in canto 3 affects the resolution of the relationship between Shabine and Maria Concepcion at the end of the poem, where, after the storm, Shabine sees "the veiled face of Maria Concepcion / marrying the ocean, then drifting away" (11.360). Shabine's relationship with Maria is transformed from anxiety and doubt into acceptance and release, as the focus of his amorous problems becomes part of "the ocean"; we might infer that the acceptance and release of Maria will allow for a corresponding acceptance and release of the political dilemma that led Shabine to lose faith in "the revolution" in canto 3.

In fact, the "young men" who mobilize against the state police and the Hotel Venezuela are described in terms similar to Maria Concepcion at the end of the poem:

> Young men without flags
> using shirts, their chests waiting for holes.
> They kept marching into the mountains, and

> their noise ceased as foam sinks into sand.
> They sank in the bright hills like rain, every one
> in his own nimbus, leaving shirts in the street,
> and the echo of power at the end of the street. (3.25–31)

At the most obvious level, this can be read as a lament for the utter defeat of mass political mobilization, emphasizing Shabine's loss of faith in organized revolution mentioned above. Also, the poetic transformation of the "young men" who (it is implied) are killed or otherwise neutralized by the government into a gentle shower of "rain" that "sank in the bright hills" or as "foam" that "sinks into sand" may be read as evading or romanticizing the pressing issues of oppression and state violence. However, in these passages Maria and the young men are not beautified so that readers may affirm or exhort their dignity or passion in the face of implacable violence. Rather, their affective transformation into a visionary or mythopoetic condition points out a glaring lack and inadequacy of both alternatives in the either-or dilemma of Trinidad society caught between the Police Marine Branch and Hotel Venezuela. Certainly the young men seem to have been chastened and routed by the repressive state apparatus, but the poem represents their "shirts in the street" and "the echo of power at the end of the street" as a legacy that haunts and disturbs the neocolonial regime, such that in "the Senate," "the judges, they say, still sweat in carmine" (3.32, 33). It is the authority figures in the repressive state who suffer, sweat, and bleed, whereas the young men have each turned into a "nimbus," an aura or glow that represents the diffusion of national consciousness, like rain falling on "the bright hills." This metaphor of rain is taken up once more at the end of the poem, where the transformed Shabine finds that "across [his] own face, like the face of the sun / a light rain was falling" (11.8–9) and invokes a similar benediction upon the Caribbean islands: "Fall gently, rain, on the sea's upturned face / like a girl showering; make these islands fresh / as Shabine once knew them!" (11.10–12). Maria, the young men, and ultimately Shabine himself are poetically rendered into motive forces: Maria is "drifting away" with her marriage to the ocean, the young men sink like foam but fall like rain over the countryside, and Shabine, after his benediction of rainfall "from this bowsprit" of the *Flight* (11.26), settles down into a state of work and rest that again recalls artwork's crystallization and field of force. This can be seen from the way Shabine ends the poem in a state of physical work and intellectual learning while blending and "cotching" (propping up against something) with the schooner's armature: "I stop talking now. I work, then I read, / cotching under a lantern hooked to the mast" (11.43–44). Walcott, in "The Schooner

Flight," renders historical and political forces into artistic and transformative figures such as Shabine and the schooner itself. In doing so, he shows us an aesthetic mode of critical nationality that does not alight upon an identity position for ethnic absolutism or cultural insiderism. Instead, it enables a literary cosmopolitics that eschews identity thinking in favor of an imagination that is not tied to any one nation but is at the same time politically and culturally engaged with the various nations Shabine encounters as he traverses the Caribbean. In *Omeros,* to which I now turn, Walcott's literary cosmopolitics shifts into a different gear, forming connections between the St. Lucian national consciousness developed in *Another Life* and North America, Europe, and Africa.

"Repeating the X of an Hourglass":
The Chiasmus of Nationalism and Cosmopolitics in *Omeros*

Despite its apparent associations with and invocations of Homer's *Odyssey*, I argue that *Omeros* is a tragic poem containing some elements of a *Kunstlerroman* enabling us to see the combination of national consciousness and literary cosmopolitics in Walcott's longest work. That *Omeros* has elements of an artist novel is evident in the figures of the British expatriate Major Plunkett and Walcott himself as he narrates parts of the poem. Both Plunkett and the narrator-Walcott are fascinated with a St. Lucian woman named Helen and are inspired by her to write, respectively, a history of St. Lucia and a poem comparing her and the island to the legendary Helen of Troy. However, these attempts to identify St. Lucia with Helen as a historically or classically accurate poetic icon come to naught. *Omeros* instead offers counterpoints to this iconification through other characters who illustrate a critical national consciousness in St. Lucia itself, and through a literary cosmopolitics expressed in the journeys of Achille the fisherman and the narrator-Walcott to Africa, North America, and Europe. At the same time, Walcott extends and revises his earlier aesthetic theories; he realizes the touch of artistic arrogance or hubris implicit in his earlier notions of the transfigured or solitary artist as well as in Plunkett's attempts to iconize Helen as St. Lucia. As part of *Omeros*'s tragic form, Walcott's narrator-self must undergo a sea change of a different sort from Shabine's. Instead of the transfiguration of the artist into the light of world (in *Another Life*) or as a solitary sailor-poet (in "The Schooner *Flight*"), the narrator-Walcott in *Omeros* becomes a character at the same level as the other figures in his poem, and it is through his transnational peregrinations that he gradually forms a commitment both to art and to his home country of St. Lucia, to which he returns at the end of the poem.

By suggesting that *Omeros* is generically more a tragedy than an epic, I am drawing on Walcott's own comments about his work as well as David Scott's discussion of romance and tragedy in anticolonial and postcolonial narratives. Although *Omeros* is written in hexametrical tercets that mostly follow the rhyme scheme of classical epic verse, the poem cleaves toward the characteristics of tragedy described by Scott, such as recursivity, temporal and historical revision, and an openness or indeterminacy in its thematic treatment of St. Lucia's culture and society. Walcott comes up against the historical contingencies and circumstances that pose limitations on his art and, in the end, departs from the anticolonial, romantic narrative of nation-building and its corresponding formation of a national identity (exemplified by Eric Williams's political rhetoric), focusing instead on the dynamic and contrapuntal relationship between a St. Lucian national consciousness and a transnational literary cosmopolitics. Most extended studies of *Omeros* treat the work as an appropriation or extension of the classical, Homeric epic in a Caribbean context (Terada; Hamner; Breslin). However, as Walcott himself observes not long after the poem was published, "It's not like a heroic epic. [. . .] since I am in the book, I certainly don't see myself as a hero of an epic, when an epic generally has a hero of action and decision and destiny" ("The Man Who Keeps the English Language Alive: An Interview with Derek Walcott by Rebekah Presson" 189). Moving from an individual and personal level to that of form and genre, Walcott later avers that he "did not plan this book so it would be a template of the Homeric original because that would be an absurdity" ("Reflections on *Omeros*" 230–31). The absurdity Walcott has in mind here is the claims by critics that *Omeros* is "a reinvention of the Odyssey, but this time in the Caribbean," because "what this implies is that geologically, geographically, the Caribbean is secondary to the Aegean" ("Reflections on *Omeros*" 232). Walcott clearly wants to avoid any sense of belatedness or derivativeness implicit in a reading of his poem as a successor to or facsimile of Homer's Greek epic, or in the idea that the Caribbean has only in the late twentieth century become capable of producing a literary work of epic length and quality. In fact, Walcott's narrator-self observes toward the end of *Omeros* that the accepted form of Greek heroic epic cannot do justice to the natural and cultural rhythms of the Caribbean, because there

> . . . The ocean had
>
> no memory of the wanderings of Gilgamesh,

> or whose sword severed whose head in the Iliad.
> It was an epic where every line was erased
>
> yet freshly written in sheets of exploding surf
> in that blind violence with which one crest replaced
> another with a trench and that heart-heaving sough
>
> begun in Guinea to fountain exhaustion here,
> however one read it, not as our defeat or
> our victory; it drenched every survivor
>
> with blessing. (LIX.I.33–43)

Walcott's description of the Caribbean Sea as an epic of erasure and rejuvenation, of the "blind violence" of "exploding surf" leading not to "defeat" or "victory" but to a cathartic "blessing" for "every survivor," highlights a formal rhythm and a set of generic qualities associated more with tragedy than the epic. Furthermore, his comments that the presence of his narrator-self in *Omeros* qualifies the poem's epic nature bring to mind David Scott's contrast between the romantic and tragic narrative forms:

> where the anticolonial narrative is cast as an epic Romance, as the great progressive story of an oppressed and victimized people's struggle from Bondage to Freedom, from Despair to Triumph under heroic leadership, the tragic narrative is cast as a dramatic confrontation between contingency and freedom, between human will and its conditioning limits. Where the epic revolutionary narrative charts a steadily rising curve in which the end is already foreclosed by a horizon available through an act of rational, self-transparent will, in the tragic narrative the rhythm is more tentative, its direction less determinative, more recursive, and its meaning less transparent. (135)

Eric Williams's speech about "Massa Day Done" and his account of Trinidad's independence from Britain is an example of an epic and romantic struggle of the oppressed under heroic leadership, for Williams casts himself as (in Walcott's words) a hero of action and decision and destiny. Both *Another Life* and "The Schooner *Flight*" also contain elements of romantic struggle and liberation, as evinced by the transfiguration of Gregorias and Walcott into the light of the world after the death of Harold Simmons, and the amalgamation of physical labor and artistic craftsmanship in Shabine as he travels through the Caribbean. But, as Scott argues, a tragic mode of thinking and feeling is more appropriate for postcolonial times, because "the critical languages in which we wagered our moral vision and political hope [. . .] are no longer commensurate with the world they were meant to understand, engage, and overcome"; tragedy is "not driven by the confident hubris of teleologies that extract the future seamlessly from the past" and it therefore "recasts our historical temporalities in significant ways" (210).

Walcott uses a bird—the sea swift—as the central motif in *Omeros* to recast the historical temporality of Caribbean culture and St. Lucian national consciousness. In contrast to the tropes of illumination and poetic seamanship in *Another Life* and "The Schooner *Flight*," the sea swift is a symbol of the natural landscape of St. Lucia and its maritime culture. Furthermore, it is a poetic figure that suggests the intertwining of national consciousness and literary cosmopolitics as well as the inversion or chiasmus that occurs in Walcott's assessments of politics, history, and culture in the Caribbean's relationship with Europe and America. This sea bird appears in every major section of *Omeros,* and "the straightened X of the soaring swift" (LXII.III.13) reminds us of Walcott's investment in the modernist aesthetic articulated by Theodor Adorno. As Gillian Rose observes, chiasmus, often represented by the letter or symbol X, is both a figure of speech and a strategy of critical thinking Adorno uses "in order to avoid turning processes into entities," and it "shows how he moves from criticism of intellectual and artistic products to criticism of society," borne out by a key example of categorical inversion such as "science misrepresents society as static and invariant; society has produced the static and invariant features which science describes" (13). As a philosophical and poetic figure of speech, chiasmus can "indicate the unreconciled and unsublated relationship between two elements that nonetheless are inextricably intertwined" (Jay, "Adorno in America" 181). This relationship can be seen at the beginning of *Omeros,* where one its main characters, Achille the fisherman, sees "the swift // crossing the cloud-surf" and "with his cutlass he made / a swift sign of the cross" (I.II.3–4, 9–10) right before he hews a tree trunk for his new canoe. The pun here on the sea swift's cross-shaped body and Achille's quick ("swift") action in drawing a cross with his cutlass plays on the contrast between the "crossing" movement of the bird as the poem begins its literary journey and Achille's rooted and stationary figure on the shores of St. Lucia. The transnational and cosmopolitical movement of the poem is thereby connected with the grounded figure of Achille the fisherman and the soil of St. Lucia itself. Furthermore, the Christian sign of the cross is juxtaposed with Achille's prayer to the spirit of the tree he has just cut down for his canoe—"Tree! You can be a canoe, or else you cannot!"

(I.II.12)—thereby placing the legacy of European religious conversion alongside the indigenous belief in natural spirits inhabiting the very landscape of the island.

Walcott's intertwining of the transnational and cosmopolitical with the national and the local, as well as the entangled histories and cultures of Europe, America, Africa, and the Caribbean, can be traced through the motif of the sea swift, which appears repeatedly as the poem unfolds and moves through different geographical regions and time periods. When the fisherman Achille embarks on his dream journey across time and space to his ancestral home in Africa and meets his spiritual father, Afolabe, it is the swift, "this frail dancer / leaping the breakers, this dart of the meridian," who prepares his oneiric path because "she could loop the stars with a fishline" and "circled epochs with her outstretched span" (XXIV.III.8–9, 10–11). In the middle of the poem, when Walcott's narrating self is living in the United States, he invokes Catherine Weldon, a white American woman who advocated for Native American rights in the nineteenth century, and her own experiences as a writer, for "like a swift over water, her pen's shadows raced" (XXXV.III.42). Through Weldon and the swift, Walcott connects the history of internal colonialism and exploitation of Native Americans in the United States with the virtual annihilation of indigenous peoples in the Caribbean. The European section of *Omeros* begins with a scene of swifts in "flight, in reverse, // repeating the X of an hourglass, every twitter an aeon / from which a horizon climbed in the upturned vase" (XXXVII.I.6–8). The emphasis Walcott places on reversal and repetition in these opening lines makes us rethink the idea of Europe as the Old World from which civilization and Enlightenment were disseminated into the New World regions of Africa and the Americas. History repeats itself, but this time in reverse like an upturned hourglass as Walcott's poetic journey turns toward a Europe that is no longer the cradle of civilization but is now (in Dipesh Chakrabarty's felicitous phrase) provincialized as the cultures of the New World climb upward like the horizons once envisioned by European seafarers in centuries past. Finally, as a coda to his poem Walcott explicitly invokes the sea swift as the motif that connects the various characters and cultures of his poem into a constellation: "I followed the sea-swift to both sides of this text; / her hyphen stitched its seam, like the interlocking / basins of a globe in which one half fits the next" and "Her wing-beat carries these islands to Africa, / she sewed the Atlantic rift with a needle's line, / the rift in the soul" (LXIII.III.1–3, 10–12). The terms Walcott uses here echo the broken, reassembled, but still scarred and battered vase featured in his Nobel Prize acceptance speech, for the swift stitches the two halves (New and Old, East and West) of the Atlantic world together without resolving them into a third, determinate whole. The metaphors of needlework and sewing draw our attention to the conjunction and relatedness of disparate parts but do not offer a formula for consolidating these parts into a reconciled entirety, because to do so would turn the poem into a tool of instrumentality rationality "defined as the unity of the features of what it subsumes" (Horkheimer and Adorno 11).

Despite Walcott's shift from romantic anticolonialism to a tragic sensibility of chiasmus in *Omeros*, Walcott's poetic vision (developed earlier in *Another Life*) for a liberating national consciousness as opposed to a state-sponsored national identity for St. Lucia is nonetheless still present in the longer work. Tourists and the disruption they cause to everyday life in St. Lucia are as ubiquitous in *Omeros* as they are in *Another Life*, as the poem opens with the wounded fisherman Philoctete explaining the island's customs to a group of "tourists, who try taking / his soul with their cameras" (I.I.2–3). These same "crouching photographers" trying "to capture the scene / like gulls fighting over a catch" with "their clacking cameras" also surround Achille after he returns from a day's fishing (LIX.III.16, 19–21), and the alliteration of "clacking cameras" coupled with the simile of gulls fighting over fish highlights the tourists' predatory and exoticizing gaze upon the locals of St. Lucia. The "waitress in national costume" who serves these tourists in *Another Life* (3575) is replaced by a male waiter "in a black bow-tie" who is "bouncing to discotheque // music from the speakers," and "determined to meet the // beach's demands," but "like any born loser // he soon kicked the bucket" (IV.III.2, 10, 3–4, 9–10, 12–13). Walcott's satire of the service industry that caters to Western tourists is clear from the mock-heroic characterization of this waiter as a "Lawrence of St. Lucia" (IV.III.10) as determined as his namesake (Lawrence of Arabia) to fulfill his mission. However, the difference is that the St. Lucian waiter is not exploring the sands of the Arab world but merely serving champagne with such incompetence that "he soon kicked the bucket"—an idiomatic phrase that highlights his physical clumsiness and his impending demise at the hands of angry tourists.

Walcott also extends his satirical pen to politicians who promise change without offering a different vision of culture and society for St. Lucia. Maljo, a candidate in a local election, promises that "a new age would begin" (XX.I.27), but his political catchphrases and slogans are as incoherent as they are ridiculous:

> "Bananas shall raise their hands at the oppressor,
> through all our valleys!" he screamed, forgetting to press
> the megaphone button. They name him "Professor

Static," or "Statics," for short, the short-circuit prose
of his electrical syntax in which he mixed
Yankee and patois [. . .] (XX.I.34–39)

The ludic anthropomorphizing of bananas raising their hands in defiance is paralleled by Maljo's inept clumsiness at forgetting to press the megaphone button, and the rhyme of "oppressor" with "Professor" in the first tercet suggests that Maljo has more in common with Euro-American governments and local neocolonial officials (such as the ministers of culture and development in *Another Life*) who exploit St. Lucia for their own profit. This connection between Maljo and foreign and neocolonial oppressors is also echoed by his mixture of "Yankee" phrases and accent with local "patois" in his political rhetoric. Just as Eric Williams's vision of discipline, production, and tolerance for his new nation of Trinidad seems to offer little by way of a cultural vision for a whole society, through the figure of Maljo Walcott argues that a politics based primarily on protest and resistance may not be sufficient for radical change, for Maljo's candidacy fails miserably and "he left as a migrant-worker for Florida," thus becoming another cog in the vast machine of economic exploitation he railed against (XX.III.27).

Maljo represents what Walcott in an earlier essay calls the "formula of politics" of the newly decolonized intellectuals and government officials, a politics of *ressentiment* in an antithetical and antagonistic relationship with the politics of exploitation practiced by the European colonizers. The other side of the coin in this formula of politics is the attempt to forge an authentic racial identity for the new nation, which, as we saw in *Another Life,* in the St. Lucian context often takes the form of an Afrocentric identity. Walcott differs with this coercive hypostatization of race and culture by engaging in a literary cosmopolitics instead, as we can see from the two sections in the middle of *Omeros* concerning Achille's dream journey to Africa. Through Achille's spiritual visit to his ancestral home in Africa and his conversation with his spiritual father Afolabe, Walcott argues that the African aspect of St. Lucian's cultural identity must be negotiated in terms of a social and historical context located in St. Lucia and the Caribbean rather than a diasporic longing for a physical or symbolic return to Africa itself. Upon Achille's arrival in his ancestral village, Afolabe challenges him to explain the meaning of his name, to which Achille replies, "I do not know what the name means. It means something, / maybe. What's the difference? In the world I come from / we accept the sounds we were given. Men, trees, water" (XXV.III.34–36). Angered by Achille's response, Afolabe voices the unbridgeable gulf between the African ancestor and his Afro-Caribbean descendant: "I am not Afolabe, your father, and you look through / my body as the light looks through a leaf. I am not here / or a shadow. And you, nameless son, are only the ghost // of a name. Why did I never miss you until you returned?" (XXV.III.55–58). That Afolabe never missed Achille until the latter's sudden reappearance implies a refusal of the nostalgia and sentimental longing implicit in a diasporic desire to return to the home- or fatherland, since the father himself never realized he ever had or missed his departed offspring at all. Furthermore, the exchange between the two men recalls Walcott's passage about "a life older than geography" in *Another Life* (1233) discussed earlier. Achille's comment that in the Caribbean "we accept the sounds we were given" rather than eschewing them and seeking a more authentic cultural identity reaffirms Walcott's prior description of "trees and men [who] / laboured assiduously, silently to become // whatever their given sounds resembled" (*AL* 1240–42). Afolabe's pronouncement that his body has become translucent ("as the light looks through a leaf") also brings to mind the double metaphor of plant and schoolbook used to describe "Africa, heart-shaped" as "the leaves of edible roots" that "opened their pages" (1234–35), with a further doubling of "leaves" as a botanical appendage as well as printed pages. Achille cannot return to an originary or primal Africa or assume such an identity symbolized by his ancestor Afolabe; the St. Lucian fisherman can only approach it as another life, not his own, through foodways and intellectual study.

Walcott's acknowledgment of St. Lucia's African heritage and his insistence that this Africanness needs to be seen as relocated in the Caribbean rather than dislocated from its wellspring can be seen in the closing sections of Achille's oneiric sojourn. After witnessing a raid on Afolabe's village and being helpless to stop the inhabitants from being enslaved, Achille observes how, as the people of each tribe are borne across the Middle Passage to the Americas, "now each man was a nation / in himself, without mother, father, brother" (XXVII.I.32–33). The term "nation" here still bears the sense of tribe or race, but immediately on the next page Walcott redefines the word, describing how the African slaves "felt the sea-wind tying them into one nation / of eyes and shadows and groans" (XXVIII.III.10–11). While this line may be read as reinforcing an Afrocentric identity marked by the suffering of the Middle Passage, the idea of "nation" here may be read as a counterpoint to the earlier use of nation in its tribal and racial sense. Moreover, we may understand the "eyes and shadows and groans" not only within the framework of slavery but also within the specific context of Walcott's discussions of nationalism in the Caribbean as a profound sense of a people learning to see themselves, and the care and pain inherent in the formation of national consciousness and cultures in the Antilles. Finally, Achille's entire dream journey to Africa culminates in a joyous return to St. Lucia that is marked by a figurative and an epistemological chiasmus. Achille gives a shout upon seeing the shores of his home island, "the shout on which each odyssey pivots" (XXX.II.7), and as he crosses the imaginary meridian that separates Africa from the Caribbean, Walcott reflects that "once that parallel / is crossed," it then "cancels the line of master and slave" (XXX.II.11–12). Achille's journey to Africa inverts and negates the colonial relationship between European master and African slave as well as the neocolonial relationship between the ministers of culture and development and the people of St. Lucia whom they wish to keep in perpetual servitude with another free ride on the Middle Passage. Achille realizes his sense of home and nation is grounded in St. Lucia, but in order to achieve this realization he must make a transnational journey across history and geography. In a similar fashion, in *Omeros* Walcott's literary cosmopolitics takes us across Africa, North America, and Europe, but returns ultimately to the Caribbean and St. Lucia. In following the "swift sign of the cross," Walcott locates his home country of St. Lucia at the intersection or pivotal point of the poetic "X" or chiasmus, securing Achille's and his narrator-self's peregrinations and homeward journey as a figure for the Caribbean's reimagining of national consciousness and literary cosmopolitics, departing from the established chronotope of ships in motion to describe the triangular connections between Europe, the Americas, and Africa in a transnational, black Atlantic circuit of colonialism, slavery, and migration.

The understanding that what makes up the nation is intimately linked to and informed by what lies outside the geographical and cultural boundaries of the nation has been a key element of Walcott's thinking as a poet and critic throughout his career. My analysis of Walcott's poetry thus accords with recent work in Caribbean literary studies that, contrary to the valorization of the region and its culture as inherently deterritorialized and transnational, argues that "within a Caribbean context being in one location by no means implies cultural homogeneity or stasis," because "the kinds of transcultural and intercultural work that [Paul] Gilroy locates as somehow exceeding and even deconstructing the nation can actually be located within the Caribbean nation, city or even village" (Donnell 87). Even though Walcott's verse may not always explicitly dramatize the Caribbean's "neo-colonial dependency, cyclical and mass migrations of population, environmental degradation, saturation by an international tourist culture, and economies that concentrate wealth in the hands of a tiny elite" (Puri 12), this does not take away from his commitment to the region and to St. Lucia as a home and an island nation. For if we concur with Alison Donnell's observation that "the particular style in which Caribbean nationalism imagined itself into being was often not narrow but already inclusive and plural, and significantly often voiced within the context of global anti-colonialism" (87), then we must also consider that a national consciousness such as Walcott's can be expressed in inclusive and plural forms that devise a new, provocative vocabulary and an aesthetic vision not confined to a narrow "formula of politics" ("Culture or Mimicry?" 4) to represent "a people who possess the land in thought and share it" ("Society and the Artist" 15).

CHAPTER 4

"Not Monological but Multilogical"

Gender, Hybridity, and National Narratives in Shirley Geok-lin Lim's Writing

SHIRLEY Geok-lin Lim, like Derek Walcott, appears at first glance to be an exemplary transnational and cosmopolitan subject, both personally and professionally. Born in Malacca, Lim grew up and was educated in the former British colonies of Malaysia and Singapore, but she is better known in the United States as an Asian American writer and critic-scholar. In this chapter, however, I argue that Lim's scholarly writing and fiction form a constellation out of her personal background as a Southeast Asian woman and immigrant and her rigorous reflections as an Asian American critic and feminist, and that these take issue with patriotic and patriarchal forms of postcolonial nationalism in Malaysia and Singapore. Lim's focus on the somatic and sentimental aspects of women's experiences negates the postcolonial state's instrumentalization of women's bodies and characters as celebrated icons of the new nation; it reimagines nationalism as a coordination of subjects and objects rather than as the control and domination of one group of subjects over others based on ethnic or racial, gender, linguistic, or religious identity. My conjunction of Lim's somatic emphasis and feminist perspective with Theodor Adorno's aesthetic theory and negative dialectics may initially appear counterintuitive, but I am drawing on both recent scholarship by feminist critics who have found Adorno's thinking useful for their analyses of gender, sexuality, and corporeality, such as Lisa Yun Lee's *Dialectics of the Body* (2005), and two edited anthologies *Adorno, Culture and Feminism* (1999) and *Feminist Interpretations of Theodor Adorno* (2006). As one anthology editor argues, "Adorno's theorizing may have unintended (by him) consequences for feminism that can only be discerned through open-ended and experimental approaches to his work, which is open and experimental in its own right" (Heberle 3), and because "feminist theorizing has become increasingly attuned to its contingent, conditional status as a field of inquiry," it is useful to consider how Adorno's "insistence on the primacy of the object encourages this nonidentitarian approach to knowledge" (Heberle 6, 7). Adorno's analysis of art tries "to say the 'unsayable,' the 'outside of language,' the mimetic, the sensual, the non-conceptual"; it "approach[es] a 'politics' which undercuts identity thinking, which refuses to engage in identitarian thinking [. . .] and remains un-appropriated" (O'Neill 29), and creates "a platform for theoretical/experiential analysis regarding the sensuousness of our experience, of our being in the world—as women and as men" (O'Neill 38). Lim's writing offers a bridge between feminist interpretations of the Frankfurt School's social theories and feminist critiques of gendered discourses of postcolonial nationalism, and this epistemological bridging reconfigures nationalism as an objective social formation rather than as a subjective identitarian concept.

In her poetry collection *Walking Backwards,* Lim describes her relationship to China as a country and a symbolic "cultural China" (Tu 12) in powerfully somatic terms: "Although she/he has been a constant / Like mother, father in memory, / China was the milk that was too heavy, That made one gag. Vomit. Like the scent / Of stinky tofu [. . .]" ("The Source" 2–6). Lim recognizes that China is a rising global power that thinks of itself as "center of the world," but she qualifies this centrality by describing the presence of China in her childhood home of Malacca in Malaysia as "a misfit, dumb / Country; and I its misfit child / Bastard and deaf, handicapped and wild" ("The Source" 10, 12–14). One cannot mistake Lim's vehement refusal of either filiative or affiliative identification with China and Chinese culture: the parental simile and geopolitical metaphor are undermined by Lim's intense physical revulsion, and the repetition of the word "misfit" emphasizes the nonidentity between Lim's objective sense of herself and the concept of China either as a nation-state or as an ethnic or cultural identity. This sentiment is expressed in more affirmative language in one of her earlier poems collected in *Monsoon History,* where she connects her father's death with Malaysia—"I light the joss. A dead land. / On noon steepness smoke ascends / Briefly. Country is important, / Is important. This knowledge I know" ("Bukit China" 3–6)—and also in *What the Fortune Teller Didn't Say* where she expresses her affinity to America through her son's uncertainties: "because I have nursed my son at my breast / because he is a strong American boy / because I have seen his eyes redden when he is asked who he is / because he answers I don't know" (13–16). These two poems suggest a different configuration of nationalism as a political consciousness and cultural critique instead of the visceral rejection of cultural nationalism and ethnic identity in "The Source," because the country (Malaysia) is important as an object of "knowledge" and (like Lim's deceased father) something to be mourned instead of celebrated as a concept that is already accomplished. Similarly, in "Learning to Love America" Lim's son's anxieties about "who he is" and his inability to supply a definite answer are part of Lim's process of *learning* to love America, a painstaking love that does not spring from the assurance of some essential identity. Although Lim invokes filiative relationships in these two poems, she does not describe this filiation in terms of some primordial characteristic that binds a homogeneous community together in a national identity. Instead, her abiding connections with Malaysia and America derive from both an intellectually sincere and an intimately sensuous relationship to these nations. Her grief over her father's death and her son's distress over who he is recall Adorno's discussion of the close connection between philosophy and pain, in which "the need to lend a voice to suffering is a condition of all truth. For suffering is objectivity that weighs upon the subject; its most subjective experience, its expression, is objectively conveyed" (*Negative Dialectics* 17–18). The suffering in these poems by Lim should be understood as the objectivity of lived experience and a critical national consciousness weighing upon the conceptual armature of the postcolonial nation. Lim suffers the nation-state but does not reject it, for she is aware that "countries are in our blood and we bleed them" ("Learning to Love America" 19), that nationalism, like blood, is constantly circulating and ought to be regarded as a sociopolitical movement rather than a consanguineous national identity.

Such an instrumental nationality, spearheaded by a patriarchal and paternalistic leadership, may be considered a culture industry that "intentionally integrates its consumers from above" (Adorno, "Culture Industry Reconsidered" 98), and it "refers to the standardization" of an ideal of femininity as well as "the incorporation of industrial forms of organization" and rationalization into the domains of gender and sexuality (Adorno, "Culture Industry Reconsidered" 100, 101). What turns women into a fetish and a symbol of the nation rather than its subject is not nationality per se, but rather the form of instrumentalized nationality. In contrast, Lim advances a critical nationality against such male-oriented nationalism through what Ketu Katrak calls a postcolonial feminist representation of "internalized exile" in which "the body [of the female protagonist] feels disconnected from itself, as though it does not belong to it and has no agency" (2). However, this sense of disconnection and exile is not absolute or determinate; Lim shows how her protagonist, Li An, becomes intimately connected with her all-female household and her half-Asian, half-American daughter, Suyin. Li An and Suyin move from being symbols of national culture and identity to pivotal members of an alternative community of women who claim the nation on their own terms rather than those set up by a male-centered postcolonial nationalist discourse.

The official national narratives of Malaysia and Singapore take up the symbolic and sociopolitical divisions created by British colonialism in order to determine their postcolonial national identities in terms of racial and linguistic purity.[1] From the intersection of three discursive fields—postcolonialism, Southeast Asian nationalism, and Asian American culture and literature—Lim's writerly subjectivity demonstrates how this strategy of purification fetishizes identity. By working through these three discursive fields, Lim articulates a literary cosmopolitics by critiquing a determinate national identity driven by a need for racial and cultural purity through "coercive mimeticism" (Chow, *Protestant Ethnic* 107). This coercive reproduction of an untainted national body is part of a larger culture industry that generates both a symbolic and a somatic effect on those interpellated by it: "The result for the physiognomy of the culture industry is essentially a mixture of streamlining, photographic hardness and precision on the one hand, and individualistic residues, sentimentality and an already rationally disposed and adapted romanticism on the other" (Adorno, "Culture Industry Reconsidered" 101). I argue that Shirley Geok-lin Lim seizes on these individualistic residues of sentimentality and inverts their association with a romantic, heroic masculine narrative of postcolonial nationalism. Lim foregrounds the sensuality of female desire and the materiality of women's physical selves, as well as the reproduction of mixed-race children, as a challenge to this coercive mimeticism, "a process (identitarian, existential, cultural, or textual) in which those who are marginal to mainstream Western culture are expected [. . .] to objectify themselves in accordance with the already seen and thus to authenticate the familiar imaginings of them as ethnics" (Chow, *Protestant Ethnic* 107). Lim's writing foregrounds and interrogates the ways in which women are interpellated as gendered subjects who must adhere to a standard of racial and cultural purity within the rubric of a postcolonial nation that

---

1. For a thorough analysis of the social, economic, and political divisions created by the British along racial lines between Malays and Chinese in colonial Malaya, see Alatas.

privileges male dominance and leadership in both politics and society. In her critical and personal essays as well as her first novel, *Joss and Gold,* Lim interweaves national consciousness and literary cosmopolitics: having migrated to the United States, Lim is keenly aware of the transnational cultural flows between Asia and America, but her appropriation of important Asian American women's literary strategies is framed within a postcolonial Malaysian and Singaporean context. Such strategies include the claiming of a female authorial figure, the recasting of immigrant narratives into a mother-daughter romance, and the critique of Asian cultural nationalism often linked to masculine figures. In Lim's novel *Joss and Gold,* Li An's and her daughter Suyin's consciousness of their desires and their sexuality are in tension with the dominant postcolonial and national narratives that focus on the foundational role of men in the process of Southeast Asian nation-building. Li An and Suyin are contrapuntal figures who claim their place within the national community and also challenge and critique the constraints and limitations of the masculine national imagination in Malaysia and Singapore, which is predicated on a concept of multiculturalism that considers different ethnic and cultural groups as equal but separate and pure.

Women in Malaysian and Singaporean Official Multiculturalism

The unequal distribution of cultural, economic, and political resources among different ethnic groups has been a problem for both Malaysian and Singaporean governments, and this problem is itself a legacy of British colonial policies that partitioned a heterogeneous population along lines that conflated ethnicity with economic status. After World War II and the gradual retreat of British colonial forces from Southeast Asia, the tensions between Malaysia's ethnic Malay population, which claims *bumiputera,* or indigenous, status, and its minority Chinese and India (South Asian) communities began increasing. The "widespread perception" among the Malay majority "that the Chinese have dominated the economy and, through various means, have inhibited Malay participation" (Mauzy 107) does not completely take into account how this ethnic and economic disparity—along with the concept of special rights for Malays and indigenous peoples—is primarily the result of British colonialism. The "paternalistic" British colonial authorities "gave the Malays certain 'special rights' involving government employment, education and lands reserves" in order "to 'protect' the Malays from being swamped by the more aggressive immigrants," and thus creating "a dual economy" consisting of "a European and non-Malay (and sometimes Malay aristocracy) modern urban economic sector, and a traditional rural Malay economy centering around rice production and fishing" (Mauzy 108). The issues of Malay rights, Malay as the national language, and economic restructuring to encourage Malay participation and businesses came to a head in the May 1969 elections, which are a pivotal event in the first section of Lim's novel. These riots ossified the communal tensions between Malays and non-Malays in the colonial and postcolonial period, and "the fiction of a government of nearly equal ethnic partners was no longer maintained. It could be clearly seen that the Malays were the hegemonic power, and intended to remain so at any cost for the foreseeable future" (Mauzy 111). In contrast to Malay hegemony in Malaysia, Singapore's multiracial policy advocates an egalitarian approach, but there are strong overtones of "Chineseness" in this policy that "could be depicted as a central building block out of which the consensual national identity was being created" (Brown 93). Multiracialism, as it is known and implemented in Singapore, differs crucially from multiculturalism in the United States. Whereas the latter is seen as "a means for 'empowering' minority ethnic and other groups," the former is "a means of disempowerment because it erases the grounds upon which a racial group may make claims on behalf of its own interests without ostensibly violating the idea of group equality that is the foundation of multiracialism itself" (Chua 36). Since its creation as a major trading port in 1819 by the East India Company, Singapore has attracted many immigrants from East Asia and South Asia. In 1963 it joined the Federation of Malaysia, but became independent in 1965 after racial and political conflicts arose. Singapore's population is exceptional because Malay Muslims—who make up the dominant majority in neighboring Malaysia and Indonesia—are a minority in the city-state, along with an even smaller minority of ethnic Indians from South Asia. To administer the management of a racially diverse population, four component racial categories were introduced: Chinese, Malay, Indian, and Others (Eurasians). This maneuver, intended by the Singapore government to depoliticize ethnicity, "pushes race out of the front-line of politics while according it high visibility in the cultural sphere" (Chua 36). The numerical and socioeconomic dominance of the Chinese in Singapore ensured that their culture—as shaped and promoted by the state—is first among equals in this new conception of Asian values and national identity.

This discourse of shared Asian values, however, has not only marginalized the role of women in Singaporean society and politics; it has also fetishized them as symbols of the nation whose meaning and value derive from a patriarchal regime. This symbolic identity, formed out of the cultural and corporeal disciplinary formations of both Malaysian and Singaporean official nationalism, serves the postcolonial nationalist project in developing a national identity that can both maintain and reproduce the biological and cultural boundaries between the different ethnic groups. As such, "it is up to a particularly male-based polity to decide upon the quality of a woman's life. The power women enjoy is but a shadow, a mirroring of power, that radiates from particular loci—coalesced under the label of a mostly male 'government' and ruling political party" (Purushotam 329). Even as women in Singapore joined the workforce in increasing numbers and attained higher levels of education after national independence in 1965, the state continually regarded women's primary roles to be those of homemakers and childbearers, "to mind their familial responsibilities, and to make more babies" in order to "best serve 'the nation'" (Purushotam 335). The Singaporean state's positioning of women within its nation-building concepts of ethnic management for economic development can be read within a larger postcolonial context:

> on the one hand, nationalist movements invite women to participate more fully in collective life by interpellating them as "national" actors: mothers, educators, workers and even fighters. On the other hand, they reaffirm the boundaries of culturally acceptable feminine conduct and exert pressure on women to articulate their gender interests within the terms of reference set by nationalist discourse. (Kandiyoti 380)

What is important here is how a masculine nationalist discourse works according to the logic of the culture industry because it subsumes women's subjectivities under a larger subject position, namely that of a national actor who must adhere to a standardized, culturally acceptable feminine conduct. Because women are regarded as "the custodians of cultural particularisms by virtue of being less assimilated, both culturally and linguistically, into the wider society," their responsibility is to "reproduce their culture through the continued use of their native language, the persistence of culinary and other habits and the socialisation of the young" (Kandiyoti 382). Following this instrumental logic, there are explicit as well as unspoken "regulations concerning who a woman can marry and the legal status of her offspring [that] aim at reproducing the boundaries of the symbolic identity of their group" (Kandiyoti 382).

In Lim's novel *Joss and Gold,* Li An and the other female characters move from Malaysia to Singapore, where job opportunities seem better for a single unwed mother running an all-female household. However, even in Singapore, women are considered symbolic figures and boundary markers in a national drama scripted by the country's male leaders as a desperate struggle for survival. The nation-state's independence from British colonial rule and its subsequent ejection from the Malaysian Federation in 1965 are indeed cast in terms of a triumphant narrative of overcoming adversity. In his autobiography, *The Singapore Story*, Singapore's first prime minister, Kuan Yew Lee, depicts his leadership of Singapore as an heroic struggle to build an egalitarian and "truly multiracial" society, what he calls "a Malaysian Malaysia, not a Malay Malaysia" that would represent all the Malay, Chinese, Indian, and Eurasian constituencies in the country (17). Lee thinks of Singapore's separation from Malaysia as a personal catastrophe and "moment of anguish" that "shattered" the "hopes of millions [he] had aroused" (650). Furthermore, this separation of "a Chinese island in a Malay sea" (23) from the Malaysian Federation is reckoned in terms of a failed marriage:

> Under Malay-Muslim custom, a husband, but not the wife, can declare "*Talak*" (I divorce thee) and the woman is divorced. They can reconcile and he can remarry her, but not after he has said "*Talak*" three times. The three readings in the two chambers of parliament were the three *talaks* with which Malaysia divorced Singapore. The partners—predominantly Malay in Malaya, predominantly Chinese in Singapore—had not been compatible. Their union had been marred by increasing conjugal strife over whether the new Federation should be a truly multiracial society, or one dominated by the Malays. (14)

The gendered terms of this description are significant because they cast Chinese-dominant Singapore as a wife who suffers unfairly at the hands of a fickle husband—predominantly Malay Malaysia. Lee's comparison of the Malaysia-Singapore separation to "a Malay-Muslim" divorce custom evokes stereotypes of Malay and Muslim culture as polygamous and misogynist (while sidestepping the possibilities that these qualities might also be present in traditional Chinese culture), thus implying that a Federation "dominated by the Malays" would regress into a state of cultural primitivism. Lee wants his reader to sympathize with a feminized Singapore spurned by a masculinized Malaysia who uses custom instead of reason to throw out his wife. By feminizing Singapore in this political separation, Lee narrates Singapore's later economic success and social stability (relative to Malaysia) as both a matter of a collective, heroic masculinity overcoming a moment of anguished weakness and of his own personal triumph and moral integrity outwitting his unsavory Malaysian opponents. The leaders of Singapore's People's Action Party "were not like the politicians in Malaya. Singapore ministers were not pleasure-loving, nor did they seek to enrich themselves" (656), and, at the end of his autobiography, Lee concludes that Singapore's story is not only a social experience in nation-building but also the narrative of his own lifelong achievements: "I did not know I was to spend the rest of my life getting Singapore not just to work but to prosper and to flourish" (663).

Adorno's Negation of the Idealized Feminine and Lim's Feminist Literary Critique

Nirmala Purushotam's and Deniz Kandiyoti's critique of the fetishization of the feminine by male postcolonial nationalist leaders such as Kuan Yew Lee accords with Theodor Adorno's examination of the instrumentalization of women in modern society. The patriarchal Lee implicitly regards the nation and its people as his most outstanding achievement and possession, and "once wholly a possession, the loved person is no longer really looked at" (Adorno, *Minima Moralia* 79). Women have their physical and cultural selves literally overwritten by a nation-building narrative that no longer looks at them as women but as "the feminine character, and the ideal of femininity on which it is modelled," and this character and ideal "are products of masculine society. [. . .] Where it claims to be humane, masculine society imperiously breeds in woman its own corrective, and shows itself through this limitation implacably the master. The feminine character is a negative imprint of domination" (Adorno, *Minima Moralia* 95). Moreover, the coercive mimeticism involved in women's self-fashioning to conform to the ideal feminine character is both an interpellation from without and a violent struggle from within, because "the femininity which appeals to instinct, is always exactly what every woman has to force herself by violence—masculine violence—to be: a she-man" (Adorno, *Minima Moralia* 96). This results in a female persona who not only is unlike a woman but who also becomes a hyphenated creature, a possession that is less than and must always be subsidiary to man. Adorno's analysis of idealized femininity as she-man recalls Kandiyoti's trenchant explication of how postcolonial nationalist movements regard women as both "'national' actors" who serve and fight alongside their male counterparts and as "custodians of cultural particularisms by virtue of being less assimilated, both culturally and linguistically, into the wider society" (380, 382). In their respective ways, both Kandiyoti and Adorno highlight how a masculine-centered project of national identity, despite its humane or humanist claims, actually turns away from a critical national consciousness and replicates European colonial rhetoric by "imperiously" determining what women should be and how they ought to behave within the framework of an exclusive and homogeneous national identity.

While Adorno seems to conclude his observation on a pessimistic note that "glorification of the feminine character implies the humiliation of all who bear it" (*Minima Moralia* 96), his analysis nonetheless suggests certain weaknesses or inconsistencies in the masculine interpellation of women. Although Adorno does not elaborate on these weaknesses, Shirley Geok-lin Lim detects and uses them as a critical vantage point in her criticism and fiction. The idealized feminine is bred by "masculine society" as "its own corrective," and this corrective construction is at once masculine society's claim of being "the master" as well as a mark of its own "limitation." The female character is thus a manifold signifier of, first, masculine society's lack and inadequacy; second, its cultural and symbolic attempts to fill this lack; and third, and most important, the limits of masculine society's cultural and symbolic power-knowledge despite its facade of completeness and mastery. Hence Adorno's pithy summation that "the feminine character is a negative imprint of domination" by masculine society rather than its *positive* embodiment, because what underlies the suturing of the feminine character to masculine society is an imprint of that society's lack and limits of its domination upon the people who make up that society. This formulation suggests that through a negating and an immanent critique of the idealized feminine, which follows and inverts the logic of masculine domination instead of rejecting it outright, a writer such as Shirley Geok-lin Lim may stage an unfeminine and de-idealized reading of women and imagine alternative social and cultural roles for and relationships between women that have not been subsumed within a determinate narrative of national *Bildung*.

The Singaporean story of nation-building is interrogated by Lim in her critical and personal essays as well as in her first novel, *Joss and Gold*, and she does so by engaging in a literary cosmopolitics that appropriates textual strategies employed by Asian American women authors for a Malaysian-Singaporean context. Patricia P. Chu discusses how Asian American writers reconfigure the *Bildungsroman* by "substituting authorship for marriage as a central trope for representing Asian American subject formation" (19). Male Asian American writers replace the *Bildungsroman*'s "well-married hero paradigm" with "the 'immigrant romance,' which recounts the protagonist's search for a white partner to Americanize him or her; the abjection of the Asian mother; the construction of Asian Americans as artist-sons engaged in oedipal struggles; and the figuring of the Asian American women as sentimental heroes" (Chu 19). But the representation of "Asian women in [Asian American] men's texts" poses an additional problem that Asian American women writers must confront, for women "are used to represent aspects of the authors' homeland or ancestral culture that are abjected from the male protagonists, the better to establish their Americanness," hence "such texts implicitly construct Asian American subjectivity as masculine" (20). Chu's discussion highlights the similarities between Asian American masculine subject formation through literary discourse and Singapore's postcolonial narrative of heroic, patriarchal nation-building through state law, and political autobiography.

Challenging this masculine subjectivity, Chu focuses on Amy Tan's *The Joy Luck Club* and Maxine Hong Kingston's *Tripmaster Monkey* to show how women writers represent Asian American subjectivity on their own terms. In Tan's novel, the immigrant romance is cast in terms of a mother-daughter narrative, where the mother stands for "an inherited core of Chineseness, or of the Chinese feminine," a core that the Chinese American daughter must integrate into "her American self" by containing this "radical difference" within a "narrative frame emphasizing the daughter's psychological work and the sentimental story of the finding of the long-lost sisters" in China (Chu 168). Chu challenges the claim that Kingston's novel misrepresents Chinese American history and culture by using surrealist techniques and postmodernist style, and argues that Kingston's appropriation of the Chinese legend of the Monkey King (which her protagonist is using as source material for his own stage play) is a way of "affirming and exploring the power and resilience of the original [text] and reinscribing it into [Kingston's] own American vision" (181). Kingston's "vision of Asian American culture as dialogic, inclusive, adaptive, and alive" is more salutary than both Frank Chin's idea of a masculine, Chinese heroic tradition and Amy Tan's evocation of "a classical Chinese past as a guarantor of present-day ethnic authenticity" (Chu 187). In short, Chu asserts that Amy Tan and Maxine Hong Kingston claim America for Asian Americans through literature by representing Asian American women's subjectivities as dialogic and contrapuntal rather than contradictory to their male counterparts.

Shirley Geok-lin Lim appropriates Tan's mother-daughter narratives and Kingston's revisioning of East Asian legends and historical tales to claim Malaysia and Singapore by interrogating their state-sponsored national identities. Through a conjunction of Asian American literary strategies and postcolonial as well as feminist criticism, Lim stresses how she inhabits "cultural worlds" that are "not monological" or dialogical "but multilogical" ("Asians in Anglo-American Feminism" 38), and such a relational, multilogical constellation is evinced by her own experiences growing up as an ethnic Chinese woman in Malaysia:

> But as an already multiply colonized subject, I do not see these oppressions as coming from a hegemonic center. Instead, I see a colonial subject as the cultural site for the contradictions inherent in the intersections of multiply conserving circles of authority. These authoritarian domains overlap each other but not sufficiently so as to preserve the illusion of totalization. Ironically, therefore, I experienced those liberatory movements precisely *where* Confucianism, Catholicism, feudalism, and colonialism intersected. [. . .] it is not these systems but their intersections that offered me points of escape. Situated as I was in Confucianist, Malay feudal, Roman Catholic, British colonial crossways, I was exposed not to systematic political oppression but to continual upheavals. ("Anglo-American Feminism" 35–36, 37, original emphasis)

Lim's essays and her novel may be read as "cultural site[s]" where "the contradictions inherent in the intersections of multiply conserving circles of authority" are exposed and critiqued, thus offering "points of escape" through reinscriptions of women's bodies and sexuality along the lines of literary tropes employed by Asian American women writers. The points of intersections and escape that Lim discusses, however, are not purely symbolic or semantic, because, as she argues in another essay, for the Asian woman writer, the act of writing is not only a political act but also a performance that engages her self somatically. Lim contends that the woman writer in Asia has traditionally been circumscribed within a male-dominated society, such that "her energies, which for writers are inscribed in writing, in the 'graphic' creations of self, must necessarily be dispersed or dispensed on material 'creations'—childbirth and childcare, the planting of gardens, preparation of meals, weaving and sewing of clothing," and because of this, "her 'bio' must largely remain on the ground floor of experience. The semiotic presses on life as experience, the daily unfolding of smells, bustle, sensations, endless movement, those pressures of personalities on the self as receiver" ("Semiotics, Experience and the Material Self" 11). While it may seem as if Lim is creating an opposition between quotidian experience and self-consciousness in which the self is a by-product of the basic, irreducible experience of daily life, Lim stresses that the realization of this slippage is the beginning of political consciousness and artistic representation rather than a normative condition. As she avers, "when the Asian woman writer becomes conscious of her own subjectivity, she becomes conscious first of the fracture between her desire for the sensual world in which her being is grounded and the isolated signifying self which grasps the social oppression of the female but cannot overcome its internalized meaning" (21). This apparent fracture between sensual desire and signifying self, between political subjectivity and domestic selfhood, is a dichotomy resulting from male-oriented social norms that circumscribe women's consciousness. Hence, in order to negate this apparent division, Lim holds that "the future of self for the Asian woman writer must lie in this vision [. . .] in which the material world emerges from its possession by males to the grasp of the woman" (24). Surprisingly, Lim finds that her own writing style falls short of the standard of "political realism" (27) she thinks necessary for her espoused principles, even describing her writerly imagination as "a myopic vision, in which feeling is foregrounded" (24). Indeed, some critics and reviewers of Lim's *Joss and Gold* express dissatisfaction with her overwhelming use of details and descriptions and the lack of plot and character development in the last section of her novel. While this may appear to confirm Lim's own deprecation of her own prose, such a lack of readerly satisfaction should not automatically be construed as a failure. I contend that Lim's style, far from being myopic, emphasizes and foregrounds affect, feeling, and somatic experience in ways that contest and invert the logic of the Malaysian and Singaporean states' instrumentalization of women as symbols and reproductive bodies. While Li An, Suyin, and Ellen do not create a space that lies outside the hegemony of the patriarchal nation-state, they are able (to use Lim's own terms) to break out of the isolated signifying self and form a community of women that survives and flourishes despite the strictures of a national identity centered on male privilege and power. It is not only the material world that is wrested from male possession and into women's hands; it is also a critical national consciousness at the level of culture and politics reimagining the nation as a community in which women are subjects rather than symbols.

Lim's sensuous and somatic treatment of her characters and the world of the novel suggests a mode of feminist critique that departs from what one critic calls the "ethnographic feminism" of Asian American women writers, in which "ethnographic myths" from East Asian folklore "are seamlessly transposed into a feminist, Westernized context" for "the American readership, whose appetite for exotic (hence ethnographic) and politically correct (hence feminist) readings is simultaneously satisfied" (Ma 12). Sheng-mei Ma highlights the ways in which Asian American writers such as Tan and Kingston use an "emplotment of immigrants' heart-wrenching and almost always 'exotic' experiences" to authenticate their narrators and themselves as ethnic subjects, while the (first-generation) immigrants "remain largely a blank, an absence" (11). Compounding this inadvertent silencing of first-generation immigrants is the stylistic tendency "to smooth away the linguistic ruptures resultant from intertextual / intercultural transposition," which Yunte Huang detects in Kingston's *The Woman Warrior* (154). This smoothing out or glossing over of such "transpacific displacement" (3) both stems from and reinforces "the deeply rooted linguistic positivism of the Western literary tradition" that "suggests that there is an extralinguistic experience—American or not—that can be captured and represented by literature regardless of the particularity of the mediating language," and this positivism has contributed to the popularity of personal narratives and autobiographies by ethnic subjects in the American education system (Huang 142). One can see the connections between Ma's and Huang's discussions of ethnographic feminism and stylistic smoothening with Rey Chow's elucidation of coercive mimeticism because, while the need to authenticate one's self-identity as an ethnic subject through these methods of "self-referentiality" appears to "finally redeem us from the fundamental and contentious binary structure of representation in which one is always (inevitably) speaking of/for something or someone else" (*Protestant Ethnic* 113), it is in effect "a socially endorsed, coercive mimeticism, which stipulates that the thing to imitate, resemble, and become is none other than the ethnic or sexual minority herself" (*Protestant Ethnic* 115). As a result, Chow argues, such well-intentioned attempts at a radical politics through the writing of self-formation and self-reference paradoxically cause ethnic and gendered subjects "to come across as inferior imitations, copies that are permanently out of focus" (*Protestant Ethnic* 127). But by imagining a female *community* instead of a female *identity* formed at the intersections of overlapping multilogical cultural worlds, Lim's critical project steps away from ethnographic feminism driven by coercive mimeticism and resonates with recent feminist interpretations of Adorno's discussions of gender in his social theory, because "while Adorno does interpret the feminine as the 'other' to the masculine, he does not suggest that the feminine is a binary or polar opposite of the masculine [...] . The feminine in Adorno's reading is of an otherness that consistently disrupts the totalizing concept of masculinity" (Lee 129). Lim's focus on her protagonists' somatic and emotional sensations underscores how critical rationality, contrary to its name, requires a combination of feeling and cognition: "the assumption that thought profits from the decay of the emotions, or even that it remains unaffected, is itself an expression of the process of stupefaction. [...] Because even its remotest objectifications are nourished by impulses, thought destroys in the latter the condition of its own existence" (Adorno, *Minima Moralia* 122). The point here is that somatic impulses and gut feelings respond to the multifaceted object that is inevitably reduced to thought-concepts of the knowing subject, such that a different language of experience and expression is required to invert "the process of stupefaction" that separates and maintains the boundaries between subject-concept and object. Hence Shirley Geok-lin Lim often represents her protagonists in terms that focus on "the mimetic, the sensual, the non-conceptual" so as to "approach a 'politics' which undercuts identity thinking, which refuses to engage in identitarian thinking—but rather crisscrosses binary thinking/territories—and remains un-appropriated" (O'Neill 29); Lim goes one step further than Adorno in showing us that these impulses, which are thought's conditions of possibility rather than its opposite, have not been utterly destroyed.

Through Li An's and Suyin's claiming of their physical and emotional selves that are not instrumentalized by masculine society's nationalist discourse of multiculturalism, Lim's novel works through and goes beyond representations of the ideal feminine as a symbol demarcating the cultural boundaries between Asians and Westerners as well as Chinese, Indians, and Malays. Lim imagines a community within the sociopolitical framework of the Singaporean nation where women can affirm themselves on their own terms instead of those already mapped out by the patriotic symbolism of postcolonial cultural nationalism. She configures a negative dialectic between America and Asia, male and female, nation and culture, such that the first term in each pair neither subsumes nor subordinates the second, in the same way that a literary cosmopolitics articulates with rather than cancels out a critical nationality within the context of Lim's novel that spans both sides of the Pacific.

"A Psychic Hinterland":
Shirley Geok-lin Lim's *Joss and Gold*

Shirley Lim's *Joss and Gold* spans two time periods and three countries. Starting in Malaysia in the late 1960s, the novel follows Li An, a young Chinese Malaysian woman who studies and teaches British literature at the national university in the capital, Kuala Lumpur. Although Li An aspires to be a writer in America, she marries Henry Yeh, a Chinese Malaysian biochemist who asks her to stay in Malaysia with him. However, during the political and racial riots between ethnic Malays and Chinese in May 1969, Li An shares a night of passion with Chester Brookfield, an American Peace Corps volunteer whose brashness and idealistic enthusiasm seem initially attractive. A disillusioned Chester returns to America after the riots, but Li An bears his child, a girl with green eyes and red hair whom she names Suyin. Henry divorces Li An upon discovering that Suyin is Chester's child, and Li An moves with her daughter to Singapore, living with her close friend Ellen and with Henry's stepmother, Mrs Yeh. The novel jumps to the 1980s, where Chester, now an anthropology professor in upstate New York, gets a vasectomy at the behest of his career-oriented American wife, Meryl. Chester finds out from an old Malaysian friend that he has a daughter by Li An, and goes to Singapore to look for her on the pretext of anthropological research. Li An is now the editor of a newsletter for an important biogenetics firm in Singapore, and grudgingly agrees to let Chester meet the twelve-year-old Suyin. Mrs Yeh's sudden death leaves a substantial inheritance for Suyin, and Henry, as her executor, comes back into the picture, treating Suyin as his daughter. The narration begins to focus on Suyin's impressions of her life in an all-female household and the puzzling predicament of having two fathers from two different cultures and countries. Li An, who realizes that her daughter must find her own answers to this complicated situation, finally agrees to let Suyin visit Chester in America. The novel concludes with Li An listening to her daughter's breathing as she sleeps, evoking in her memory Gerard Manley Hopkins's poem "The Leaden Echo and the Golden Echo."

Most reviewers of *Joss and Gold* adopt an ethnographic perspective, focusing on the effects of American imperialism on postcolonial societies and the problems of gender and race in Malaysia and Singapore. The book is read as a "coming-of-age novel" that is "dominated by strong, independent, and goal-oriented women wrestling with individual development issues within the larger framework of a society also in transition" (Haggas 2087). *Publishers Weekly* praises Lim for her "keen eye for the effects of American imperialism" and her "acute, realistic detail" but also faults her for providing so much detail that the narrative becomes "burdensome" and requires "judicious editing" (52). Another reviewer remarks how "the plot wears thin toward the end and touches little on the relationship between Chester and Li An after their reunion. Instead, Lim brings Suyin to the forefront, keeping the story open for a possible sequel" (Quan 162). These reviewers' dissatisfaction with certain plot and stylistic issues of Lim's novel stems from a reading of the novel as a realist *Bildungsroman,* but we must understand that *Joss and Gold* is, instead, a cosmopolitical and (to use Lim's own word) multilogical narrative. Certainly, it begins as a conventional coming-of-age narrative centered on Li An and offers incisive commentary about race, gender, and politics in Malaysia and Singapore—these two elements are never absent from the text. But Lim's novel is also in conversation with Asian American women's writing, for it uses the mother–daughter relationship and the rewriting of cultural nationalism in order to critically confront the heroic masculinity of Malaysian and Singaporean nationalism. As Peter Nazareth astutely points out, there is a symbolic connection between Lim's novel and the memoirs of Singapore's first prime minister, Kuan Yew Lee: "The country has no hinterland, Lee reiterates—and the [Singaporean] writers know it consequently has no psychic hinterland, which they must create" (Nazareth 139). The "psychic hinterland," for Lim, turns out to be both Malaysian-Singaporean and Asian-American, for her novel, like Singapore itself, "reshapes the resources of a multinational world" (Nazareth 139). Lim's novel stages a multinational, transpacific dialogue: if, in a novel by Amy Tan, the mother's essential Chineseness must be abjected in order for the daughter to fully claim her Americanness, then in Lim's novel, it is not abjection but reproduction and miscegenation that are foregrounded through Li An's affair with Chester Brookfield and through Suyin, her daughter who has both white American and Chinese Singaporean blood. Through Li An and her hybrid daughter Suyin, *Joss and Gold* presents the reader with the negative imprint of masculine society's domination of women by turning an idealized feminine character and her daughter into boundary-transgressing figures of impurity who undermine the strict racial and cultural boundaries of instrumental nationality. Moving between Malaysia and Singapore and the United States, Lim stages a literary cosmopolitical encounter between national consciousness on both sides of the Pacific Ocean.

Li An, as the protagonist of the novel, challenges the Chinese ideal of a mellow woman and dutiful wife both in her profession and in her personality. When Li An is a student and tutor of English literature at the university in Kuala Lumpur, her relationship to language is embodied in the somatic sensations of her being rather than as intellectual capital or cultural *Bildung*. At the novel's beginning, Li An prepares a prose passage from D. H. Lawrence for her seminar on practical criticism, where "she read it aloud, relishing the overflow of sibilants like spiced chickpeas in her mouth" (*Joss and Gold* 4). She spends her time sitting in the library "reading old copies of *Scrutiny* and copying fine phrases by F. R. Leavis, occasionally tearing off her sweater and running outside in the blazing sun to the back of the faculty lounge, where she bought sizzling flaky curry puffs and smoked two cigarettes in a row" (4). Certainly, Li An's emphasis on practical criticism and her choice of D. H. Lawrence for her students carry strong overtones of Leavis's own literary tastes, including his proposal that the study of English contributes "towards remedying those disorders of civilized society" ("'English,' Unrest, and Continuity" 105) by creating a "collaborative community" within the classroom that serves as "the model or paradigm of the ideal [. . .] educated public that (ideally) makes possible at any time a performance of the function of criticism" ("'English,' Unrest, and Continuity" 109). This "collaborative community" formed through literary study is why, in Li An's own words, English literature matters for postcolonial, postindependence Malaysia: "What literature does is connect things, even the most unlikely things. [. . .] That's what we have to do with our lives, connect with others" (*Joss and Gold* 9). What Li An does not realize, however, is that Leavis's humanistic conceptualization of English literature cannot be appropriated to the Malaysian and Singaporean postcolonial context without extensive modification.

In fact, Li An's own reactions to Leavis's philosophy belies the ideal of community and collaboration she explicitly avows, as if she embodies the sensuousness she reads in Lawrence's prose against Leavis's moral principles. Lim's prose emphasizes the physical, sensuous aspect of Li An's literary learning, unlike the moral edification which Leavis argues is the reward for studying literature. Li An's body language is bold and unfettered: she is "a swaggering teddy boy" who rides "her bike bent over the handlebars" (*Joss and Gold* 5); she likes "roaming on her motorbike like a boy," and "her tight jeans showed her thighs and calves, and her smoking made her conspicuous among a crowd" (10). Despite Li An's own avowal of literature's mission to connect and create a microcosm of an ideal educated public or social body, her own body and behavior make her stand out rather than blend in: "She was like a Western girl—bold, loud, and unconcerned about her reputation" (10). Lim's novel suggests that the Leavisian idea of a literary, collaborative community, which Li An espouses, cannot be formed within dominant structures of Malaysian or Singaporean nationalism and society because Li An (the foremost proponent of this idea) stands in contrast to rather than in connection with the Malaysians around her. Her very attachment to literary language and a community of readers causes her physical carriage and body language to appear as an exceptional deviation rather than a normative aspiration. Furthermore, this Leavisian ideal cannot be realized because of the racialization of the Malay and English languages. Li An's university classmate and friend Samad is a Malay nationalist who argues that Malay is the "national language" of Malaysia, whereas English is "a bastard language" that only one percent of Malaysians who will have contact with the rest of the world really need to learn (*Joss and Gold* 56). Lim undercuts the corporeal notion of literature shaping a national *Bildung* and the Leavisian idea of a moral community formed through shared literary learning because in postcolonial societies such as Malaysia and Singapore, these ideas enforce a sense of cultural purity and separatism among the ethnic Malay and Chinese communities that also carries with it an interpellation of women and their bodies as idealized feminine characters.

"Better that like stay with like":
Henry's Chinese Way and Abdullah's Malay Rights

Li An's marriage to Henry Yeh, a Chinese Malaysian biochemist who is the son of a rich businessman, marks her interpellation by this discourse of cultural purity and idealized femininity, or what Shirley Geok-lin Lim calls the overlapping authoritarian domains of Confucianism, Malay feudalism, and (resistance toward) British colonialism. When Li An expresses her desire to go to America and become a writer, Henry's reaction reveals his commitment to a heroic, patriarchal nationalism. Henry argues that Malaysia "has just become a nation" and "is like an experiment," an experiment that a scientist such as Henry is conducting in order to "discover that truth which no one else has ever found" (*Joss and Gold* 11). Despite Henry's assurance that he and Li An are on par with each other as "the important people in the country because we are the people with brains" (11), his vision of Malaysia as a scientific experiment corresponds to his own scientific vocation—Henry sees himself as the one who can search for and discover the truth that will make Malaysia work as a nation. Li An is keenly aware of her own marginalization as a Chinese Malaysian woman, but seems unable to do anything about it at this point in the novel, for she laments that she wishes she "were a man and a scientist. Then there would be a place for [her] here" (13). Furthermore, Henry's physical movements as he proposes to Li An and asks her not to leave reveal how he idealizes her as a feminine and maternal figure rather than as a woman with her own ambition and sense of self: "he put his arms around her and put his head on her hair. He was like a little boy silently demanding her attention" (13). Simultaneously, Henry thinks of his and Suyin's roles in their marriage as that of male breadwinner and dependent woman:

> Marry me, and stay with me. You won't have to teach. I'll pay off your government bond, and you won't be forced to go back to your town. You don't have to work if you don't want to. [. . .] You could write, Li An. I'll let you write. You say it's time for Malaysians to write about themselves. You can't write about Malaysia in America. (*Joss and Gold* 13)

For Henry, Li An's position in the marriage is defined by what she will *not* do: she "won't have to teach," "won't be forced to go back to [her] town," and "won't have to work." Li An's writerly ambitions will be indulged by Henry at his sufferance, and his idea of good writing is tied to a nativist identity because for him Malaysians can only "write about themselves" in Malaysia, not in America. Although Henry castigates Li An's desire to go to America as "a selfish way of acting" (*Joss and Gold* 11), his marriage proposal is framed by his own self-interest and the interest of a Malaysian national identity.

However, Li An's interrogation of this national identity reveals the fault lines of race and gender within this collective representation. Soon after her marriage, Li An interrupts a discussion about race and language between her Chinese husband and their two Malay friends Abdullah and Samad. After his friends leave, Henry chastises Li An for contradicting Abdullah: "You have become too Westernized. First, you must accept what people say. If you cannot agree, you must still be quiet. Men get upset when women contradict them" (*Joss and Gold* 57). Henry insists that Li An use her "intelligence for agreement, not for arguing. That's the Chinese way. Even the men follow the rule" (57). Li An's feminine character is defined as a nurturing participant in the national collective (a mother succoring her childlike husband Henry); she also must "articulate [her] gender interests within the terms of reference set by nationalist discourse" (Kandiyoti 380). Li An's final rejoinder to Henry's admonishment that she must learn her place as a Chinese woman—"But I'm not Chinese! I'm Malaysian!" (*Joss and Gold* 57)—is especially important. Li An's direct, emphatic statement reveals the limits of the liberatory national narrative constructed by both Chinese and Malay Malaysian leaders in their idealization of a feminine character, because this narrative positions Malaysian women (of any ethnicity or culture) in the ambivalent position of being both standard-bearers of cultural purity (in Li An's case, being Chinese) and standards of national progress (being intelligent and writing about Malaysia for Malaysians).

Furthermore, if Henry represents "the Chinese way" of social conventions and decorum, then his friend Abdullah represents the dominant Malay view of what Malaysia should be—namely a multiculturalism in which Malay culture is the dominant standard to which all other ethnic groups should adhere. Abdullah's views express the terms of reference set by a Malay nationalist discourse, for he is a journalist working for a newspaper that "published daily editorials demanding special rights for Malays" (*Joss and Gold* 44–45); Li An finds this disturbing, because "reading it made her feel she was in danger of attack in an alien country" even though she was born, has grown up, and lived in Malaysia all her life (45). Even though Abdullah is, in person, a courteous and charming intellectual whom Li An finds persuasive, the novel's description of their intellectual conversations expresses the ambivalence of his argument:

His position was quite clear, but he argued with her subtly, like a good partner observing the patterns and courtesies of an elaborate dance. She didn't feel threatened when he explained the need for Malay special rights intelligently and elegantly; he made it seem fair and just, a readjustment to the fundamental design of the dance. She liked the idea of the Malaysian future as this gentle weaving readjustment and had asked Abdullah why his paper did not present its position in that light. He answered that it did, she was simply not reading it correctly. (*Joss and Gold* 45)

At first glance this passage suggests that Li An finds Abdullah's argument for Malay special rights, as the *bumiputera*, or indigenous people who make up Malaysia's demographic majority, reasonable. Although Abdullah presents Malays and Chinese as being "good partner[s]" in "an elaborate dance" of Malaysian nationalism, Lim raises the question about the exact significance of the dance metaphor. Is the dance referring to (according to Abdullah) the dominant Malay culture that is the "fundamental design" that Malay special rights will make "fair and just," or is it (according to Li An) "the idea of the Malaysian future" that will be readjusted through this "gentle weaving," that will create a nation of Malaysian citizens and not just Malays and Chinese? Pushing this metaphor of a courtly dance even further, we must ask: who is leading this dance, and is "a good partner" someone who is on par with the dance leader, or someone who merely follows the leader well? Li An seems to believe in the former, whereas Abdullah's stance is the latter, whereby Malays are the leaders in multicultural Malaysia. In this light, we can see that Abdullah's idea of a good partner is not too different from Henry's idea of a good partner: a wife who does not have to do anything and who uses her intelligence for agreeing rather than arguing. Abdullah's comment that Li An "was simply not reading [his newspaper's views] correctly" on the subject of race relations is similar to Henry's comment that Li An ought to follow the unspoken "Chinese way" of decorum. Henry assumes that Li An is too Westernized and needs to be more Chinese, while Abdullah implies that Li An is too Chinese and cannot correctly comprehend the Malay perspective. Lim places Li An in this quandary in order to highlight how these gendered and purist demands made by national identities create an impasse in a postcolonial society that is trying to be simultaneously modernized or Westernized and traditional or native.

These identities premised on ideas of racial and cultural purity hierarchize different groups in Malaysia, as we see in Abdullah's assessment of the tragic fate of Paroo and Gina. Paroo is an Indian (South Asian) Malaysian who is dating Gina, a Chinese Malaysian woman, against the wishes of both their families, who frown on interracial relationships. They attempt a joint suicide by overdosing on sleeping pills; Gina dies, but Paroo survives. Abdullah gives his analysis of the tragic situation to Li An:

> Better that like stay with like. Indian and Chinese cannot mix, too many differences—food, custom, language. To be husband and wife must share same religion, same race, same history. Malay and Chinese also cannot mix, like oil and water. Malay have many *adat,* Islam also have *shariat.* All teach good action. Chinese have no *adat,* they eat pork, they like gamble, make money. [...] Of course, Chinese also have their own religion. But they must become like Malay if they want to marry Malay. (*Joss and Gold* 46)

Abdullah translates what would be normally be considered ethnic differences—differences in "food, custom, language"—into indelible and incommensurable disparities such that the Malays, Indians, and Chinese in Malaysia cannot share the "same religion, same race, same history," hence people from these various groups cannot intermarry and become "husband and wife." What is more striking is Abdullah's use of Paroo and Gina's failure at becoming "husband and wife" as an analogy for the incompatibility of "Indian and Chinese" and "Malay and Chinese." In each case, "Chinese" is the secondary term, just as "wife" is the secondary term in the first pairing of "husband and wife." Abdullah's word choice reveals his unspoken assumption of Malay superiority: he begins by discussing Paroo and Gina, an Indian–Chinese pairing, but his analysis quickly turns into a comparison of how Malays are superior to Chinese and how Malay culture is the standard that must be adhered to. For Abdullah, Malays have "*adat,*" or traditional prohibitions, whereas the Chinese have none, hence the Chinese are inferior. While it is possible for a Chinese woman to marry a Malay man, the insurmountability of ethnic difference that underwrites the idea of "better that like stay with like" suggests it is impossible for any Chinese to truly become Malay. In either case, Abdullah (like Henry when he proposes to Li An) assumes that the Chinese woman and wife plays a secondary, subservient role to the Indian, Malay, or Chinese man and husband. Unlike Henry and Abdullah, Li An was optimistic that Paroo and Gina's mixed marriage gestured toward a Malaysian future, because "as [school]teachers, Gina and Paroo would serve as models of a new kind of Malaysian" and Gina "would have light-brown children who would look both and neither Indian and/or Chinese, the new Malaysians" (*Joss and Gold* 41). The union of Paroo and Gina fails tragically in the first part of the novel, but Shirley Geok-lin Lim uses Li An's attachment to the English language as a way of foreshadowing her future role as the mother of a mixed or hybrid Eurasian girl, because Abdullah remarks that English is "a bastard language," and that only Malay is the truly "national language" of Malaysia (56). Li An's emphatic rebuttal of Henry's demand that she adhere to a traditional Chinese way of behavior, and her instinctive uneasiness about the slippage between Abdullah's reasonable explanation of Malay indigenous rights and his newspaper's fiery denunciation of other ethnic communities, suggests a critique of masculine society's cultural and purist national identities advanced from a feminist perspective that combines rational interrogation and emotional introspection centered on a female assertion of selfhood. Furthermore, because Li An is an English-speaking, English-teaching Malaysian Chinese woman, her affair with the white American Peace Corps worker Chester Brookfield challenges these tightly policed racial and cultural boundaries by claiming that both her language and her child are legitimate rather than bastard offspring of the nation.

The Burden of the White American Man:
Chester Brookfield

Chester Brookfield, when he first appears, seems to be a refreshing change from the authoritarian realms of Chinese tradition and Malay nationalism that Henry and Abdullah represent. However, Chester's actions toward Li An suggest that both he and a Malay nationalist such as Abdullah expect Malaysians to hold fast to a purified native identity tied to a specific culture and language. An American Peace Corps volunteer who majored in anthropology at Princeton, Chester prefers anthropology to literature because he does not "think [he] can learn as much about people from books as from the things they make and use every day" (*Joss and Gold* 33). As such, he tries to spend "as much time as he could with Malaysians" (30) by teaching woodworking at a vocational school in Kuala Lumpur, living with Malay roommates (Abdullah and Samad), and taking Malay lessons in his spare time (29). Chester also tries to become as native as possible, eating "spicy food in huge gulps without any complaints," joking that "perhaps [he] was a Malay in another life" (31), and echoing Abdullah's idea that "Malay is the only real culture in this country" (33). But Chester soon discovers that Malaysians are not as naïve or as native as he would like them to be. "Only three students" take his woodworking class because "no one wanted to be an artisan-carpenter in Malaysia" (29), and these students persistently ask him questions about America (30). Chester soon finds himself grudgingly teaching English-language classes at the school, because the headmaster "says what he really needs now is another English teacher, not a carpenter" (36). Lim's novel points out, however obliquely, that the students themselves—the next generation of Malaysians—are more interested in learning a language that gives access to and symbolizes modernization and development. They thus thwart or frustrate the ambitions of both the Western anthropologist and the local nationalist to create an immutable, uncontaminated identity based on an unchanging language or culture.

As racial and political tensions rise in Malaysia, Chester finds the local charm fading quickly, for "the longer he stayed with Abdullah and Samad [. . .] the more he realized how different he was from them. He was tired of drinking rose syrup and of having chilies in his food" (*Joss and Gold* 64). Instead, he uses his friendship with Li An to expound on the virtues of American culture and literature, virtues he regards as inherently and universally democratic. On the one hand, Chester vehemently espouses anticolonial and anti-British views; he scoffs at Li An's love of English literature, arguing that the Americans "had a revolution and threw them out with the tea bags" and that Li An should be teaching her "own culture" (33), which, for Chester, can only be Malay culture. But while Chester exhorts Li An to be more culturally authentic, he also takes her to the "United States Information Service Library" and insists that Li An read American literature for inspiration, because American writers are "modern writers" who speak "for a democratic American vista," namely the ideal of the United States as "a melting pot" where "everyone melted into the American middle class" (64). Therefore, Chester concludes, "English has left with the British," and Li An "should really emigrate to the States" (64), since Li An's own vision of an egalitarian, truly multicultural Malaysia makes her "almost sound like an American" (35). Ironically, Chester does not realize he is substituting one form of Western hegemony for another: the British colonizers may have left, but Chester represents an American imperialism trying to incorporate various postcolonial nations into its own post–World War II ambit. Chester assimilates Li An's vision for Malaysia—a vision that tries to ameliorate the conflicts between essential cultural or racial identities—as a characteristically American "democratic vista" or "melting pot," rather than considering Li An's vision on its own terms as a critical form of postcolonial national consciousness trying to undo the effects of British colonialism. Chester's paradoxical insistence that Li An be traditionally authentic and teach her own (i.e., Malay) culture and at the same time read modern American writers to keep up with the times also echoes the demands of postcolonial nationalists who want women to be both symbols of cultural essence and emblems of national progress. Chester's exhortation that Li An "should really emigrate" to America since her personality already seems American is therefore similar to the two forms of interpellation we have seen from Henry and Abdullah: the concept of a "Chinese way" that all ethnic Chinese Malaysians should automatically and naturally obey, and the separate-but-equal idea of "better that like stay with like."

Despite the similarities between Chester's American thinking and Henry's and Abdullah's attitudes, Li An is deeply attracted to Chester. After sleeping with him on the night of the racial riots of May 13, 1969, Li An "knew he was planning something for them, something wonderful," because she felt "no man could touch a woman as he had her without love, and love had inevitable consequences" (*Joss and Gold* 86). However, contrary to his confident and breezy manner, Chester turns out, like Henry, to be uncertain, childlike, and reluctant to take responsibility for his involvement in local affairs. Dashing Li An's hopes, Chester reveals that he will be going home with the rest of the Peace Corps, because, as he says, "our parents were after the embassy people to make sure we were safe, and we were warned not to get involved with the local trouble" (87). Chester further emphasizes that "the Peace Corps is concerned about its volunteers in Malaysia, and is urging us to consider our options. It isn't good for Americans to get in the middle of foreign national politics" (87–88). Chester distances himself from and absolves himself of responsibility for Li An and Malaysia, and his flight from Malaysia reveals the limits of the apparently attractive American alternative to Chinese traditional behavior and Malay cultural nationalism. Li An, despite sounding "almost like an American" with her democratic ideals, cannot be incorporated into American society despite Chester's insistence that she would fit in perfectly there. Chester's attitude and involvement (despite his avowal of detachment) in Malaysian affairs is characteristic of an Orientalist approach toward other cultures. Asia, and more specifically, Malaysia, becomes a commodity that enriches the knowledge and life experience of Chester, who is an anthropologist at heart and by training. After his own marital disappointments eleven years later, Chester begins yearning for Malaysia, Li An, and the daughter he has never met. After the events of 1969, Lim's novel jumps to 1980 and the location changes to upstate New York, where we find that Chester has obtained a Ph.D. in anthropology from Columbia University. But Chester is assigned to teach sociology at a small liberal arts college for women, where his students "showed almost no curiosity about actual foreign countries" and "thought of Asia and Africa as primitive and unbearably savage" (115). He undergoes a vasectomy at the behest of his American wife, Meryl, who argues that "there's no way [they] can have a baby and be fair to everyone" since she is rushing to finish a thesis for her master's degree and is applying to be "the first woman commissioner in the history" of the New York City Parks Department (102). Confronted with an unsatisfying career, the loss of his biological ability to father a child, and the determined ambitions of his wife, Chester begins to remember his time in Malaysia with a mixture of fear and fascination:

> It was a kind of panic, like the panic he felt when he saw the black smoke the night of the riots of Kuala Lumpur, a sensation of falling through space not knowing that there would be a landing. The same panic he felt when he read Paroo's letter about Li An's baby, and counted the dates and found that they matched. He had suppressed the panic each time and come through. After all, neither the riots nor Li An's baby had been his business. He could leave and he did. (*Joss and Gold* 110–11)

Despite the overtones of turmoil and discord in the word "panic," Chester seems to relish this panic as a surmountable emotional obstacle, something that he can suppress "each time and come through" because, as an anthropologist, he sees himself personally and professionally as an observer rather than a participant, hence "the riots and Li An's baby" were not "his business" at all. The privilege he enjoys as a white, male, American anthropologist to come and go freely is predicated on his anthropological training: "to be white, to *know* one was white, to find anything else peculiar and uncomfortable, was no sin—it became, in fact, the basis for curiosity and inquiry, one's fate" (*Joss and Gold* 153, original emphasis). Chester, in the end, is fascinated more by differences than similarities, and commits himself "to study difference, not overcome it," and to do so "guiltlessly" (154). Furthermore, Chester's desire to travel to Singapore to see Li An and his daughter Suyin is driven by "curiosity" to "see what the child's like" (159) rather than a sense of responsibility toward Li An. This suggests that Chester's professional acumen is premised on an essential racial identity of being "white" that parallels Henry's Chinese traditions and Abdullah's Malay nationalism, and it undermines the idea of the "melting pot" and "a democratic American vista" that Chester extolled earlier. Chester's professional and personal curiosity and inquiry is, in postcolonial terms, a "vantage point outside the actuality of relationships among cultures" that confers "the epistemological privilege of somehow judging, evaluating, and interpreting the world free from the encumbering interests and engagements of the ongoing relationships themselves" (Said, *Culture and Imperialism* 55). *Joss and Gold* critiques this American Orientalist epistemological privilege and the essentialist discourses of race and culture that underwrite official Malaysian multiculturalism. Lim's novel presents Henry,

Abdullah, and Chester as representatives of their similar discourses of race, language, and cultural identity; the novel offers a "multilogical" critique of these "authoritarian domains [that] overlap each other but not sufficiently so as to preserve the illusion of totalization" ("Anglo-American Feminism" 35).

"She would never again be unburdened or alone":
Li An, Suyin, and an Alternative Community of Women in Singapore

Joss and Gold, however, is more than an exposition of masculine society's cultural nationalist and Orientalist domination of women, for Lim does not think of these interpellating systems as absolutely dominating. The illusion of totalization is broken when the systems coincide and overlap, and "it is not these systems but their intersections that offered [. . .] points of escape" ("Anglo-American Feminism" 37), allowing Li An and her daughter Suyin a way out of the instrumental rationality of masculine postcolonial nationalism in Malaysia and Singapore. In the last part of *Joss and Gold*, Lim's narration focuses on Li An and her surrogate family made up of her close friend Ellen (now the principal of a high school in Singapore) and her mother-in-law, Second Mrs Yeh (Henry's father's second wife, whom he acknowledges as a mother), and her half-Chinese, half-American daughter, Suyin. By increasingly focusing on Li An's relationship to her daughter Suyin to the point where Suyin overshadows her mother as the protagonist of the novel's latter half, Lim engages in a cosmopolitics of the female body, extending what Ketu Katrak calls "the politics of the female body" in her study of postcolonial women's writing that "includes the constructions and controls of female sexuality, its acceptable and censored expressions, its location socioculturally, even materially, in postcolonial regions" (8). Lim's writing is cosmopolitical because in this last section she foregrounds the literary connections with Asian American women's writing, especially through the tropes of mother-daughter narratives and revisions of East Asian myths and folktales discussed by Patricia P. Chu. The symbolic instrumentalization of women in the culture industry of a heroic masculine postcolonial nationalism is interrupted and negated by these transpacific connections between one feminist literary context and another. These connections "are undertaken with self-consciousness and remarkable creativity that decides to take risks and confront domination selectively and strategically in the interest of self-preservation," as "women resist bodily oppressions by using strategies and tactics that are often part of women's ways of knowing and acting" (Katrak 3, 8). Invoking

Asian American women writers' literary strategies within a Malaysian-Singaporean context, Lim employs the mother-daughter narrative and reworking of East Asian myths to challenge the nationalist exhortations that (on one hand) women should "mind their familial responsibilities" and "make more babies" in order to "best serve the 'nation'" (Purushotam 335), and that (on the other hand) women have a duty to "reproduce their culture through the continued use of their native language, the persistence of culinary and other habits and the socialisation of the young" (Kandiyoti 382). In the final section of *Joss and Gold,* Lim takes up the logic of pure biological and cultural reproduction and challenges them on their own grounds through Li An's creation of an all-female surrogate family, her profoundly physical connections to both her daughter and literary language, and finally through Suyin herself and the mythical figure of Madam White Snake, a female snake spirit in Chinese mythology who enters a forbidden romance with a human scholar and is punished for eternity because of this transgression. Furthermore, Lim's cosmopolitical critique of both Malaysia and Singapore focuses on the technocratic and instrumental use of language and race in these societies driven by the pursuit of global capital. This final section reveals how all the characters we saw in 1969 in Malaysia end up as successful entrepreneurs and professionals in Singapore twelve years later. It seems, on the surface, as if race, language, gender, and culture are not as important once everyone migrates to Singapore. But Lim also points out how a dominant Chinese identity—and with it, a male-dominant concept of race and identity similar to the ones espoused by Henry and Abdullah back in Malaysia—nonetheless underscores Singapore's economic progress and social fabric.

Singapore's economic progress is apparent in the last section of the novel, and all the characters who in 1969 held immutable views on race, culture, and identity seem to have changed their tune in 1981. Abdullah and Samad, the two Malay nationalists, are "now living in Singapore" and have become "VIP CEOs" (*Joss and Gold* 165) there, and because of their success they "also have big houses in Malaysia" (166). Abdullah was also part of the leading Malay political party in Malaysia, UMNO, "before joining OKM—Overseas Koranic Majulis—[a] big-time travel company [to] bring Muslims to *hajj* in Mecca" (166). Abdullah, despite his earlier emphasis on special Malay rights and Malay indigeneity, studied journalism in the United States, and his "English had become New England; two years at Harvard had done what almost twenty years of British education had failed to do" (188). Furthermore, in 1981 Abdullah is about to fly back to Kuala Lumpur to open a new mosque, a symbolic act to "show the fundamentalists that we can make money and also be good Muslims at the same time" (189). Abdullah even concedes that "Li An was right" and that "the national language [Malay] is the soul of our country, but English is the language of money for Malaysia and Singapore. The goal of Malaysia is to make money. So English is the destiny of our country" (249). Abdullah's emphasis on "money" and on "mak[ing] money" suggests that underlying the seemingly color- or race-blind economic ethos of Singapore there is an aspect of ethnic Chinese culture that Abdullah himself castigated in 1969: "Chinese have no *adat*, they eat pork, they like gamble, make money" (46). Beneath Abdullah's comment that he is opening a mosque in Malaysia to prove that money-making Malays can also be good Muslims is an anxiety that making money is an inherently Chinese trait, and that his Malay identity and language—"the national language [that] is the soul of our country" (249)—is slowly being eroded by English—"the language of money"—as well.

Furthermore, the newsletter Li An edits for her company, BioSynergy, holds an important place in Singapore's economic climate, for "it was a hot document studied by investors, shareholders, and the Monetary Authority of Singapore for clues to the company's health and future" (*Joss and Gold* 176). Li An's choice of the newsletter's logo suggests a strong Chinese cultural symbolism: it consists of "two Ss" that "suggest the shapes of the dragon and the phoenix" (259), implying "the dragon's harmonic meanings and the phoenix's regenerative energies," and even though it resembles "something European and medieval, yet it was clearly Chinese in origin" (260). Chester, upon his arrival in Singapore in 1981, is also astounded by how, on the one hand, "The Chinese were everywhere, but they had English names" and "Anglo-Chinese was the norm," yet on the other hand both the Singaporean state and its people are pushing for a "Chinese-Chinese [identity] to be the norm" (200). Li An's logo design for her company's newsletter emphasizes this conjunction of Anglo-Chinese normativity couched in Chinese-Chinese cultural terms. Henry's idea of the "Chinese way," which, in the Malaysia of 1969, suggests propriety and knowing one's place, has become, in the Singapore of 1981, an instrumentalized ethnic and cultural identity that allows the state to compete actively in global business. However, the beneficiaries of this new conjunction of identity and globalization are clearly male. Li An's boss, Ang Swee, who is the chief executive officer of BioSynergy, is ethnically Chinese but holds an Australian citizenship simply because it has "more cachet" (224), and "he never worried about being superior" but "simply enjoyed the condition" (224) of being both Chinese and Westernized. Similarly, Abdullah and Samad are "VIP CEOs" (165) owning large properties in Malaysia but have chosen to settle and work in Singapore; they move frequently between the two countries while their wives and children remain in Singapore. In contrast, Li An's move to Singapore is not of her own volition; it is necessitated by her abandonment by her husband, Henry, after Suyin's birth.

Even in this climate of cultural Chineseness and economic success, Lim's novel shows us how Li An creates a family composed completely of women who can nurture her half-Chinese, half-American daughter Suyin, who in Chinese-Chinese Singapore becomes the brunt of racist remarks such as "chap cheng kwei—mixed breed devil" (*Joss and Gold* 255). Ellen, Li An's close friend from college, becomes an older-sister figure who "swore at" Li An for "crying" over Henry's abandonment; she instead urges Li An to put "all [her] strength into nursing the baby" (205). Lim's novel emphasizes that Ellen, who remains single and dedicated to her career as a schoolteacher and later headmistress of a high school, does not exhibit romantic or erotic feelings for Li An; her love for Li An is expressed in terms of friendship and guilt for not preventing Li An's romantic liaison with Chester: "I only do this for old friend's sake. Otherwise I will feel too guilty for words" (181). Ellen is not a surrogate lover but rather an older sister for Li An and "a second parent" for Suyin. Ellen serves as the role model of a strong-willed, independent woman for Li An; from the latter's point of view, Ellen is "like a minor goddess" busy "rearranging their lives," helping Li An and Suyin look for an apartment in Singapore and then finding "Li An the job as a part-time copy editor in the communications department in BioSynergy," which eventually leads to Li An's high-ranking executive position in the present (181). Once they move to Singapore, "Auntie Ellen" becomes a "second mother" (205) who "picked Suyin up from school, supervised her homework, and then went home, many evenings only after Li An got home from work" late at night (196). Ellen becomes a second maternal figure who maintains her own independent vocation outside of the family unit, thereby reconfiguring the conventional norms of the nuclear family in which a child must be cared for by two parents of different sexes. Ellen, in her role as a minor goddess, offers an assertive female role model that differs from the heroic masculine narratives put forward by fathers of the nation such as Singapore's Kwan Yew Lee.

If Ellen is a role model, an older sister, and a second parent, then Second Mrs Yeh serves as the matriarch of this reconstituted family of women. Second Mrs Yeh, the second wife of Henry's father, gives Li An's daughter legitimacy under the Yeh family name by adamantly claiming Suyin as her granddaughter. Second Mrs Yeh is the one who "picked the name [for Li An's child] months before she was born" and urges Li An to keep Henry's family name (Yeh) to make life "more safe" for Suyin in the future (*Joss and Gold* 169). Second Mrs Yeh, or Grandma Yeh, shares a physical bond with the infant Suyin that is comparable to Li An's own bond with her daughter:

"She's Henry's baby," Second Mrs. Yeh crooned to the infant, her visits unchecked by Henry's absence. Humming her song, she rubbed olive oil onto the carapace where the skull bones had not closed, the light brown hair twisting over the tender spot where only skin protected the brain. "Ah Pah's [Henry's father's] granddaughter," she breathed over the membrane, fingers stroking the green oil into the scalp. [...] Invisible, unerasable. Second Mrs. Yeh's granddaughter. (*Joss and Gold* 170)

Despite Suyin's obvious physical appearance, Grandma Yeh insists that Suyin is her own granddaughter. This insistence flies in the face of conventional genealogy, and might be read as stubborn self-denial or sheer naïveté. But we may understand Grandma Yeh's actions as her way of exercising her power as secondary matriarch within the Yeh family to protect Suyin. Mr Yeh himself was killed during the May 1969 riots in Kuala Lumpur (*Joss and Gold* 83–84), and the novel does not reveal the whereabouts of his first wife and her family. It is clear that Henry, born of Mr Yeh's first wife and heir to the Yeh family name, is the new male authority figure in the Yeh family, and Grandma Yeh urges Li An to keep Suyin's last name as Yeh, thus acknowledging that power of patrilineal descent. However, we can also read Grandma Yeh's use of the Yeh family name as a female appropriation of Henry's patriarchal power. This masculine discourse presupposes that women will maintain racial and cultural purity by reproducing legitimate offspring, but Grandma Yeh subverts it by claiming legitimacy through the letter or the logic of conjugal relations rather than through blood or biological relations. Grandma Yeh reasons that if Suyin (however racially mixed) is Li An's daughter, and Li An is her own daughter-in-law and Henry's wife (despite their divorce), then Suyin is therefore the granddaughter of herself and her deceased husband, Mr Yeh. Grandma Yeh asserts Suyin's place within the Yeh family through her own position as second wife, which, though secondary, is nonetheless symbolically and financially powerful. She turns the Yeh family name into a signifier that she shrewdly deploys for her own purposes to safeguard Li An and Suyin's future within a society that values patrimony and racial purity.

Symbolically speaking, Grandma Yeh's rubbing of olive oil on the infant Suyin signifies her grand-maternal blessing of the child, making Suyin not just "Henry's baby"—a biological product—but, more importantly, the legitimate "granddaughter" of "Ah Pah" (Mr Yeh), a status which is "invisible" but also "unerasable" through Grandma Yeh's matriarchal invocation. The passage quoted above emphasizes the physical details of Suyin's infant body, especially "the carapace where the skull bones had not closed" and "where only skin protected the brain." While Suyin's body may not yet be completely formed, with Grandma Yeh's blessing, her identity as a member of the Yeh family is formed completely, and she is thus protected and made "more safe" for the future. This blessing becomes financially significant toward the end of the novel, when Grandma Yeh dies and leaves all the money she inherited from her husband, Mr Yeh, to Suyin (*Joss and Gold* 254). Henry has to honor Grandma Yeh's will and become the executor of her legacy. In doing so, he finally has to acknowledge that he is Suyin's father, something that Grandma Yeh "had wanted him to say all these years, and with her death, he could finally say it" (262). Grandma Yeh's foresight in keeping Suyin's last name as Yeh, and her insistence (against common sense and convention) over the years to "everyone" that Suyin is her granddaughter and therefore Henry's daughter, finally proves effective, because even though "Suyin was a backward family bond," Henry, "being now a good Chinese father [himself], would not refuse that bond" (262–63). Suyin can now claim a father, even if belatedly, and Henry's presence protects Suyin from her schoolmates' bullying and name-calling.

Despite her ostracization by her classmates as a mixed-blood demon, Suyin is also an object of desire by both Asian and Western characters. Suyin embodies the cross-cultural, cross-racial nightmare of cultural purists in Malaysia, Singapore, and America, but at the same time she also represents the logical outcome of the multicultural and melting-pot ideals these same purists uphold as an important part of their respective national consciousness. When Chester sees Suyin for the first time he notices the physical features of her mixed heritage, "red-gold hairs shining" on her arms, and "her dark hair [that] gleamed with russet streaks" (*Joss and Gold* 222). Chester is then overcome by "shame that was like a different kind of love—the first time he had loved so shamefully—as he watched his daughter walk away" (222). Chester's ambivalence—fierce love paired with intense shame—comes from his conflicted desires as an American Orientalist anthropologist: although he has chosen "the bland clean shampooed middle-class reality that bright energetic Meryl promised" (222), that same reality has also taken away his reproductive power thanks to Meryl's insistence on his vasectomy. Chester's only offspring, therefore, is this half-Chinese, half-American girl who disrupts the comfortable life he had constructed for himself in upstate New York. Abdullah also discusses Suyin's hybridity in similarly ambivalent terms when he talks to Chester about his experience as a refugee-camp officer in the 1970s when Vietnamese boat people landed in Malaysia: "[Suyin] is beautiful. That is the way with Eurasians. Allah is merciful. These children will always have problems, so beauty is the gift to sweeten their path. [. . .] There I met some of the *bui doi,* children of the dust. Beautiful children! Golden skin, golden hair, face like *orang puteh* [white person], soul like Asian. But no one wants them" (189). From Abdullah's point of view, the beautiful "golden skin" and "golden hair" of Eurasians or mixed-blood children such as Suyin is compensation for their illegitimacy and bastard status, because "no one wants them" as part of their family, society, or nation. Abdullah presents this as a *fait accompli,* simply "the way with Eurasians," much like Henry's insistence on a conventional "Chinese way" (57) or his own earlier admonishment, "better that like stay with like" (46). But mixed in with Abdullah's rejection of these hybrid children as legitimate members of a national community is a fascination with their existence, with their "face like *orang puteh*" and "soul like Asian"—a realization that these children are products of physical and cultural contact between Asia and the West that cultural nationalists such as Abdullah want to disavow. Henry, after Grandma Yeh's death, and as executor of her legacy to Suyin, also wants "her, Suyin, Grandma's beloved granddaughter, his own daughter, to understand what he was doing and why" (254), despite having earlier abandoned Suyin and Li An. Grandma Yeh's matriarchal influence forces Henry to come to terms with this multicultural, multiracial child as his own daughter, thereby challenging the masculine society's essentialist belief that one's legitimate offspring must be of the same race, ethnicity, or culture.

But Lim's novel also challenges this masculine discourse of cultural purity through Suyin's role as the mythical Madam White Snake in her school's Chinese drama performance. Lim's inclusion of this myth and Suyin's participation in it echoes Maxine Hong Kingston's revision of the Chinese folktale *Journey to the West* and the adventures of the Monkey King that is part of a "vision of Asian American culture as dialogic, inclusive, adaptive, and alive" (Chu 187). Lim puts the myth of Madam White Snake to similar use, claiming it as a narrative of transgression and the liberating power of female sexuality that challenges the circumscription of women's bodies and sexuality within official nationalist discourses. Suyin's "Mandarin was bad," but "with her green-brown eyes, reddish hair, and dramatic height, the Chinese language teacher had insisted on putting her on stage for Chinese drama night" (*Joss and Gold* 207). Suyin has the most important but absolutely speechless part, that of Madam White Snake herself. Despite the Chinese teacher's assurance to Li An that the role was about how "Madam White Snake was breaking the laws of propriety and of ascribed position by changing into a human" and that "Suyin's slinky silence was supposed to represent a divine spirit, not her failed Mandarin" (207–8), Li An is fearful and anxious that her daughter will have to be "dressed in white tights and tee, sequined and spangled" and "wriggle on stage" as a "female, snaky, hissing, nonhuman, non-Chinese-speaking freak of Cho Kang Secondary School" (207). The experience reminds Li An that "in Singapore Suyin would never be Chinese. She would never be the lead actress, and she would learn to enjoy the eyes of the boys as her body moved, sinuously exaggerated" (229–30). Here, Suyin's sinuous performance and incompetent Mandarin signify her inability to meet Singaporean standards of racial and cultural purity; she will be placed on stage as an exotic spectacle, as a "nonhuman, non-Chinese-speaking freak" who serves as an implicit warning to any who dare think of "breaking the laws of propriety and of ascribed position." This reading of the Madam White Snake performance as a humiliation of Suyin is certainly correct, but Lim also suggests that Suyin's "slinky silence" and her nascent sexuality that "got her attention from the boys" (229) may have a more positive, transgressive aspect in the future. As Auntie Ellen reminds Suyin toward the end of the novel, "she could decide whatever she wanted to once she was eighteen" and that "very soon, she would be eighteen and a woman like [Ellen and Li An]" (257). For Li An, Suyin's sexuality can only be exploited by men as a fetish. Suyin's consciousness, her sexuality, and the fetishization of her body are distinct in Li An's thinking, such that Suyin "enjoys" the "eyes of the boys" as "her body moved"—her body becomes dislocated from her own sense of self. But from Suyin's point of view, she is the actor and subject of her performance who can employ her physical self to her benefit, hence "she had quickly discovered that wriggling her body got her attention from the boys" (229). To claim that Suyin grasps a form of female agency would be an overstatement, but if we consider the radical aspects of the Madam White Snake legend—"a divine spirit" who breaks the "laws of propriety and of ascribed position"—then Suyin's growing awareness of the power of her hybrid body represents a move away from "the identification of women as privileged bearers of corporate identities and boundary markers of their communities" toward "a language of identity which allows for difference and diversity without making women its hostages" (Kandiyoti 388). We should remember that the "attention" Suyin receives in the last section of the novel is not just the erotic gaze of high school boys, for she is also the recipient of two forms of paternal attention: Chester's intense (albeit shamed) love, and Henry's meticulous (albeit belated) affection as the executor of her estate. While Suyin is not fluent in Mandarin, the officially designated mother tongue of Chinese Singaporeans, and thus cannot be considered Chinese enough to be a Singaporean on linguistic grounds, Lim's novel suggests a different kind of language, one that is not deployed by instrumental nationality to construct a carefully policed gendered and cultural national identity. It allows Suyin to be a Singaporean through the legitimation of her hybridity through both her American and Chinese fathers. Postcolonial nationalism's male-centered cultural purity through a separate-but-equal multiculturalism is negated through the figure of Suyin. Even while Suyin is ensconced and framed by the male gaze, her hybridity transgresses the laws of propriety that govern the boundaries of racial and cultural purity.

Language and literature also become important for Li An in the last part of the novel, where her previously held ideals about literature's relationship to life and community undergo a dramatic change because of her job and her daughter. Despite Li An's emphasis on the scientific and community-building power of literature, Lim's novel stresses how she responds to literary language at a deeply physical level that cannot be reduced to "the real science of life" (*Joss and Gold* 8). When Chester reads a poem by A. E. Housman, clearly "making fun of the poem, declaiming the words *spires* and *farms* with mock relish," Li An "couldn't help appreciating the music of the English words" as "the killing air came out of the words and echoed in her body even as Chester and Henry were smiling at the absurdity of the ideas" (32). Li An's body resonates with Housman's poem even though Chester is mocking it, because for her English is more than an instrumental language to be used for scientific analysis (according to Henry) or for making money (according to Abdullah): "the English ingested through years of reading and talking now formed the delicate web of tissues in her brain. Giving up her language would be like undergoing a crippling operation on her brain" (56). The English language and English literature become an avenue through which Li An asserts her sense of self as both a woman and a Malaysian. Li An, using her analytical skills, rebuts Abdullah and Samad's arguments that "Malay is good enough for this country" since only one percent of Malaysians need to learn English (56). Li An silences them by asking "who will choose the one percent" and "what about Malaysians who may want to strive to join that one percent" (57). After this heated conversation, Li An further rejects Henry's insistence that she should be less Westernized and adhere to Chinese feminine decorum by arguing that she is "not Chinese" but "Malaysian" (57). On the night of the 1969 riots, when she sleeps with Chester, Li An's body is resonating with the political, racial, and sexual tension, such that "her body was vibrating quietly. The vibrations, she recognized, were a natural motion of her body. Every body was constantly vibrating. The breath, pulse, heartbeat, set up a ceaseless motion, a tension of desire that was life" (80). Lim emphasizes here that Li An's desire for Chester is not simply erotic; it is an extension of her body's resonance with the turbulent political and racial climate in Malaysia, just as the "killing air" of Housman's poem "echoed in her body." Li An's body resonates somatically with the problems of the Malaysian and Singaporean communities in ways that exceed the framework of wifely and maternal responsibilities ascribed by official nationalist discourse. Language and literature do not allow her to connect with Henry, Abdullah, or Samad, but they play an important part in Li An's consciousness and assertion of herself as a woman rather than an idealized feminine character.

In Singapore, faced with brutal economic necessity, Li An appears to change her attitude to language and literature when she becomes the editor for BioSynergy's newsletter. Li An seems to give up her idealistic view of literature and settles for producing commercialized, neatly packaged informational writing: "immaculate layout, letter-perfect editing, careful content control. A company organ, a mouthpiece, slick, glib, superficial, glossy" (*Joss and Gold* 179–80). But even Li An's rejection of the empowering value of literature is couched in literary terms. She switches from a humanist view of language to a modernist one, such that she "no longer read significance, merely the acts. No ideas but in things, the poet William Carlos Williams had said. That had been the hardest poem for her to learn, to embrace the empty depth in the glittering surface of things" (179). This approach to literature, however, is more in accordance with her own somatic resonance with language that belies her earlier humanist mind-set, for her body is not an "empty surface" beneath "the glittering surface of things," but rather a thing in itself that is full of "ideas," brimming with "a ceaseless motion, a tension of desire that was life" (80). Far from abandoning literature for slick superficialities, as an editor Li An gains a new grasp of the immanent connection between content and form not only in literature but also in her intimate and somatic connection with her daughter, Suyin. Nursing her infant daughter, Li An finds that

> sensations flowed and filled the cavities in [her] body: her infant's mass, the baby hair texture, fine as cocoon threads, the odor of baby—a milky powdered sweetness, perfume of the newly born, her blessed existence. Li An was surfeited by those moments, which shaped that compact space encompassing Suyin and herself, and which sufficed, she felt, forever. (*Joss and Gold* 208–9)

Just as reading Lawrence's prose gives Li An physical relish and hearing Housman's poetry makes her body resonate with language's musicality earlier in the novel, Suyin becomes a work of art that fills Li An's senses with "milky powdered sweetness" and the "perfume of the newly born" rather than the spicy sibilance of chickpeas or the killing air of England. The "blessed existence" that Li An celebrates with Suyin recalls Grandma Yeh's blessing of

Suyin as she bathed the infant in olive oil, paying attention to the baby's head and her light brown hair. Through Suyin, Li An creates "a compact space" of maternal love that is not anchored to wifely responsibility, and surrounding this compact space of mother and daughter is the close-knit and alternative family structure including Ellen and Grandma Yeh.

Reading Suyin as a work of art does not dehumanize her, because it allows us to answer the question that Liew Geok Leong raises in her afterword to the novel: why does Li An insist on having Suyin rather than getting rid of the baby before or after her birth? Just like Grandma Yeh's legitimation of Suyin as a member of the Yeh family, Li An's decision to keep Chester's child seems to defy common sense. Leong suggests that Li An keeps the baby because her own emotional yearning for a child matters more than a consideration about the baby's troubled future as a racially mixed child (271). While this may be so, the conclusion of *Joss and Gold* takes this maternal yearning one step further: it emphasizes the crystallization of literary reading together with the experience of being a woman and a mother in a postcolonial, male-centered society where language is seen as a tool of instrumental nationality, and women are constantly hailed as cultural paragons and boundary markers. Li An, after a heated conversation with Ellen about allowing Suyin to visit Chester in America, realizes that it is Suyin herself who must "answer these questions" (*Joss and Gold* 264) about the sudden presence of not one but two fathers from different countries and cultures. As Li An stands, "imagining the slow regularity of her daughter's breathing," she retraces the important events of her life that have led up to this moment: "marriage, love, whatever she shared with Henry or Chester, might have ended, but the traces had not disappeared. Nothing she lived through was ever finally over" (264). She then picks up a copy of *The Oxford Book of Modern Verse*, "the only book she had kept with her from her student days" (264–65), and

> settled down to read the poems again, pulled in by a music of feelings that had remained set in print, even as the pages had yellowed and turned brittle. A muse of feelings she thought she had forgotten, more than words, more than poetry, returning to the spaces inside her body its silent and eloquent touch. For the moment, standing again before Suyin's bedroom door and listening to the golden echoes in her daughter's breathing, she did not ask for more. (*Joss and Gold* 265)

At one level, the conclusion of *Joss and Gold* signals a departure from the mother-daughter narratives in Asian American women's writing where (in the case of Amy Tan's *Joy Luck Club*) the Chinese mother stands for a "radical difference," or "an inherited core of Chineseness" that the Chinese American daughter must in some way abject or reconcile with her American subjectivity so that the daughter can "share with other Americans an enriching access to a matrilineal heritage of protofeminist individualism and enterprise" (Chu 168). But instead of having the mother (Li An) contained or abjected by the daughter (Suyin), Lim's novel creates a sentimental coordination of maternal and feminine affection that is also critical of masculine politics of cultural nationalism. The relationship between Li An and Suyin embodies a kind of sentimental longing and fulfillment that Rey Chow observes in East Asian films and that Theodor Adorno points out in his discussion of artworks, figurative language, and historical conditions. The sentimental, for Rey Chow, is

> *an inclination or a disposition toward making compromises and toward making-do with even—and especially—that which is oppressive and unbearable. [. . .] the sentimental is rather about what keeps and preserves, what holds things together. For this reason, the sentimental is perhaps best described as a mood of endurance, a mode whose contours tend to remain fuzzy rather than sharply delineated and whose effects may more easily be apprehended as (a prevailing) tone.* (*Sentimental Fabulations* 18, original emphasis)

This mood or mode of endurance is a double-edged sword, however, because on the one hand "as *wenqing* or accommodation, the sentimental is ultimately about being accommodating and being accommodated, about the delineation and elaboration of a comfortable/homely interiority" (Chow, *Sentimental Fabulations* 19), but on the other hand "*at the heart of Chinese sentimentalism lies the idealization of filiality*," which "is not simply a matter of respecting one's biological or cultural elders but an age-old cultural apparatus for interpellating individuals into the hierarchy-conscious conduct of identifying with—and submitting to—whatever preexists them" (22, original emphasis). *Joss and Gold* stages an encounter between *sentimentalism* as the idealization of filiality and *sentimentality* as a mode of accommodation and perseverance through Li An's endurance of cultural nationalism's patriarchal expectations. Certainly, Grandma Yeh's concern with Suyin's retention of the Yeh family name and the reemergence of Chester and Henry into Suyin's life suggests that filial piety is an important part of the novel's positioning of its female characters within the larger Singaporean social order. But at no point does this accommodation between Li An's sentimental and domestic circle of Suyin, Ellen, and Grandma Yeh with the dominant social order create the worst-case situation where "the gravest problems arise [. . .] when the homely—what is inside—too, is revealed to be oppressive and unbearable—indeed, uninhabitable" (Chow, *Sentimental Fabulations* 19). Chester's unexpected visit to Singapore, Grandma Yeh's death, and Henry's return into Suyin's life do not cause the life Li An, Suyin, and Ellen have built for themselves to become unbearable or uninhabitable. Of course, Li An realizes that even if, "for the moment" (*Joss and Gold* 265), there is a close connection between her and her daughter symbolized by the "golden echoes" of Suyin's breathing, that may change depending on how Suyin answers the questions regarding her dual patrimony from Chester and Henry. But the novel's conclusion registers this concern while making it recede into the background; instead, what is foregrounded is a sentimental retracing of Li An's life, her "marriage, love, whatever she shared with Henry or Chester [. . .] Nothing she lived through was ever finally over." This in turn triggers a literary turn to Li An's sentimental musings as she reads *The Oxford Book of Modern Verse*. This sequence of memories and sensations—Suyin's breathing, Li An's memories of her love and life with Chester and Henry, and finally the buried-but-unforgotten sensations of literary reading—can be read as the artistic process of longing, neediness, fulfillment, and change that emerges out of an artwork's engagement with the historical conditions of its creation. As Adorno argues, "there is no valid artwork without longing," but artworks can "transcend longing" through "the neediness inscribed as a figure in the historically existing. By retracing this figure, they are not only more than what simply exists but participate in objective truth to the extent that what is in need summons its fulfillment and change" (*Aesthetic Theory* 132). Suyin, born of the historically existing encounter between Li An and Chester, a Chinese Malaysian woman and a white American anthropologist, is a figure who inscribes the neediness and the necessity of racial and cultural mixing in the postcolonial world, an objective truth that is vehemently denied or rejected by masculine authority and cultural nationalism.

Through Li An and Suyin, Lim performs a chiasmatic maneuver that first takes up the social and cultural interpellations of women as the idealized feminine in postcolonial Malaysia and Singapore and subsequently inverts them in order to show the limitations of this masculine discourse and other possible, alternative relationships. The chiasmus is a characteristic move in Adorno's critical thinking, an example of which is his paradoxical pronouncement that "masculine society imperiously breeds in woman its own corrective, and shows itself through this limitation implacably the master. The feminine character is a negative imprint of domination" (*Minima Moralia* 95). But such chiasmatic thought is also appropriated by gender theorists and, as Judith Butler argues, it is crucial to reformulating the terms of raced and sexed subject positions called into being by regimes of power:

> the temporal structure of such a subject is chiasmatic in this sense: in the place of a substantial or self-determining "subject," this juncture of discursive demands is something like a "crossroads" [. . .] . There is no subject prior to its constructions, and neither is the subject determined by those constructions; it is always the nexus, the nonspace of cultural collision, in which the demand to resignify or repeat the very terms that constitute the "we" cannot be summarily refused, but neither can they be followed in strict obedience. (383)

As a woman who bears a hybrid child, Li An functions as a nexus of cultural collision, fulfilling her role as woman and mother by inverting the strictures regarding the phenotypical and cultural purity of women and their offspring in postcolonial Malaysia and Singapore. That Li An does so without asking for assistance from either Henry or Chester or migrating to another country where life as a single mother might be less strenuous suggests that Lim is staking a claim on the national consciousness of both countries by asserting a female right to social and familial agency against prevailing cultural norms regarding female gender roles. Masculine society's interpellation and repetition of the ideal feminine upon a woman such as Li An cannot, to use Butler's terms, be summarily refused, but at the same time the very terms of this interpellation preclude or prevent the strict obedience of those who are hailed by it, hence women's position as the negative imprint of male domination. Suyin, Li An's daughter, represents the potential for reworking the discourse of cultural authenticity and idealized femininity when she takes on the role of Madam White Snake, which gradually makes her self-conscious of her difference from mainstream Chinese Singaporean society but simultaneously awakens her nascent physical and sexual sensibilities. The way in which Lim's novel emphasizes Suyin's physical growth and maturation and Li An's rediscovery of her sensual love of literary language may certainly be read as part of a female *Bildungsroman,* but, more importantly, it evinces the sentimental endurance expressed in Li An's struggle against a patriarchal society that becomes more than a personal triumph over an authoritarian and chauvinistic national formation. It is also an exposition of how an alternative and equally legitimate community of women can exist within the national framework without acceding to the demands of racial, cultural, and linguistic purity as grounds for inclusion within the nation. By revealing the roles and positions that can be claimed by women, Lim performs an immanent critique of nationalism as an identitarian narrative that determines and objectifies women as cultural symbols and reproductive bodies. This mode of criticism is immanent because even as she interrogates women's symbolic and corporeal objectification, there is within the cosmopolitical frame of her thinking an abiding attachment to Malaysia and Singapore as nations negotiated through political consciousness and cultural politics. It is an attachment that discloses and rethinks, rather than identifies with or rejects outright, the raced and gendered terms of coercive mimeticism that fetishize a postcolonial national consciousness into a patriotic and patriarchal national identity.

CHAPTER 5

Ethnographic Tactics and the Cosmopolitical Aesthetic in Contemporary Malaysian Fiction

I N 2008, Salman Rushdie's *Midnight's Children*, which won the Booker Prize in 1980, was given an additional honor by the prize committee when it was selected for the Best of the Booker award. When asked about the qualities of a Booker-Prize-winning novel, one of the prize organizers candidly replied that "the key is literary tourism—taking the reader somewhere they are not familiar with" and "giv[ing] people information and feeling about something they knew very little about indeed" through "a description of something that most of us don't know anything about" (Dowd para. 2–4). That Rushdie's sprawling, dense, and highly stylized prose should be considered an almost transparent account offering readers in the West a touristic glimpse of India, giving them information and feeling about a faraway place that was once the jewel in Britain's imperial crown, suggests that even an author and a novel often considered formative of anglophone postcolonial literature and criticism may run afoul of what one critic calls the "anthropological exotic" that turns even an ironic and self-reflexive text such as *Midnight's Children* into "a surrogate guidebook" that "has been exploited, directly or indirectly, for the Raj nostalgia it despises" (Huggan 37, 115). While Graham Huggan argues that a "strategic exoticism" on the part of postcolonial writers both resists and is symptomatic of the anthropological exotic (32), in this chapter I revise this characterization of the postcolonial literary marketplace as a site in which the veil of exoticism is overlaid by Euro-American readers and publishers onto writers from postcolonial societies. I depart from the notion that the anthropological exotic functions as an inevitable interpellation by the West of the Rest, in which writers and texts from the latter are seen as either symptoms of or struggling against the hegemony of the exoticizing literary marketplace. Instead, I conceptualize the anthropological exotic of the postcolonial literary marketplace according to what the Frankfurt School critics call the culture industry and argue that in the twenty-first century, writers who depict their cultures and societies with a high degree of literary verisimilitude are working through a cosmopolitical (as opposed to a geopolitical) aesthetic that revises realist historical fiction through the use of ethnographic tactics and techniques. These ethnographic tactics both evoke and interrogate the exoticism existing in Western perceptions of postcolonial societies as well as the ideologies of homogenous collective identity in their own national cultures often promulgated in official accounts of national history. Perceiving the anthropological exotic as a culture industry sheds light on the fetishization of postcolonial writers and their texts for mass consumption and conceptualizes it as a field of productive forces that may be traversed and articulated rather than as a determinate interpellation of Third World otherness by First World selves.

If one important aspect of postcolonial literature is (to paraphrase Salman Rushdie's famous phrase) the empire writing back to the metropole, then what we are seeing in the novels of Twan Eng Tan and Preeta Samarasan is the postcolonial diaspora writing *back-to-back,* responding to both the metropole and their nation-state, transforming the oppositional countermovement in the dialectic between the (former) colony and metropole into a negative dialectic that triangulates the metropole, the postcolonial nation-state, and diasporic cultural space. This triangulation is cosmopolitical because diasporic Malaysian writers such as Samarasan and Tan draw on literary resources and predecessors in Anglo-American writing and their own national milieu in order to interrogate the discourses of cultural absolutism and exoticism both in the global literary marketplace and in their own society. Samarasan and Tan engage in a literary cosmopolitics as they position themselves as diasporic subjects who nonetheless maintain abiding attachments to Malaysia precisely by critiquing the nation through their literary representations. Their self-positioning as diasporic writers is a literary tactic advancing a critical national consciousness in contrast to Malaysia's dominant cultural discourse that relegates them to a secondary or marginalized position. I examine Samarasan's *Evening Is the Whole Day* and Tan's *The Gift of Rain* in the context of Malaysia's cultural politics and official nationalism, which define Malaysian national culture in terms of an indigenous Malay ethnic identity in spite of the historical and contemporary presence of sizable ethnic Chinese and Indian communities in the country. Furthermore, Malaysian national literature is also defined as a body of works written in the Malay language, excluding literature written in Chinese, Tamil, or English. I argue that, in their novels, Samarasan and Tan (who are of South Asian and Chinese descent respectively) combine an ethnographic approach to Malaysian culture and society together with literary tactics used by writers elsewhere in the South Asian and Chinese diaspora in order to accomplish two objectives. First, they interrogate metropolitan or First World conventions of consuming postcolonial or Third World literatures as exoticized representations of distant and different cultures; second, they critique the "ethnic absolutism" (Gilroy 2) of a Malay-centered national culture established by their home country.

Graham Huggan's conceptualization of strategic exoticism provides the point of departure for my formulation of a cosmopolitical aesthetic in Samarasan's and Tan's novels. Both writers draw on the dramatic realism of historical fiction to depict important moments in Malaysia's colonial and postcolonial past, but this historical veracity is revised through their use of ethnographic tactics, an interrogation of the anthropological exotic from within the dominant field of the global literary marketplace. Avrom Fleishman explains that the historical novel fleshes out the "domestic detail" of "a specific past situation in all its concreteness," and that as a "genre [it] is unashamedly hybrid: it contemplates the universal but does not depart from the rich factuality of history in order to reach that elevation" (8). While Samarasan and Tan certainly fill their narratives with rich and vivid details of colonial Malayan and postcolonial Malaysian society, they depart from Fleishman's conclusion that "a historical story must become a heroic (or antiheroic) plot" and finally culminate in "the ultimate subject of the historical novel" that is "the human life conceived as historical life" (10, 11). Furthermore, Fleishman's contention about historical fiction closely resembles the kind of literary tourism touted by the organizer of the Booker Prize, because "the form of historical fiction" is "to interpret the experience of individual men [. . .] in such a way as to make their lives not only felt by the reader as he would feel his own existence were he to have lived in the past, but understood as only someone who had seen that life as a completed whole could understand it" (12–13). More recent studies of history in contemporary fiction have moved away from such an experiential and holistic purchase on the past; Eric Berlatsky suggests that postmodern historical fiction "critiques narrative's tendency to obscure our access to the past" but, despite the apparent rejection of epistemological certainty in more extreme glosses of postmodernism and poststructuralism, also "suggests alternative forms as more effective means of accessing the real" (15). These forms "cannot be found in narrative ordering but only in the contingent and the fragmentary," in the moments where circumstances and events become "that which rises up to take us by surprise and which therefore has the capacity to change" existing relations of knowledge and power (18, 19). Berlatsky's discussion of postmodern historical novels' ability to "complicate and problematize notions of reference precisely in order to suggest a subtler, and therefore more compelling, model of mimesis" (8) accords with the ethnographic tactics at work in Samarasan's and Tan's novels, a mode of mimesis that rehearses the veracity of historical reality through the inflections of contingent and fragmentary events and forces that rise up with surprising momentum. These novels do not dismiss historical reference but rather use such references tactically to trace a cosmopolitical aesthetic; put differently, they employ figurative language toward an "ethnography of global connection," performing "an exploration of ethnographic methods for studying the work of the universal" through the twists and turns of historical fiction (Tsing 1). Universals, for Anna Lowenhaupt Tsing, are general concepts such as capitalism, social justice, and modernity, and nationalism can certainly be regarded as a similar universal aspiration, "a chance to participate in the global stream of humanity" (1). Tsing's particular approach to the ethnography of the global, which departs from metaphors of fluidity and freedom, emphasizes what she calls "friction" to describe the "heterogeneous and unequal encounters [that] can lead to new arrangements of culture and power," highlighting how even as universal patterns of "domination and discipline come into their own" they may not necessarily do so "in the forms laid out by their proponents" (5). Samarasan and Tan engage with the domination and discipline of the anthropological exotic intrinsic in both the global literary marketplace and postcolonial nation-state, and their ethnographic tactics represent the friction between diasporic perspectives on national culture and strategies of cultural exoticism and national identity.

As Rey Chow argues, drawing on the work of cultural critic Michel de Certeau, despite the apparently radical bent of globalism, the global moment nonetheless maintains "essentialist notions of culture and history" and "conservative notions of territorial and linguistic propriety and the 'otherness' ensuing from them"; these notions are "new solidarities" and "are often informed by a *strategic* attitude which repeats what they seek to overthrow" (*Writing Diaspora* 17, original emphasis). For this reason, "interventions cannot simply be thought of in terms of the creation of new [strategic] 'fields.'

Instead, it is necessary to think *primarily* in terms of borders—of borders, that is, as *para-sites* that never take over a field in its entirety but erode it slowly and *tactically*" (*Writing Diaspora* 16, original emphases). Following Chow's thinking, Samarasan's and Tan's literary interventions are better characterized as tactics originating from the para-sitical interstices between hostland and homeland rather than strategies of resistance and solidarity coming from a determinate location or position. The critical thrust of their fiction writes back not only to the former colonial and Western centers but also rebounds back to the Malaysian nation-state as well. The difference here is not contradictory but contrapuntal: the strategic representation of oneself and one's culture as exotic is, as some critics astutely observe, a recurring feature in the work of an earlier generation of postcolonial writers such as Salman Rushdie, V. S. Naipaul, and Derek Walcott in which their self-reflexive authorial voices simultaneously acknowledge and ironically comment on their own entry into and reception within the global literary marketplace.[1] In this sense, their self-reflexiveness is a form of what Mary Louise Pratt calls "autoethnography," a form of writing "in which colonized subjects undertake to represent themselves in ways that *engage with* the colonizer's own terms. If ethnographic texts are a means by which Europeans represent to themselves their (usually subjugated) others, autoethnographic texts are those the others construct in response to or in dialogue with those metropolitan representations" (7, original emphasis). My formulation of ethnographic tactics builds upon and extends this postcolonial autoethnography of strategic exoticism, which is an initial response of cultural self-representation and self-assertion "usually addressed both to metropolitan readers and to literate sectors of the speaker's own social group" (Pratt 7). Whereas their mid- and late twentieth-century predecessors such as Naipaul and Rushdie deployed self-exoticism strategically in order to stake out a position and be read and recognized in a literary field still dominated at the time by British and American authors and texts, twenty-first-century writers such as Samarasan and Tan tactically traverse an entire field or constellation of anglophone and postcolonial writing that has been growing steadily since the end of World War II and official European colonialism. This body of English-language writing has been variously named Third World, Commonwealth, postcolonial, and, more recently, world or global literature. Cosmopolitical writers adapt the resisting and reflexive strategies of their postcolonial predecessors and weave them immanently into the texture of their novels. This does not mean

---

1. See Walkowitz, Hayward, and Brouillette for extensive discussions of Rushdie, Naipaul, and Walcott, respectively.

that Samarasan and Tan have superseded the postcolonial; instead, it means that postcolonial thematics and tropes have become a staple of their literary vocabulary, and that they use these tropes to perform a cognitive mapping of the cosmopolitical force field of social, cultural, and political relations. Fredric Jameson makes a related point in his discussion of a geopolitical aesthetic in late twentieth-century cinema that maps out the world-system of late capital. While Jameson's formulation is provocative, his gloss of the geopolitical as the late capitalist world-system runs the same risk as Graham Huggan's conceptualization of the anthropological exotic in that it tends to see the economic workings of either the world-system or the global literary marketplace as a determining instance in visual or literary interpretation. A cosmopolitical aesthetic differs from a geopolitical one in that it cognitively maps out the negative dialectic between metropole, nation, and diaspora that folds the autoethnographic reflexiveness of postcolonial writing into its own ethnographic tactics and style. Critique is no longer assayed through an authorial avatar that intervenes as the narrative unfolds; instead, critique itself becomes a trope or figurative turn that is folded into the warp and woof of the literary narrative. In order to grasp the contours of their critical intervention, in the next two sections of this chapter I discuss the historical and political context of Malaysian cultural nationalism as well as the cultural discourses of diasporic subjectivity in which Samarasan and Tan both implicitly or explicitly position themselves.

The Cultural Politics of Malaysian National Identity

While my previous chapter focused on the heroic masculine narratives of nation-building in Malaysia and Singapore, in this chapter I wish to highlight historical dimensions of this nation-building process that Samarasan and Tan allude to in their novels, as well as the literary and linguistic dimension of the formation of a racialized, cultural national identity. Formerly colonized by the Portuguese, the Dutch, and finally the British up until the mid-twentieth century, the country that is today called Malaysia is made up of various ethnic groups that include a majority Malay population, as well as communities of Chinese, Indian, Peranakan (ethnic Chinese who have assimilated to Malay culture and language), Eurasians (people of mixed European and Southeast Asian descent), and indigenous groups such as the Orang Asli. As historical and sociological studies of race relations in Malaysia from the colonial period up until the present day have shown (Alatas, Abraham), a pervasive sense of Malay social, cultural, and economic decline and dissolution was developed by British colonial authorities in the nineteenth century as part of their economic and political governance of the local Malay population. This sense, that Malay identity and social standing were under siege, was exacerbated by the influx of immigrants from southern China and southern India with the growth of the rubber and tin industries toward the turn of the century. The British assigned these new immigrants to various economic sectors (small businesses and tin mining for the Chinese, rubber plantations for the Indians), while the Malays were responsible mainly for agricultural production. The historical and contemporary perception that the Malays were intrinsically lazy and suited only for farmwork, while the Chinese and Indians were by nature more industrious and enterprising in their various businesses, is thus largely determined by the colonial economic system and its resulting social hierarchy. World War II and the Japanese occupation of British Malaya (from 1942 to 1945)—the central historical time frame of Tan's *The Gift of Rain*—compounded the tensions between these communities: many Malays and Indians collaborated with the Japanese in hopes of getting rid of their British colonial masters, while the Chinese community bore the brunt of the Japanese military's aggression because of their association with and financial support for mainland China, which was also at war with Japan. With the end of World War II and the formal end of British colonialism in 1957, Malaysia became an independent nation-state, and various power-sharing strategies were attempted between the three main ethnic groups. However, these attempts at forging a just and equal society for all Malaysians ran into insurmountable obstacles, because "the lower economic status of the Malay majority did not generate [. . .] a compelling critique or movement to address social inequalities," such that "the UMNO [the dominant Malay political party] together with its alliance partners propagated a political strategy designed to secure ethnic privilege. Consequently, the integrity of self-understandings about ethnicity nurtured during colonial rule and its relationship to economic exploitation were preserved intact" (Nair 88–89). This unbroken linkage of ethnic identity and economic roles came to a head in May 1969, when after a general election, deadly race riots broke out between the Chinese and Malays in the capital city of Kuala Lumpur. In its wake, Malay leaders established a set of economic and cultural policies that would secure for the Malay community the privileged status of *bumiputera* (literally "sons of the land"), and it is this post-1969 Malaysia that Samarasan depicts in *Evening Is the Whole Day*. These policies created, among other things, economic and educational advantages for the Malays so as to redress their perceived backwardness caused by British colonialism as well as Chinese and Indian economic competition. However, the *bumiputera* policy ends up privileging ethnic and cultural rather than economic aspects: despite the fact that some minority groups such as the Orang Asli have an equal claim to indigenous status, they have not been recognized as *bumiputera;* while many ethnic Chinese and Indian families have lived on Malaysian soil longer than new immigrants from the neighboring country of Indonesia, the latter are recognized as Malay and *bumiputera* while the former are not (Ooi 451). At the same time, Malaysia's national culture and national language were equated with Malay culture and language; while the other ethnic communities were allowed to retain their local languages, instruction at all levels of public education was to be conducted in the Malay language.

These post-1969 cultural and linguistic policies meant that Malaysia's national literature was defined as literature written in the national or Malay language, that "Malay culture should form the foundation of the national culture" (Tham 58). After 1969, various state-sponsored literary congresses affirmed that Malaysia's national culture "must be based on the culture of the indigenous [Malay] communities of Malaysia" and that "literature may act as a channel for the transmission of views, thoughts, and descriptions of modern social life in order to change and modernise Malaysia" (Tham 51). However, literary works written in English, Chinese, or Tamil were considered "sectional literature" (Quayum and Wicks x), and the upshot was that Malaysian writers "in English and other languages were denied an active engagement in nation building and the formation of national culture. They were moreover denied official recognition and public acclaim in their country of birth and citizenship," leading to a "profound experience of marginalisation and feelings of alienation" (Quayum and Wicks x). These policies regarding culture, language, and literature "inscribe Malay culture and ethnic identity as constitutive of the nation, in contrast to a more politically inclusive nationalism" (Nair 91), and have led many non-Malay Malaysian writers to move overseas while still maintaining familial, cultural, and literary connections to Malaysia from afar, writing about Malaysia in their fiction and poetry. The biographical note in *Evening Is the Whole Day* tells us that Preeta Samarasan moved to the United States after finishing high school in Malaysia, and now resides in France; according to a similar thumbnail biography, Twan Eng Tan divides his time between Kuala Lumpur, Malaysia's capital, and Cape Town in South Africa. Both Samarasan and Tan are thus doubly diasporic writers: not only are they part of a larger Chinese and South Asian diaspora, respectively, they are also members of a growing community of diasporic Malaysian writers that includes Shirley Geok-lin Lim (United States), Ee Tiang Hong (Australia), and Tash Aw (Britain). Both their novels about Malaysia are also published by presses based in the United States (Weinstein Books for Tan and

Mariner Books for Samarasan), which makes their writing part of a growing body of anglophone postcolonial literature written by migrant or diasporic writers, published by major presses in the West, and intended for both a Western and an Asian readership.

Diasporic Subjectivity, Ethnographic Tactics, and the Cosmopolitical Aesthetic

However, despite the physical and emotional distance from their homeland of Malaysia, both Samarasan and Tan evince abiding attachments with their nation-state, and it is precisely their distance that allows them to make a diasporic intervention that critiques the state of their nation and its official cultural nationalism. Diasporas, by nature of their physical distance and cultural dispersion from their homelands, are often considered in opposition to the nation, because they are "emblems of transnationalism" that "embody the question of borders, which is at the heart of any adequate definition of the Others of the nation-state" (Tölölyan, "The Nation-State and Its Others" 6). Furthermore, studies of diasporic identities have often focused on hybridized cultural identity and deterritorialized cross-border mobility as important attributes that enable diasporic subjects to interrogate and escape from the homogenous and authoritarian national regimes (Appadurai, Clifford). My investigation of Samarasan's and Tan's simultaneously transnational and national literary representations of Malaysia dovetails with another area of diaspora studies that focuses on the abiding sociocultural connections between diasporas and nations, such that "diasporas may criticize their homelands but not chastise them [. . .] at its best the diaspora is an example, for both the homeland's and hostland's nation-states, of the possibility of living, even thriving, in the regimes of multiplicity which are increasingly a global condition" (Tölölyan, "Rethinking Diaspora(s)" 7). The regimes of multiplicity of a global condition in which the homeland and hostland nation-states find themselves enmeshed and connected to one another through the mutual critique and mediation of diasporic writers such as Samarasan and Tan is another way of glossing the force field of social, cultural, and political relations mapped out by such writers in the cosmopolitical aesthetic.

Samarasan's and Tan's diasporic status enables their participation in a metropolitan exoticization of postcolonial or Asian countries such as Malaysia as well as their negation of such exoticism through ethnographic tactics evinced in their idiosyncratic prose style. In representing Malaysia to a Euro-American audience, both writers are, to some extent, part of a global literary marketplace that packages writers and texts from other countries and cultures as mass commodities for consumption in the West. Furthermore, given their detailed and evocative descriptions of the physical and cultural landscape and everyday life in Malaysia, at first glance their prose may be seen as a form of "anthropological exotic" that "invokes the familiar aura of other, incommensurably 'foreign' cultures while appearing to provide a modicum of information that gives the uninitiated reader access to the text and, by extension, the 'foreign culture' itself" (Huggan 37). However, this exoticized representation can be problematized and understood as a critical subversion of the commodifying power of the global literary marketplace if we consider Tan and Samarasan in light of their status as diasporic writers rather than naïve and native informants. Anthropological exoticization is premised on a subjective as well as a textual mode of identity and identification: it identifies the writer with the society and culture he or she is from, and also identifies or equates the writer's textual representation with a faithful or authentic image of that sociocultural reality. Although, as Huggan points out, such anthropological exoticization is pervasive in the Euro-American marketing and reception of postcolonial literature, I argue that in the context of post-1969 literary and cultural politics, this ethnographic mode of reading and conflating imaginative writing with social and cultural realities is also part of the official Malaysian definition of national literature. This can be seen from the insistence, on the part of the nation's Malay leaders, that Malaysian national literature and culture be limited to Malay-language writing and based on Malay culture because of that community's indigenous status and—by extension—organic link with the national imaginary; we see this also in the view (espoused by similar authorities) that literature should serve as a channel for transmitting thoughts and views, placing an "emphasis on sociological and political themes with a view to developing values and attitudes considered conducive to the objective of nation building" (Tham 43).

The cultural position of diasporic writers, however, complicates this one-to-one correspondence of subject to society and representation to reality and allows Samarasan and Tan to map out a cosmopolitical aesthetic wherein the metropolis and the national homeland are connected together through the space of diasporic cultural articulation. Stuart Hall, in the context of the Caribbean and African diaspora, argues that "cultural identities" are "unstable points of identification" and "not an essence but a *positioning*" ("Cultural Identity" 226, original emphasis); furthermore, "diaspora identities [. . .] are constantly producing and reproducing themselves anew, through transformation and difference" ("Cultural Identity" 235). Similarly, Brent Hayes Edwards suggests that "the use of the term *diaspora* " does not offer "an easy recourse to origins, but [. . .] forces us to reconsider the discourses of cultural and political linkage only through and across difference" (64, original emphasis). Edwards argues for the simultaneously articulated and disjointed nature of diasporic subjectivity not simply as a concrete or substantial cultural identity but also as "a difference or gap in time (advancing or delaying a schedule) *or* in space (shifting or displacing an object)" (65, original emphasis). The combination of Hall's positional and transformative concept of diasporic identity together with Edwards's more deconstructive gloss are part of the ethnographic tactics of Samarasan's and Tan's novels. Both writers appear to act as native informants and provide ethnographic or anthropologically exotic depictions of an essential and authentic Malaysian society and culture. On the other hand, they are also diasporic subjects who produce and reproduce their identities through transforming and differentiating various symbolic and cultural resources from both their homelands and hostlands.

Samarasan and Tan achieve this transformation and differentiation by employing the ethnographic conventions of the literary marketplace in ways that fulfill a desire for the authentic and the exotic, but also reveal the disarticulations and displacements, or the gaps and fault lines, inherent in this mode of reading and consumption. Their tactics of ethnographic writing embody and highlight the critical sutures and gaps that become visible once we recognize the overlapping national and transnational frameworks that are the conditions of possibility for their writing, and within which their novels are circulated and read. The politics of postcolonial literary space have been discussed by several critics who point out that the category of postcolonial literature is a "niche developed in tandem with general market expansion in the publishing industry," such that "talk of saving literature from 'reduction' to commodity status is now scarcely possible" (Brouillette 3). In this global literary marketplace, the author-figure is part of the commodity marketed along with a work of fiction, and we should "understand strategic exoticism, and likewise general postcolonial authorial self-consciousness, as comprised of a set of literary strategies that operate through assumptions shared between the author and the reader, as both producer and consumer work to negotiate with, if not absolve themselves of, postcoloniality's touristic guilt" (Brouillette 7). This holds true for postcolonial writers with a higher readership in metropolitan countries such as Salman Rushdie and J. M. Coetzee, whom Brouillette examines in her study. However, because Samarasan and Tan are writing for both a Euro-American readership and an audience in Malaysia, ethnographic tactics make a further step toward a stylistic critique of the culture industry of the global literary marketplace as well as the national (Malaysian) scene of cultural nationalism. The culture industry neutralizes style, understood as the relation or slippage between the parts of an artwork and its whole, such that "operating only with effects, it subdues" the individual parts of an artwork "and subordinates them to the formula which supplants the work. It crushes equally the whole and the parts," and "the whole confronts the details in implacable detachment, somewhat like the career of a successful man, in which everything serves to illustrate and demonstrate a success" (Horkheimer and Adorno 99). This can be seen from the way Salman Rushdie's *Midnight's Children,* which is critical and subversive of the way in which nation-states reproduce themselves and police their boundaries through the totalizing use of narrative and historiography, can be read as a work of literary tourism with implacable detachment once it receives the accolade of the "Booker of Bookers." The detailed parts of Rushdie's questioning of narrative authority and historical totality are lost when the novel becomes a commodified whole that is marketed as a story that gives metropolitan readers exciting experiences and ethnographic information about India. Ethnographic tactics negate and invert the fetishizing power of the anthropological exotic not by opposing it with a more genuine or authentic style or thematic, since "the concept of a genuine style becomes transparent in the culture industry as the aesthetic equivalent of power"; thus a directly oppositional text would also, in turn, fetishize the idea of the authentic and the genuine (Horkheimer and Adorno 103). Instead, ethnographic tactics take up Horkheimer and Adorno's suggestion that "in every work of art, style is a promise" rather than a realization, and this promise or vision is worked out through "its struggle with tradition" that eventually negates and steps beyond given reality and the status quo:

> The moment in the work of art by which it transcends reality cannot, indeed, be severed from style; that moment, however, does not consist in achieved harmony, in the questionable unity of form and content, inner and outer, individual and society, but in those traits in which the discrepancy emerges, in the necessary failure of the passionate striving for identity. (Horkheimer and Adorno 103)

The discrepancies, excesses, and apparent failures reviewers find in Samarasan's and Tan's novels should be read in terms of the negation of the anthropological exotic's desire for an achieved harmony and a unity of form and content, while at the same time these discrepancies and excess testify to the novels' struggle with the tradition or earlier works of postcolonial and national literature, together with their passionate striving toward a critical nationality that imagines the nation as a potentially just and egalitarian social formation rather than a unified community determined by a particular ethnic or religious identity. To put this another way, if Clifford Geertz (in his study of twentieth-century ethnographic writing) suggests that the ethnographer often approaches the textual representation of other cultures as both "a pilgrim and a cartographer" (10), then Samarasan and Tan write about Malaysia through the eyes of a *pilferer* and a cartographer. Rather than absolving or expatiating touristic guilt, these two writers' selection and adaptation of various tropes and devices from earlier ethnographic as well as literary texts in the form of historical fiction are tactics that map out a cosmopolitical aesthetic critical of global and national narratives of collective identity premised on cultural authenticity.

The cosmopolitical aesthetic takes seriously the claims that postcolonial studies and postcolonial literature have as critical discourses always been global in their scope and vision rather than belatedly interrogating or beholden to a historical break with European colonialism. As Stuart Hall points out in a cogent survey of the field, "the term 'post-colonial' is not merely descriptive of 'this' society rather than 'that,' or of 'then' and 'now.' It re-reads 'colonisation' as part of an essentially transnational and transcultural 'global' process—and it produces a decentred, diasporic or 'global' rewriting of earlier, nation-centered imperial grand narratives," and the global, Hall further elaborates, must be understood as "lateral and transverse cross-relations" that "supplement and simultaneously dis-place the centre-periphery" as "the global/local reciprocally re-organise and re-shape one another" ("When Was the Post-Colonial?" 247). However, the global rewriting of imperialism in postcolonial texts that are supposed to be exemplars of world literature does not do away with nationalism or the nation-state, as Simon Gikandi argues: "no reading of these seminal texts is complete without an engagement with the nation-state, its history, its foundational mythologies, and its quotidian experience. To the extent that they seek to deconstruct the foundational narratives of the nation, these are world texts; yet they cannot do without the framework of the nation" (632). The paradox of supposedly world or global texts that are still animated by the framework of the nation or the impulse of nationalism is a situation Fredric Jameson explains through a geopolitical aesthetic that "attempts to fashion national allegory into a conceptual instrument for our new being-in-the-world" (3), a form of cognitive mapping that "would pose the principle that all thinking today is *also*, whatever else it is, an attempt to think the world system as such" (4, original emphasis). However, in the geopolitical aesthetic, which is an amplified version of Jameson's earlier and highly controversial argument about national allegory, the nation vanishes amidst the tensions and flows between the global and the local, between "the most random, minute, or isolated landscapes" on the one hand and "a host of partial subjects, fragmentary or schizoid constellations" that "stand in allegorically for trends and forces in the world system" on the other (5). Instead of a geopolitical aesthetic that emphasizes the emergence of landscapes, subjects, and constellations as figures through which we may trace the world-system of late capital, a cosmopolitical aesthetic focuses on the tactical positioning and articulation of these landscapes, subjects, and constellations as negations or inversions of conventional tropes of identity through which we may trace the critique of the anthropological exotic. The residual nationalism that Gikandi detects in world or global fictions should be read not as a specter to be exorcized but rather as the active presence of a cosmopolitical aesthetic that, while deconstructing the foundational narratives of the nation and national identity, evinces a critical nationality that recasts and reshapes the nation within a world or global context.

Father Figures and Diasporic Daughters in *Evening Is the Whole Day*

The cosmopolitical strand of Indian writing in English, or IWE (Ghosh 2), is an important literary resource that Preeta Samarasan draws on to interrogate both the anthropological exotic and Malaysian cultural nationalism. Her novel *Evening Is the Whole Day* shows a strong ethnographic slant as it focuses on the lives of one family in a minority community in Malaysia, tracing their rise and fall over three generations. The Rajasekharans are a family of South Indian descent living in the city of Ipoh in northern Malaysia. The father, Raju (or Appa), is a lawyer who campaigns with a socialist party for a multicultural Malaysia in 1969, but after the May 1969 riots he is politically marginalized and becomes a public prosecutor instead. His wife, Vasanthi (or Amma), is a working-class girl whom Raju wanted to mold into an educated and intellectual woman, but she is more concerned with the material trappings of middle-class life. Vasanthi is scorned and ridiculed by Paati, Raju's mother, who lives with the family in the peacock-blue house her husband bought from a departing British rubber estate owner. Paati is looked after by Chellam, a servant whose dissolute father takes all her wages for alcohol, leaving her penniless. Chellam is also a surrogate older sister for the two younger children, Suresh and Aasha, after their real sister Uma cuts herself off from her family even as she prepares to depart for Columbia University. As the novel moves backward from 1980 to 1978 (with brief expository detours into the early and mid-twentieth century), we discover the reason for Uma's silent withdrawal: she is physically molested one night in 1978 by a frustrated and desperate Raju, who, it turns out, also keeps a Chinese mistress, with whom he has two children. Two years later Paati, who turns her back on Uma after seeing her victimized by Raju, dies from a fall after being pushed by her eldest granddaughter; Aasha protects Uma by framing Chellam, the servant, who is fired, sent back to her father, and later commits suicide. The novel begins with Chellam's departure in disgrace from the house, and ends with Uma's departure for the United States a week earlier.

Samarasan's novel responds to a transnational, diasporic body of South Asian English-language writing by luminaries such as Salman Rushdie and Amitav Ghosh as well as its own national literary predecessors in Malaysian anglophone literature. Unlike Twan Eng Tan, who is rather coy about his politics, Preeta Samarasan makes no secret of her own convictions. As she says, in Malaysia "Indians have neither the support of the government nor of a strong, successful community" (*Bostonist* para. 12), and that one of her "biggest motivations for writing the book" was to address several factors that have created "the culture of fear that has defined Malaysian life since 1969" (*Bostonist* para. 19). Additionally, Samarasan avers that her "expatriate status" in the United States enables her to achieve a critical and productive distance from Malaysia (Bakar, "Bibliobibuli" para. 14). The transnational aspect of Samarasan's authorial subjectivity is emphasized by her acknowledged connections to other South Asian writers who have achieved international acclaim. Samarasan acknowledges that she has been "inspired by [Rushdie] on many levels" (para. 2), and, as Bishnupriya Ghosh argues in her study of contemporary Indian novelists, writers such as Rushdie and Amitav Ghosh are aware that "despite the glare of international visibility" due to their prize-winning books, they are nonetheless keen to "engage in a literary politics that interrupts their own global circulation and rejects an overt fetishistic localism" (20), which is a cognate term for what Graham Huggan calls the anthropological exotic. These cosmopolitical writers perform a "sustained interrogation of these strains of virulent nationalism that shatter the social imaginary of democratic self-rule" by "unraveling forms of reactionary cultural nationalism" (Ghosh 124) and "cutting and splicing histories" (169) as well as featuring ghostly or spectral characters in their narratives, thereby producing "uncanny discourses" that are "aimed at dislodging spatio-temporal assemblages that might culturally emplace some subjects at the cost of others" (173).

Evening Is the Whole Day shows that Samarasan not only resists the fetishizing localism of global literary circulation by employing the uncanny tropes used by other cosmopolitical South Asian writers; she also uses these tropes to extend and reimagine a national consciousness expressed by a Malaysian novelist, K. S. Maniam, whose work Samarasan also recognizes as an important influence on her formation as an Indian Malaysian subject and writer (Borpujari para. 3). Maniam, a writer of Indian descent who writes in English, argues from his experience as both a child growing up in post–World War II Malaysia and a writer of fiction that the English language is a crucial and connecting medium in a polyglot postcolonial society. Although as a child Maniam attended a school where the "Anglophile Headmaster could abolish the use of languages other than English," this headmaster "could not interfere with the kind of bridging that happened between boys who came from various home languages and cultures. In a strange sort of way, the English language on our young and flexible tongues, did bring us together, the children of the various communities in Malaysia on some neutral ground" ("In Search of a Centre" para. 9). Moreover, despite the fears of the Malaysian government that English would dilute or degrade the native cultures and languages of various ethnic communities, Maniam—in terms that recall Shirley Geok-lin Lim's discussion of multilogical rather than monological worlds—asserts that his schooling in English made him aware "that it wasn't possible to have just one centre in our lives. In the school compound we spoke and wrote in English. [. . .] When we left the school compound for the day, we left one centre behind and re-entered another: the centre ruled by our own languages and cultures" ("In Search of a Centre" para. 10). The multilingual and polycentric situation of Maniam's childhood and education in Malaysia proves central to his identification as a Malaysian subject rather than an Indian or South Asian diasporic individual when he studies abroad in Britain in the 1960s, because "the community in that Malayan Teachers' College [in Britain] was truly a Malaysian society in that everyone, irrespective of race, religion and culture shared the common spirit of living together. There were hardly any racial or cultural prejudices. For a would-be writer, this experience was not only necessary but vital, for it allowed him entry into other personalities, cultures and languages," and this was possible because "it was the English language that forged that close and common bond among" Maniam and his fellow Malaysian teacher-trainees in Britain ("In Search of a Centre" para. 15–16). The common bond that Maniam feels with his fellow Malaysians while studying abroad in Britain expresses a critical nationalism that works through religious, cultural, and linguistic differences in an effort to share a common life, and it contradicts the state mandate that "Malay culture should form the foundation of the national culture" (Tham 58). However, while Maniam maps out an autobiographical trajectory for the

Malaysian writer that moves from diaspora toward nationalism, this move runs the danger of conflating national consciousness with national identity as Maniam's writerly persona becomes identified with the nation as a whole at the expense of other voices or communities that may be playing an active role in the political and cultural process of negotiating the nation. Samarasan parts ways with her literary predecessor by insisting that the nation needs to be imagined not only by those inside it but also by those who maintain a critical and diasporic distance outside it; she eschews Maniam's autobiographical trajectory of national narration in favor of intrinsic and extrinsic ethnographic tactics.

Evening Is the Whole Day, like novels by other diasporic South Asian writers, has been read ethnographically and exotically: a *New York Times* reviewer praises Samarasan for giving readers "the long slow banquet of a fine novel" that promises more than "news, history, [and] travel blogs" about "far away locales" (Goodman para. 1). Similarly, a Malaysian reviewer celebrates the novel as one that "embraces you entirely, seizing your senses and emotions" (Manickam para. 1) with "rich imagery" (para. 2). *Evening Is the Whole Day* indeed offers evocative descriptions of the landscapes and lives of Malaysia and its people, and the opening passage has the tone of an ethnographic study offering the reader a literary tour of Peninsular Malaysia, the landmass of which is described as "stretching delicate as a bird's head" (Samarasan 1). Samarasan also offers a vivid account of Malaysia's tropical rainfall and its effect on people's everyday life that bears quoting at length to show its full sensory and kinesthetic details:

> These are the most familiar rains, the violent silver ropes that flood the playing fields and force office workers to wade to bus stops in shoes that fill like buckets. Blustering and melodramatic, the afternoon rains cause traffic jams at once terrible—choked with the black smoke of lorries and the screeching brakes of schoolbuses—and beautiful: aglow with winding lines of watery yellow headlights that go on forever, with blue streetlamps reflected in burgeoning puddles, with the fluorescent melancholy of empty roadside stalls. (Samarasan 1)

A concise yet highly evocative sketch of ordinary city life in the midst of a tropical downpour that takes us from the choking heat of day to the quiet solitude of night, this opening passage displays Samarasan's considerable ethnographic flair, but a stylistic twist surfaces in the deft personification of the rain-soaked cityscape as at once "blustering and melodramatic" as well as "beautiful" and "melancholy." Malaysia is a seething landscape of intensities and affect that cannot be leisurely consumed as an ethnographic tableau. Moreover, at the end of the passage we are reminded that "every day appears to begin with a blaze and end with this deluge, so that past and present and future run together in an infinite, steaming river" (1). Such a summation would not seem significant were it not for one of the epigraphs of the novel taken from British writer Graham Swift's Booker-Prize-winning 1984 novel *Waterland:* "History begins only at the point where things go wrong; history is born only with trouble, with perplexity, with regret. So that hard on the heels of the word Why comes the sly and wistful word If" (106). Swift's novel, set in the marshy region of northeast England known as The Fens, is regarded as a landmark work of historiographic metafiction, a genre of contemporary writing in which fiction self-reflexively comments upon and brackets historiography in order to achieve "not a transcending of history, but a problematized inscribing of subjectivity into history" (Hutcheon 117–18). Samarasan uses the slyness and wistfulness of the conditional "If" in her epigraph from Swift to point toward her exploration of alternative narratives and subjectivities that are unacknowledged by official versions of postcolonial history and cultural nationalism. Her evocation of Swift's novel is an act of literary cosmopolitics that draws on the cultural capital of *Waterland* and its popularization of historiographic metafiction among an Anglo-American reading public. Her ethnographic tactics literally take a leaf out of Graham Swift's book of historiographic metafiction, inverting the anthropological exotic's simultaneously distancing yet familiarizing gaze through the problematized inscribing of her subjects in an ethnographic mode.

The ethnographic gaze was one powerful means of knowledge production and sociocultural control the British colonizers exerted over their subjects, and Samarasan's strategic thrust in her novel is aimed at the residual but unattenuated presence of such a colonial ethnography and its derivative ideas of racial and cultural superiority or inferiority even in postcolonial, independent Malaysia. These ethnographic stereotypes continue to inform the nation-state's official cultural nationalism and the formation of its national identity, and it is to their lingering existence, rather than the failure of a critical national consciousness, that the social tensions in present-day Malaysia may be attributed. Immediately after the highly evocative opening paragraph, the novel reveals that "in truth, though, there are days that do not blaze and rains less fierce," and how the sight of "grey mist" and "glowing green hills [. . .] must have reminded the old British rulers of their faraway country" (Samarasan 2). The sudden reference to Malaysia's old British rulers in a section that is time-stamped "September 6, 1980" (1) signals that British colonialism and its legacy continues to haunt the nation even after official independence in 1957, and that the novel is less a historically realistic presentation of Malaysian life and culture than a narrative of the past represented through a mist of memories and desires. The persistent presence of British colonialism and its aftereffects in Malaysia are represented by the physical structure of the Rajasekharans' Big House, the ghosts who inhabit it, and the use of racial stereotypes by the different ethnic communities against each other during the May 1969 riots. The Rajasekharans live in a house bought by Raju's father from Mr McDougall, a rubber estate owner who despises the locals and leaves Malaysia just before independence. McDougall is part of the British governing class, who, "like God [. . .] had watched their word take miraculous material form, [with] Malay and Chinese and Indian stepping up unquestioningly to fill the roles invented for them" by the colonizers (21), thus foreshadowing the racial riots that would take place in 1969 as a result of the inability of the newly decolonized community to break free of the roles created for them by the British. Against this unrelenting colonial bigotry, Raju's father, Tata, tries to efface McDougall's "conservative taste" (26) by adding his own architectural extensions, but the consequence of Tata's renovations is that the house "metamorphosed into something out of an Enid Blyton bedtime story" (23). This reference to the famous British author of children's literature suggests that Tata's attempts at assimilating the house to a local Malaysian aesthetic are not only childish; they also disguise the fact that something British stubbornly remains beneath the renovated surface of the Big House and the new nation of Malaysia. Furthermore, echoing the hubris of Mr McDougall's godlike observational stance, Tata's purchase and installment of electric lights in the Big House is closely connected to the birth of the new nation-state of Malaysia. At the very moment of midnight on August 31, 1957, when "Tunku Abdul Rahman [Malaysia's first Prime Minister] raised his right arm high on a colonial cricket ground and saluted the country's new freedom," Tata flips a new switch in the Big House and "there was Light," with the biblical allusion repeated at the scene of national independence: "The blazing Light of a dozen fluorescent streetlamps, the crackling Light of a hundred flashing cameras, the (metaphorical, now, but no less real) inner Light of pride and ambition that shone in a million patriotic breasts just as it had shone in other breasts at other midnights" (25). In this passage, Samarasan's literary cosmopolitics frames a critique of national identity with the allusion to Salman Rushdie's historiographical interrogation of India's national independence in *Midnight's Children*. The capitalization of the word "light," with its connotations of biblical truth and universal enlightenment, is both foreshadowing and ironic. In contrast to the beauty and melancholy of the ambient city lights in the opening passage, here we see the conflation of the blazing, crackling light of streetlamps and camera flashes with pride and ambition associated with patriotism rather than nationalism or national consciousness, foreshadowing the future clashes between Malays and Chinese over the pride and privilege associated with ethnic or cultural nationalism rather than critical nationality. Light becomes instrumentalized as spectacle, just as the nation becomes an identity rather than a social formation.

Nowhere is this residual and pernicious aftereffect of British colonial power more evident than in the novel's stylized description of the May 1969 riots, during which the racial profiles used by the British resurface with a vengeance as various ethnic groups in Malaysia turn against each other in the wake of an election that saw Raju's, or Appa's, coalition party making substantial political gains against the dominant Malay majority faction. Unlike Shirley Geok-lin Lim, who traces the indirect effects of the riots through her protagonist Li An's thoughts and feelings while she spends a night of passion with Chester, Samarasan captures the frenzied anger and violence of the entire country, depersonalizing the events by paradoxically anthropomorphizing the growing social tensions through two figures, Rumor and Fact: "three days after the election, Rumor and Fact burst forth into the noonday Kuala Lumpur heat, Rumor in a red dress, Fact in coat tails, and together they began a salacious tango in the streets" (120). The salacious tango here alludes to a reference made by Li An in Shirley Geok-lin Lim's *Joss and Gold*, in which she remarks that her friend Abdullah's explanation of Malay special rights in a multiethnic country seemed "like a good partner observing the patterns and courtesies of an elaborate dance" (*Joss and Gold* 45). In *Evening Is the Whole Day*, however, this elaborate dance of race relations between willing and well-behaved partners spins dangerously out of control, as "the stories that Rumor and Fact spun together poured like lava through the city" and these stories, which seem to have no discernible source and no means of verification, heighten the animosity between the Malay and non-Malay communities as each begins to intensify its stereotypes of the others:

> fourteen non-Malay opposition members had been elected in the state of Selangor alone; these Gerakan and Democratic Action Party victors were going to strip the Malays of their God-given scholarships and housing loans and job quotas, [. . .] the Chinese were going to grab Selangor for themselves, just as they'd grabbed Singapore, as if their pockets weren't bulging enough already; the frightened gomen [government] had gunned down a Chinese Labor Party activist for no reason. And the Indians? They'd staged a drunken midnight demonstration, an excuse for a brawl, really, so typical of those bloody booze-guzzling estate coolies. (Samarasan 121)

Through the use of semicolons, Samarasan presents the hatred and violence sweeping through Malaysia with an ethnographic turn that reveals how these racial and racist sentiments are discursive forces for which one person or group—whether Malay, Chinese, or Indian—cannot be held culpable. Rather than providing a detailed, objective study of contemporary race relations or tracing the tumultuous events through the eyes of one or a few characters, Samarasan pulls us back from the raw intensity of the racial violence and instead draws our attention to the wellspring of Malaysians' racist vocabulary:

> every man, Chinese, Indian, and Malay, forgot his contempt for the views of the departed British and savored the taste of his old masters' stereotypes. *Coolie*, they hissed. *Village idiot fed on sambal petai. Slit-eyed pig-eater.* They'd been given a vocabulary, and now, like all star pupils, they were putting it to use, relying on the old, familiar combinations, patting each other on the back to applaud their own initiative, encouraging the back rows of the classroom to rise to the challenge. (Samarasan 121, original emphasis)

The analogy of Malaysians as students schooled in the vocabulary of racial stereotypes in the classroom of British colonialism underscores how "the concept of independence and of Malaysia itself was configured by the colonial project. Both the British and the Malay political community found themselves in a defensive position and the political discourses that grew out of that period [. . .] were expressions of such a state of mind" (Ooi 459). In a literary inversion of the pride and ambition of patriotism displayed in 1957 at the earlier moment of national independence, the May 1969 riots illustrate the defensive belligerence of the Malays, Chinese, and Indians that stems from the colonial discourse of ethnocentric chauvinism and economic exploitation. To read this as a failure of the national project would, however, be erroneous. The novel suggests that anticolonial nationalism has not so much failed as it has not been given a chance to succeed or properly take shape. The unyielding power of the racial and economic divisions created by the British colonial system prevented an economically equitable and socially egalitarian national community from emerging, instead installing an instrumental, cultural nationalism that was focused on producing and reproducing a national identity of Malay dominance.

The official narrative of national independence and progress is centered on Raju Rajasekharan, who, like the Prime Minister Tunku Abdul Rahman, went to university in Britain, earned a law degree, and enters politics with the fervent hope of creating "a Malaya for all Malayans" regardless of their ethnic origins (Samarasan 44). However, Samarasan reveals the problems inherent in such nation-building projects centered on heroic and masculine figures. While Raju hopes to create a better society, he also harbors an equally strong desire for self-aggrandizement: "Marriage was part of his first five-year plan, which was itself every bit as determined, purposeful, and specific as the nation's own. [. . .] To Malaya, the Party would bring prosperity and peace, and to Appa, great glory both public and private" (44). Raju sees his domestic prosperity as synonymous with his nation-building project to the extent that his choice of Vasanthi as his wife, because of her "awkwardness" and "simplicity," stems from his belief that marrying her would mean "taking on the real work of nation-building" (62). Vasanthi's "lack of experience" and apparent innocence makes her the perfect candidate to "bloom under his expert tutelage" (54) and his "power to exalt and educate" (93) her in romantic and intellectual matters. Raju's equation of nation-building with wife-molding is critiqued by Deniz Kandiyoti's study of women and nationalist movements; such movements often "reaffirm the boundaries of culturally acceptable feminine conduct and exert pressure on women to articulate their gender interests within the terms of reference set by nationalist discourse" (380) and associate "women with the private domain" in a way that "reinforces the merging of the nation/community with the selfless mother/devout wife," thus hindering "their emergence as full-fledged citizens" (382). However, Vasanthi has no interest in national politics or intellectual edification and is keener on entering the fashionable world of the Malaysian middle class, adopting the motto that *"in the end all that matters is money"* (Samarasan 102, original emphasis). Raju's unsuccessful educational project at home is paralleled by his political failure after the May 1969 riots and the disbanding of his party, and he chooses "personal glory" over "the last of his ideals," swallowing his pride to become a public prosecutor for the government (135).

The triumphant narrative of an independent and multiracial Malaysia, represented by patriarchal figures such as Raju, his father Tata, and the Prime Minister (Samarasan 20), is disrupted and undermined by the haunting inequalities left behind by colonialism in the specters of Mr McDougall's daughter and Paati, whose stories are left out of the official narrative of national independence and who "figure a nonsynchronism that is opposed to the empty homogenous time of history proper" (Ghosh 167). These two ghosts haunt the Big House and remind us of the spectral residue of colonialism: the first is Mr McDougall's daughter with his Chinese mistress, and the second is Paati herself, Raju's mother. When the Scotsman who originally owned the Big House refused to acknowledge his Chinese mistress and her daughter before he returned to Britain, the Chinese woman drowned herself and the little girl in a double suicide (Samarasan 18, 270). The nameless little girl's haunting of the Big House is a reminder of the subordinate status and inferior treatment of local women by the colonizers, and of the rejection of hybrid children of mixed parentage who are the inevitable products of the colonial encounter. Paati's ghost also attests to this ineradicable colonial presence, for in life she was extremely sympathetic toward the British, weeping "for the Englishmen who would be booted out unceremoniously for the supposed sins of their fathers" and saying on the eve of Malaysian independence that "when the British are really gone for good, we'll miss them" (23).

Samarasan's critique of this apparently selfless but actually self-serving patriarchal nationalism is further underscored by her cutting and splicing of Raju's story with those of two other women: Chellam, the servant, and Uma, Raju's daughter. In the first chapter of the novel, Samarasan compares and contrasts the two. "Chellam is eighteen years old, the same age as Uma," but the differences in their education, economic, and social status quickly become obvious. It is only after the novel details the departure of these two women that Raju's rise and fall as a political figure is revealed, and as the novel moves back toward 1978 from 1980, Samarasan exposes Raju's moral bankruptcy as both the head of the household and an employer. Raju gives all of Chellam's monthly wages to her drunkard father, Muniandy, in order to avoid a scene that would tarnish his middle-class respectability (Samarasan 255), an act which goes against his original socialist principles and smacks of cowardice (168–69). Uma, on the other hand, is the apple of her father's eye, whose "heart was as beautiful as her face" (283) and exudes an inner strength that Raju "loved," "admired," and also "feared" (284). Uma appears to be the female paragon that Raju wanted to turn his wife Vasanthi into, and she becomes the object of Raju's desire in ways that emphasize his need to control and shape those around him. As he molests his daughter, Raju detects a "childlike smell" from her "that was his most devastating punishment, this reminder that what he'd done, he'd done to the child Uma had once been, the child she still was" (301). Through Raju's actions, Samarasan criticizes a version of nationalism that appears to be egalitarian and committed to social justice but inevitably privileges male subjects who govern the country as they do their families. This version of nationalism portrays women "as victims of their societies' backwardness, symbols of the nation's newly found vigour and modernity or the privileged repository of uncontaminated national values" (Kandiyoti 388), and ultimately fails by either turning against itself and committing violence against the women who symbolically exemplify its virtues (in Uma's case), or by ignoring or rationalizing the plight of the poor and underprivileged as a necessary part of the nation's social stratification (in Chellam's case). Furthermore, Raju's incestuous assault on his own daughter is Samarasan's scathing judgment on a cultural nationalism that strictly polices the boundaries between the Chinese, Indian, and Malay communities. If, as Kandiyoti argues, women are identified as "privileged bearers of corporate identities and boundary markers of their communities" (388), then Uma's victimization at her father's hands takes the endogenous logic of cultural nationalism to an extreme but inevitable conclusion: the best way to maintain the homogeneity and purity of one's community is to reproduce it with those who are closest in blood and lineage.

Samarasan's critique of Malaysian nationalism becomes clearer if we understand *Evening Is the Whole Day* as a response to *The Return*, a novel written by an older Indian Malaysian writer, K. S. Maniam. Maniam's novel, like *Evening*, follows a three-generation immigrant Indian family through the narration of Ravi, a schoolteacher, who recalls the arrival from India of his grandmother, Periathai. Periathai builds a house and carves many scenes from the Indian epics of the Ramayana and Mahabharata onto its pillars. After she dies, the municipal authorities want to demolish the house, and her son (Ravi's father) Naina tries, in vain, to stop them. Naina immolates himself in a final act of defiance, and the novel closes with English-educated Ravi writing an elegiac poem commemorating his father. *The Return* stages a symbolic turn away from diasporic Indian toward a national, Malaysian identity through the deaths of Periathai and Naina and the destruction of the house with its carved pillars, along with Ravi's anglophone and anglophile education. Ravi is "representative of the boy growing into adulthood with unquestioning loyalty to whatever is new" (Maniam, "Fiction into Fact" 266), and his "personality represents an aggressive, intellectualised attitude and consequently is reductive in its scope" (Maniam, "Fiction into Fact" 267), as opposed to the double consciousness of his grandmother and father, who try to adapt Indian cultural practices to Malaysia. Ravi represents, like Raju in *Evening*, a new national consciousness, but whereas Maniam expresses a cautious optimism that the turn away from a diasporic identity will help ethnic Indians better integrate into Malaysian society, Samarasan is less hopeful because of the prevailing social order that still emphasizes impenetrable racial boundaries. Therefore, it is no surprise that Uma, who represents the next generation after Raju and Ravi, leaves for Columbia University in America, turning away from the nation and becoming part of the diaspora. Uma's selection of a double major in biology and theater on her college application form (Samarasan 325) marks her decision to break out of the biological determinism of racial identity and "ethnic absolutism" (Gilroy 2) in Malaysia toward a more performative and flexible concept of identity. As her sister Aasha remarks upon seeing Uma's application form, "Uma's won. Uma's going to do what she pleases and there's nothing anyone can do about it" (Samarasan 325). Uma's theatrical aspirations recall the dramatic vocabulary Stuart Hall uses to describe diasporic identity: identity is not "an already accomplished fact" but a "'production,' which is never complete, always in process, and always constituted within, not outside, representation" ("Cultural Identity and Diaspora" 222), and "subject to the continuous 'play' of history, culture, and power" (225). Although the novel ends without any exposition of Uma's time in the United States, Uma's imminent adoption of a diasporic subjectivity offers a glimmer of hope in a novel otherwise shot through with unrelenting disillusionment and despair about the politics of Malaysia's cultural nationalism. But the novel is, in the end, still closely linked to Malaysia, even if Uma leaves the nation behind. As Samarasan says in an interview, *Evening Is the Whole Day* is to a large extent "Appa's [Raju's] story. The story of his disenchantment and apathy—which is the story of middle-class Malaysian Indians" (Stameshkin para. 32). Samarasan ultimately points out that the project of creating a Malaysian nation-state based on social justice and equal opportunities for all its constituent groups is not yet complete even with the end of British colonialism and the achievement of formal independence. Other perspectives and voices, such as those of the underprivileged Chellam and the diasporic Uma, must be taken into account in order to balance and revise the patriarchal nationalist discourse of father figures such as Raju.

Claiming the Nation through Hybridity in *The Gift of Rain*

If Preeta Samarasan is in dialogue with cosmopolitical South Asian as well as nationalist Indian Malaysian writers, Twan Eng Tan rehearses a historically rich tradition of anthropological writing as well as contemporary British literature in his novel *The Gift of Rain*. Penang, a city on a small island located off the western coast of Malaysia, is the setting for the novel, which moves between two time periods: first, 1939 to 1945, during which British-held Malaya was conquered by the Japanese Imperial Army, which in turn surrendered to the victorious Allied forces at the end of World War II; second, the late 1990s, during which Penang is a rapidly modernizing city. Philip Hutton, the narrator, is the child of a British businessman and a Chinese woman, and his mixed parentage causes him to be isolated in both the European and Asian communities in colonial Malaya. In the later time frame Philip, the sole surviving member of the Hutton family, is an old man who is about to retire from his family's trading company but who uses his wealth for the historical restoration of many colonial-era houses in Penang. A Japanese woman, Michiko Murakami, visits him and reveals that she once loved his good friend and mentor Hayato Endo, or Endo-san. Philip reminisces and narrates the earlier time frame of the story, in which he is a sixteen-year-old who befriends Endo-san, the Japanese vice-consul in British colonial Malaya. Philip learns *aikido* and the Japanese language from Endo-san while unwittingly passing along strategic information about Malaya that eventually helps the Japanese military defeat the British in 1942. Because of his fluency in various local languages and Japanese, and out of a desire to protect his family, Philip becomes Endo-san's lieutenant in the new regime. He unwillingly assists the Japanese secret police in their atrocities against the locals, but secretly helps save as many civilians as he can by passing on information to the resistance made up of Malayan Communist forces and the British-led Malaya People's Anti-Japanese Army. His espionage is discovered, but his father asks to be executed by Endo-san in his stead while Philip is placed under house arrest. He is finally released when British troops arrive to reclaim Malaya in 1945. However, the novel takes a spiritual turn: Philip and Endo-san were lovers in their past lives, and they are locked in a romantic but deadly cycle of reincarnation in which Endo-san always ends up killing Philip. By training Philip in *aikido* and the Japanese language and making him his assistant, Endo-san tries to break this cycle of love and destruction by reconciling their two lives, but with the defeat of Japan and his imminent trial as a war criminal, Endo-san asks Philip to kill him instead, thereby breaking the fateful circle by reversing their roles. Philip does so, and retreats into a semi-reclusive existence, alternatively hated and admired by the people of Penang, who view him either as a cowardly traitor or as a pragmatic survivor who defied the Japanese. The novel ends in the present day with Michiko's death (from radiation sickness caused by the atomic bombing of Nagasaki) and Philip contemplating his remaining days.

While at first glance appearing to fulfill the anthropological exotic of the global literary marketplace, *The Gift of Rain* evokes but also inverts important literary and cultural tropes and stereotypes associated with ethnographic narratives and colonial adventure stories and travelogues about the Orient and the Far East. Tan's novel gestures toward two literary traditions. First, as one reviewer observes, it evokes Joseph Conrad and other fin-de-siècle British fiction about the decline of the British empire in Malaya[2] with its "exotic Eastern location," "rich lushness," and "good old-fashioned,

---

2. The term "Malaya" is used here to refer to the territory under British colonialism, whereas "Malaysia" denotes the country after its formal independence in 1957.

masculine, ripping yarn" (Jordison para. 6). Second, it is also part of a large body of work about the Japanese occupation that combines "familiar horrific stereotypical" descriptions of "the brutal image of the fierce Japanese warrior" (Klein 176) with a "sympathetic portrayal" of the "human side of the soldiers as well as the benevolence of many of the civilians" (177). Ronald D. Klein argues that this type of writing, as a record of the horrors of war as well as of the "tactics of survival and the character it produced," plays an important part "in the forging of a national identity" in both Malaysia and Singapore (179). Furthermore, Tan's novel echoes ethnographic accounts of the Japanese such as Ruth Benedict's *The Chrysanthemum and the Sword* in its descriptions of their social mores. Many Japanese characters are presented in an ethnographic fashion with perplexingly contradictory traits: Goro, a military officer, has a "sublime" taste for classical music matched by a sadistic desire for violence, killing an innocent man for not showing an antique piano "proper care" (Tan 296, 297); Saotome, the Japanese ambassador, is both a philosopher who enjoys his Zen rock garden and a pederast who enjoys young Chinese girls and lusts after Philip himself (287–88). Finally, Endo-san repeatedly stresses the importance of duty to the Japanese: "*If we fail in our duty, we fail our country, and our family,*" he tells Philip, and continues, with an air of resignation, "It has always been so in our way of life. One cannot escape it" (89, original emphasis). These descriptions of the Japanese, a mixture of social obligations with wanton violence and decadent perversion, appear to be an index of how the Japanese think and behave, and they highlight how different the Japanese are from both the colonial British and the local Malays, Chinese, and Indians. Read in this light, Tan's writing echoes Ruth Benedict's anthropological study of the Japanese that explains how "the Japanese themselves saw certain violent swings of behavior as integral parts of a system" (19) and "examines Japanese assumptions about the conduct of life" (13). The ethnographic gaze also extends to the non-Japanese characters in the book by highlighting aspects of their personalities that correspond to cultural or racial profiles. Kon, Philip's Chinese friend and fellow *aikido* exponent, is a hot-blooded youth and son of a powerful Chinese triad (gangster) boss who joins the resistance against the Japanese, but is ultimately betrayed by the Chinese girl he loves and killed by the Chinese resistance leader, who is afraid of losing "face" or honor because of Kon's growing popularity (Tan 383–84). Noel Hutton, Philip's father, refuses to leave Penang with the rest of the Europeans out of a British sense of fair play and dignity; as he says to Philip, "We'll keep the flag flying. We'll keep our family name untainted, and we will not lose face" (273), displaying the "stiff upper lip" attitude often associated with gentlemanly British behavior. Tan also sprinkles impressive descriptions of the Malayan landscape that contribute to this ethnographic effect: on the opening page we see "rain [. . .] smearing the landscape into a Chinese brush painting" and how "the scent of grass wove through the air like threads entwining with the perfume of flowers, creating an intricate tapestry of fragrance" (1), and at the end of the novel the elderly Philip experiences a flash of insight, which he experiences "with the delicacy of a butterfly entering the reveries of the venerable Chinese philosopher, as though alighting on the most fragile of petals" (431). Even the homoerotic affection between Philip and Endo-san is described in terms of a fierce duel between honorable warriors: "that evening he used his *katana* against me in his violent ways and I responded in kind. [. . .] My sword received his force with equal hunger and I opened myself up to him as clouds open up to the sun" (308). The effect of the abundance of historical detail and rich, Orientalist descriptions has not gone unremarked: one reviewer observes that it is a "Malaysian novel aimed at an international readership" and, as such, makes itself accessible by providing "a great deal of information on the complex social background of the country" (Bakar, "It's a BIG Book" para. 8) and also "unashamedly draw[ing] on romantic Oriental elements like the deliberate *chinoiserie* of the imagery [. . .] and the delicate motifs of insects" (para. 11). Another reviewer, also noting that Tan's descriptions and *chinoiserie* are "psychotically tasteful" (Lake para. 7), even goes so far as to propose that the novel "might perhaps have been more naturally realised in a decent Manga production" (para. 8). The idea that Tan's book might be better suited to the medium of Japanese graphic novels suggests that *The Gift of Rain* succeeds—perhaps too well—in fulfilling a Western or metropolitan readership's desire for the anthropological exotic in fiction about East Asian cultures and countries.

However, the comment that Tan's descriptive prose is "psychotically tasteful" suggests that there is more afoot than a simple anthropological exoticization of colonial Malaya for an audience hungry for foreign fare. Tan acknowledges Kazuo Ishiguro as a model for his own writing (Tam para. 32), and Ishiguro admits that his Booker-Prize-winning novel *The Remains of the Day* is very much a work of posed ethnicity because it "has the tone of a very English book, but actually [he is] using that as a kind of shock tactic" to create "a super-English novel. *It's more English than English*" (Vorda and Herzinger 12, original emphasis). Ishiguro uses this affected style of super-Englishness to criticize the "enormous nostalgia industry" in Britain during the 1980s (Vorda and Herzinger 14). Similarly, Tan's *chinoiserie* and "stilted dialogue" (Law-Yone para. 6) are a self-conscious critique of the essentialism inherent in the anthropological exotic of the global literary marketplace and that also exists in the present-day Malaysian government's racialization of national literature and culture that subordinates Chinese and Indian communities in favor of Malay interests. Just as Ishiguro creates a narrator in Stevens the butler who seems quintessentially and excessively English, Tan uses the principles of *aikido* in the novel for his own tactic of foregrounding but also simultaneously inverting the anthropological exotic. Endo-san advises Philip to face an opponent by not "meet[ing] the force of the strike head-on," and instead "step[ping] to the side to avoid the blow," and "redirect[ing] the force"; if Philip can "deflect, distract" his opponent, "even agree with him," then Philip can "unbalance" his opponent's mind and "lead him anywhere [he] want[s]" (Tan 52). The psychotic edge of Tan's tasteful descriptions and his stilted dialogue correspond to the anthropological exotic but actually unbalance it, redirecting the momentum of his readers' desire for the exotic back at them, just as Endo-san reminds Philip: "*Redirect your opponent's momentum back into himself*" (164, original emphasis). In other words, in *The Gift of Rain* Tan has created a super-exotic novel, one that is more Oriental than the Orient, and his reviewers' complaints about Tan's descriptions and dialogue must be considered in light of this deliberate excess of Orientalist signification rather than as a failed attempt at cultural authenticity.

Tan's super-Oriental exoticism unbalances the fetishizing power of the anthropological exotic with its treatment of historical fact and Philip Hutton's fictitious role in events of World War II. The novel would have us understand that Philip passed along information to Endo-san about accessible roads through the local jungle (Tan 265) and the ocean tides and weather pattern along Malaya's coast (300) that enabled the Japanese army's swift advance and victory. Philip is also present at the formal surrender of Penang to the Japanese military (278–79), and his collaboration with the Japanese regime echoes the cooperation that took place between many Malayans (especially among the Malays and Indians) and the Japanese forces (Andaya and Andaya 258–61). Furthermore, Philip's own family background links him to another period of historical upheaval. His maternal grandfather, Wu An Khoo, is supposed to have been a tutor and friend to an emperor of China, Wen Zu, who preceded the last Manchu emperor Pu Yi, but "all records and traces" of Wen Zu were destroyed by the Empress Dowager such that "he never existed in history" (Tan 123). Grandpa Khoo mysteriously disappears into the Malayan hills after giving Philip a jade pin he used to test for poisons in their food (365–66); this jade pin was originally possessed by one of the Five Ancestor monks who were disciples of Bodhidharmo (119), the legendary monk who brought Buddhism to China and Japan and vanished "after ten years of continuous meditation" (111). This mixture of historical fact with religious mysticism seems credible enough, as one reviewer praises the novel for "describing a place and time that is at once vividly real and fantastically alien" and "instantly transport[ing] the reader to a destination that only exists in fading memories and imagination" (Donaghy para. 3). However, in his author's note at the end of the book, Tan reveals that he has "taken certain liberties with events": the surrender of Penang (and by extension Endo-san and Philip Hutton's role in the war) and the "Forgotten Emperor" Wen Zu are all products of Tan's "dramatic license" (433). The success of the anthropological exotic depends on a seamless combination of the familiar and the strange: the strangeness here being the supernatural love story of Philip and Endo-san locked in a cycle of love and death, as well as the legend of Bodhidharmo, the Forgotten Emperor, and Grandpa Khoo's disappearance; the familiar is brought to us by the historical time frames of the novel (British colonial Malaya, World War II, China's Qing dynasty). But Tan's ethnographic tactics invert this anthropological exotic, and this discomfiting inversion can be seen from complaints that his prose is psychotically tasteful, that the characters' dialogue is stilted, and that certain passages sound "like a cut-and-paste from Wikipedia" (Jordison para. 9) or like "clumsily introduced historical explanations" (para. 10). Rather than seeing these as flaws in Tan's writing style, we should understand the overwrought and ostentatious parts of the novel as disarticulations or interruptions in the textual body of the Orient created in the imaginations of metropolitan readers. These disarticulations haunt and disturb the anthropological exotic, because they remind readers that there is no essential or authentic Japan or Malaya lying behind or beneath the novel's ethnographic detail and atmospheric vividness. This deconstructive thrust can be seen from a key episode in the middle of the novel, where Philip experiences a moment of pure enlightenment, or *sartori*. While visiting Philip's room, Endo-san remarks that Philip has copied one of his own paintings of the monk Bodhidharmo (Tan 218), but Endo-san's painting is itself a copy of a painting by Musashi Miyamoto (42), which is itself a graphical rendition of a monk who vanished into thin air, out of history and into legend. Philip suddenly experiences a moment of "complete clarity and total contentment" that he will seek to recapture for the rest of his life (219). The complete clarity that Philip experiences and hungers for parallels the transparency and unmediated nature of the anthropological exotic that "gives the uninitiated reader access to the text and, by extension, the 'foreign culture' itself" (Huggan 37). But in Tan's novel, what lies at the heart of this search for total contentment is a series of representations pointing toward a constitutive *absence* that cannot be grasped or filled—Philip's enlightenment is centered upon a copy of a copy of a painting of a monk who vanished into thin air. In contrast to Ruth

Benedict's ethnographic account of the Japanese, Tan's ethnographic tactics in *The Gift of Rain* do not explicate a core set of features or characteristics of the Japanese or Malayan way of life to its readers, nor do they transport us to a vividly real and fantastically alien time and place. Instead, the novel uses our desire for what is foreign and exotic to evoke plausible and conventional Orientalist and historical impressions and then unbalance the momentum of our reading. It is a moment not of complete clarity or contentment but of diasporic disarticulation within a cosmopolitical aesthetic. It is a conjoining of Kazuo Ishiguro's posed ethnicity and super-English writing style with historical events in colonial Malaya and postcolonial Malaysia and with national and cultural stereotypes that interrupts and withholds any fulfillment of exotic expectations and questions the terms upon which we as readers desire knowledge of and fetishize other cultures and peoples through our reading.

This cosmopolitical thrust of Tan's fictional critique of the anthropological exotic in the global literary marketplace is matched by an equally unbalancing critique of the logic and politics of official cultural nationalism in postcolonial Malaysia from a queer diasporic standpoint. It is important to note that the novel's half-British, half-Chinese narrator, Philip Hutton, is not only biracial but also queer, as he and Endo-san are lovers who have been locked in a cycle of death and rebirth across centuries. Philip is a narrator and protagonist who inverts the heteronormative and reproductive roles promoted by official nationalism, as he never marries or has any children, and his lover is one of the generally reviled and demonized Japanese imperial aggressors. Philip is situated both within and without the colonial history of Malaya, as he is a character who exists in the time frames presented by the novel as well as a reborn soul "stepping out of the flow of time" (Tan 11) who thus offers the possibility or promise of unsettling and reconceptualizing what Benedict Anderson (citing Walter Benjamin) calls the "homogeneous empty time" of the nation (Anderson 24). Moreover, in addition to his British and Chinese heritage and his fluency in the local tongues of Hokkien and Malay, Philip turns out to be Japanese as well, for in his past life he was executed by his friend and lover Endo-san because he "betrayed the Shogun's government by providing information to the rebels" in the same way that he now passes information to the anti-Japanese resistance fighters in occupied Malaya (Tan 307). While the novel describes Endo-san's and Philip's relationship as a complex layering of affection between father and son, teacher and student, and romantic lovers, their emotional and physical intimacy is always haunted by and mixed in with the fearful dilemma of remaining loyal to and betraying their respective communities and countries, while at the same time making an "attempt at redemption" while locked in a "cycle of pain" (218).

Endo-san wishes to train and recruit Philip as his protégé so that Philip may work for the Japanese imperial government in Malaya and thus break the cycle of death and rebirth; Philip decides to become a collaborator with the Japanese in order to keep his own British family alive and to secretly assist the local Malayan resistance and save civilian lives by sending along information regarding the purges conducted by the Japanese secret police. Although Endo-san admonishes Philip in grand and tragic terms to remember their love "even when [they] appear to be fighting to the death" as mortal enemies on two opposing sides of the war (218), within the context of contemporary Malaysian literary representations of the Japanese invasion, Philip's love for Endo-san also inverts the dominant perception in Malaysia and Singapore of the Japanese as militaristic sadists during World War II. While this does not excuse the violence and atrocities committed by the Japanese military, *The Gift of Rain* may be considered part of a category of works about the Japanese occupation that shows "a more human face of the Japanese" who arrived after the initial military attack "to form a civilian government, take over the running of businesses, and staff Japanese-language schools" (Klein 156).

At the same time, Philip's hybridity and queerness suggests that *The Gift of Rain* may be read as a literary intervention into Malaysia's cultural nationalism from a queer diasporic perspective. As Gayatri Gopinath argues, "queer incursions into diasporic public culture reterritorialize the home by transforming it into a site where non-heteronormative desires and practices are articulated and performed," and "rather than doing away with home and its fictions of (sexual, racial, communal) purity and belonging, queer diasporic literature engages in a radical reworking of multiple home spaces. The queer diasporic body is the medium through which home is remapped and its various narratives are displaced, uprooted, and infused with alternative forms of desire" (164, 165). Philip embodies the multiethnic and polyglot admixture of peoples and cultures that makes up colonial and postcolonial Malaysia. When Philip and his siblings were growing up, his father "instructed that [they] were to be addressed in the dialect of Hokkien by the Chinese servants, and Malay by the Malay gardener. Like many of the Europeans who considered Malaya their home, he had also insisted that all his children receive their education locally as much as possible," such that Philip and his siblings "grew up speaking the local languages," an education that "would bind [them] to Penang forever" (27). These emotional and linguistic bonds with Penang run deeper than Philip's biracial heritage, as he avers: "This is my home. Even though half of me is English I have never hungered for England. [. . .] I have lived on this island all my life, and I know I want to die here too" (19). The fervent and passionate tone of Philip's declaration may seem oddly sentimental unless we regard him as a figure who can serve as a way of imagining a balanced relationship between the different and conflicting social and cultural elements that make up Malaysia, a role Philip feels has been given to him through his time and training with Endo-san: "in strengthening my body Endo-san was also, as he had promised, fortifying my mind. It was a process that offered me the ability to bridge the conflicting elements of my life and to create a balance" (181). Philip's hybridity, queerness, and posed ethnicity challenges the essentialist understanding of race and culture in postcolonial Malaysia that undergirds the state's official *bumiputera* policy and reconceptualizes the idea of ethnicity as a posture and a process that can reach across different cultures rather than reinforcing the boundaries between them. The ethnic Chinese in Malaysia, like their counterparts in the United States of America, are often regarded as a minority community that occupies a superior economic niche but that is circumscribed politically and culturally. In the context of Asian American literature and cultural representation, Lisa Lowe argues for an understanding of Asian American cultural practices as hybrid, one that "does not suggest the assimilation of Asian or immigrant practices to dominant forms but instead marks the history of survival within relationships of unequal power and domination"; the history that Lowe speaks of is also "multiply determined by the contradictions of capitalism, patriarchy, and race relations" (67). Philip Hutton is a narrator and protagonist whose life is marked by such contradictions, and he, unlike his friends and family members, survives by virtue of his multiple determination by various histories of migration, diasporic contact and liminality, British colonialism, and Japanese imperialism. Philip's half-British, half-Chinese parentage prevents him from being "completely accepted by either the Chinese or the English" (Tan 28), but the skills he learns from Endo-san, his polyglot fluency, and his collaboration with the Japanese, which leads to both his lionization and his vilification after the war, point to his ability to survive within relationships of unequal power and domination. Through Philip, Tan illustrates how the demographic and cultural makeup of Malaysia has always been heterogeneous and hybrid. Tan's critique of Malaysia's state-sponsored national identity works through the same logic of unbalancing and redirecting the anthropological exotic, only this time it is the cultural essentialism underlying the racialized stratification of Malaysian society that is thrown and turned against itself as Tan reterritorializes the idea of Malaysia as home and nation through the queer and hybrid Philip Hutton, expressing a critical nationality through an alternative form of desire and reproduction that is not predicated on the maintenance of ethnic purity and authenticity.

This critical nationality is illustrated through Philip's key role in restoring old historical buildings in Penang, and his donation of his father's collection of ceremonial Malay daggers along with Endo-san's and his own Japanese swords to the Penang Historical Society. While walking around Penang, the young Philip finds it remarkable that he lives in "a Malayan country ruled by the British, with strong Chinese, Indian, and Siamese influences," and that he "could move from world to world merely by crossing a street. [. . .] One could easily lose one's identity and acquire another just by going for a stroll" (Tan 66). After the war, Philip notices many old buildings in the city that were "abandoned by their owners" and "bought by companies that tore them down to build modern shops," and is filled with a keen "sense of loss"; thus, the adult Philip uses the wealth from his father's company to set up "the Hutton Heritage Trust" and "saved countless buildings from disappearing, from the shophouses of Georgetown to the mansions along Northern Road," with a special emphasis on "using craftsmen from China and England" with "materials as close to the originals as I could" (169). In undertaking this important role in preserving and reproducing the urban space and architecture of Malaysia's multicultural heritage and history, Philip exercises the economic power of his combined British and Chinese heritage to neither threaten nor criticize the interests of the dominant Malay community, but rather to preserve for society at large the shared and diverse heritage of Malaysia's past. What is significant here is that Philip's sense of belonging to Penang and Malaysia is based on cultural *practice* rather than cultural *essence:* in his youth he experiences the multiple communities by strolling around the city and adopting identities, and as an elderly philanthropist he commemorates the past by restoring old houses rather than dwelling in his own memories. In this way, the novel challenges the fear of Chinese economic dominance that is one of the principal factors behind the national policy of *bumiputera* privilege for the ethnic Malay community. The city spaces Philip restores are not simply a recreation of British colonial Malaya, nor are they—like the "modern shops" that spring up after the war—signifiers of a modernity centered on economic progress and development; they are a reminder that Penang, like many other cities in postcolonial Malaysia, is made up of different ethnic cultures and enclaves that can be inhabited and crossed over by those who live there. Philip's painstaking restoration of these historical buildings can thus be read as a challenge to both the British colonial and the postcolonial Malaysian state's segregation of city and society according to ethnicity and economic roles. Tan's representation of Philip offers an implicit critique of the logic of cultural essentialism that underlies this doctrine of official nationalism: if one were to follow this logic, which is itself a legacy of British colonialism that conflates one's culture with one's economic acumen, then the imbalance between the different communities in Malaysia will be unresolvable, since Malays are always in a state of decline vis-à-vis the Chinese and the Indians, who are in turn naturally more enterprising and industrious as a result of their immigrant background. If we recall Ronald D. Klein's observation that the literature about the Japanese occupation serves as way of thinking through "the tactics of survival" and as a means of "forging a [post–World War II] identity" (179), then Tan's novel goes one step further by unbalancing the status quo of racial hierarchy and cultural essentialism in the national identity of present-day Malaysia.

Furthermore, at the end of the novel Philip is honored by the Penang Historical Society not only for his role in preserving the city's architectural heritage but also for his generous donation of two sets of weapons: the first is his father's collection of Malay *keris,* or ceremonial daggers; the second is a pair of Japanese *katana,* or samurai swords, that belonged to Endo-san and himself, respectively. The Malay *keris* is an important "cultural talisman" that "is used in a symbolic and ritualistic way, thus assuring the wearer of proper status as a Malay" (Frey 2). In addition to being a symbolic confirmation of the wearer's Malayness, the *keris* is also an important weapon wielded by the legendary hero Hang Tuah, whose exploits are recorded in the "national epic" known as the *Hikayat Hang Tuah,* and who stands in the "Malay community" as "a symbol of their power and glory as a people" (Piah et al. 232–33). When Philip's father bought his last *keris* from a Malay sultan who had been recently deposed (possibly by the British colonial authorities), the weapon was desacralized because it was passing into the hands of a British amateur Orientalist: "But because it was being passed to a European, the sultan had assured him that the soul of the *keris* had been removed by a *bomoh,* a Malay warlock" (Tan 161). By returning this *keris* and others in his father's collection to the Penang Historical Society, Philip takes these artifacts out of a private Orientalist collection and restores them as important symbols of Malay ethnic and cultural heritage into the public sphere of Penang's history; however, his actions invert the exclusive and essentialist connotations of the *keris* with Malay cultural pride and supremacy, because it is not the epic Malay hero Hang Tuah but a hybrid and queer traitor-hero existing inside and outside of the nation's homogeneous empty time who restores the *keris* into the public time and space of Penang that he has also played a key role in restoring through the Hutton Heritage Foundation. The *keris* and the *katana* no longer exist as instruments of violence, warfare, and ethnic and cultural pride; they are no longer part of an instrumental nationality that valorizes one ethnic identity or community over others as the foundation for the nation-state. Instead, they are recognized as objects through which an alternative claim can be made by Philip upon Malaysia as home and nation through his hybridity and queerness, which is borne out by his donation of the *keris* and *katana* to the Penang Historical Society and his decision to allow the Historical Society to announce his "full name"—Philip Arminius Khoo-Hutton—for "the first time" (430). In so doing, Philip fulfills what his grandfather saw in him during his youth: "Accept the fact that you are different, that you are of two worlds. [. . .] you are used to the duality of life. You have the ability to bring all of life's disparate elements into a cohesive whole" (234); Philip draws together the various Malayan and Malaysian histories of colonization and conquest, immigration and diasporic existence, into a cohesive but not necessarily harmonious whole.

Summary:
Diasporic Interventions, National Returns

Evening Is the Whole Day and *The Gift of Rain* evince the intertwining of a literary cosmopolitics and a critical national consciousness through a tactical employment of ethnography and historical realism. These characteristics mark their affiliation with and appropriation of literary tropes used by other diasporic or immigrant writers of South Asian or East Asian descent, an important transnational connection that is enabled by and also critical of the field of global literary production and consumption. At the same time, the commodification of anglophone postcolonial literature is, as Graham Huggan and Sarah Brouillette remind us, an inevitable outcome of this transnational movement of people, capital, and cultures in the late twentieth and early twenty-first centuries, bringing with it an increased metropolitan desire for the culturally foreign and the anthropologically exotic. But Samarasan and Tan, drawing on but also extending their South Asian and East Asian counterparts' endeavors, employ ethnographic tactics that evoke and invert the conventions of the anthropological exotic through the cutting and splicing of official histories with minoritarian narratives and the foregrounding of hybrid subjectivities as opposed to pure, unsullied communities. The friction between their attachment to the national homeland and their consciousness of its limitations and possibilities marks them as diasporic subjects who do not make "a physical return but rather a re-turn, a repeated turning to the concept and/or the reality of the homeland and other diasporan kin" (Tölölyan, "Rethinking Diaspora(s)" 14). In place of a cosmopolitan subjectivity and deterritorialized mobility, these writers trace a cosmopolitical aesthetic grounded in an abiding and a critical attachment to their homeland of Malaysia.

CONCLUSION

Nation, Narration, Negation

> As the negation of practical life, [art] is itself praxis, and indeed not simply on the basis of its genesis and the fact that, like every artifact, it is the result of activity. Just as its content is dynamic in itself and does not remain self-identical, in the course of their history the objectivated artworks themselves once again become practical comportments and turn toward reality.
>
> —Theodor Adorno, *Aesthetic Theory* 241

LIKE Adorno's posthumously published *Aesthetic Theory*, the work of postcolonial nationalism is unfinished and, although seemingly dated, stands in need of reinterpretation for the global moment as a sociopolitical formation imagined through literature as aesthetic form and cultural discourse. In this conclusion I discuss literary criticism's recent turn away from the nation and nationalism as both an intellectual topic and a conceptual framework in favor of analyses of state power and sovereignty, exemplified by a 2008 special issue of the leading journal *Contemporary Literature*. The editors of this special issue "refuse to see the state as a merely negative bugbear, purely affirmative category, or relic of bygone modernity" (Hart and Hansen 494), arguing that it is no longer the nation but the state that, though "weakened as analytic paradigm" by increasingly transnational forces, nonetheless "remains fundamental to political modernity" (497). In separating the state from the nation, however, they regard the latter as a distillation of "concepts of consanguinity and folk heritage" that attenuates "the political meaning of 'nation' as indicating a group of citizens organized under a single government" (505); furthermore, "these notions of ethnolinguistic consanguinity" are "of declining significance today, when the contingent tie between language, literature, and nation is coming undone in the face of the global movement of peoples and books" (506). Hart and Hansen's definition of nationalism as ethnic, linguistic, and consanguineous homogeneity is an identitarian gloss I hope this book has problematized and unpacked as but one mode of understanding what the nation is—and a rather limited mode at that. Hart and Hansen's analysis of state sovereignty draws on Antonio Gramsci's "dialectical vision" of class hegemony and coerced assent to "imagine other forms of governmentality, other forms of state power" (499); if they see any redeeming qualities in nationalism, it lies in their reading of Mohsin Hamid's novel *The Reluctant Fundamentalist* as a text that shows how "national difference [. . .] risks becoming mere nostalgia" and must be countered by a nationalism that "is neither religious nor ethnopoetic" but distinctly "political" (510). Their argument that Gramsci's vision offers a dialectical and political nationalism is similar to my own invocation of Theodor Adorno's negative dialectics and aesthetic thinking to understand nationalism in postcolonial literature as critical and cosmopolitical rather than instrumental, as a national consciousness that refuses the allure of religious or ethnopoetic nostalgia that replicates and manipulates identitarian thinking for its own sake. My point is that we need not, as Hart and Hansen imply, define nationalism purely in ethnolingusitic or consanguineous terms in order to step outside its apparent confines to discuss state sovereignty; we may do so from a position that is immanent to or within the logic of nationalism itself, for the very project of critical nationality assayed by the writers I have examined in these pages shows us that national consciousness actively engages with the vicissitudes of both authoritarian states and transnational capital and cultural flows.

While critics of contemporary literature might be eager to overlook the nation as they focus on the state, my argument for a reassessment of nationalism in postcolonial writing is consonant with the work of political scientists examining the fraught and shifting relationship between nation and state in the late twentieth century. With respect to South Asia, Tariq Amin-Khan maintains that national struggles in former European colonies have fallen short of their liberating goals not because nationalism is inherently flawed but because the colonial state "intensified the antagonisms between different colonized groups, laying the trajectory for a peculiar kind of national identity formulation—one that is rooted in conflict—and having an afterlife in the post-colonial state" (38). This problem was compounded by the uneven distribution of power and resources immediately after national independence, such that "most postcolonial states became *multinational* states led by a dominant nation," resulting in a situation where "a centralized and authoritarian unitary state structure was entrenched" that did not represent or recognize the varying needs of its citizens (109, original emphasis). Therefore, the current immiseration of many countries in the global South should not be attributed to a resurgence of virulent tribalism or ethnocentrism; it ought to be understood as a legacy of European colonialism that, in its neocolonial guise, has persistently hamstrung the postcolonial state's ability to establish and maintain a viable, stable, and egalitarian social formation, which is exactly what a critical nationality strives toward. Similarly, Michael Keating's study of national claims that do not involve statehood in Quebec, Catalonia, and Scotland shows us that political nationalism and self-determination need not always aspire to sovereign power, that "national identities are not always monolithic and exclusive" but can be "plural, contested, and shifting" (3, ix). Instead of understanding nationalism as a teleology that culminates in a sovereign and territorially bounded nation-state, Keating sees "nationality conflicts as a form of politics to be negotiated continually, rather than as a problem to be resolved once and for all"; instead of "a primordial view" of the nation as "a self-evident sociological category or an immanent community of fate," it is more productive to regard it as a political entity, "historically constituted as a self-governing community" in which "its people see themselves as a nation and wish to determine their future as a collectivity" (3). Amin-Khan and Keating regard nationalism as a sociopolitical project imbricated in and negotiating with colonial and neocolonial state power and global capital and cultural flows; it need not always be construed as a primordial identity or ethnic absolutism that we must dismiss or transcend in order to examine the authority of the sovereign state or the uneven network of global power relations. My own argument about national consciousness and literary cosmopolitics interpreted through Theodor Adorno's aesthetic theory and negative dialectics is in line with their contributions; whereas political scientists focus on juridical discourse and governmental systems, as a literary scholar, I have focused my objects of inquiry on fictional and poetic narratives and philosophical aesthetics. As Adorno reminds us in the epigraph, a literary text, as an artwork, is a "negation of practical life" that "does not remain self-identical" but through the history of its writing, circulation, and reception "become[s] practical comportments and turn[s] toward reality" without reducing or regimenting its formal complexity (*Aesthetic Theory* 241). Just as anticolonial national consciousness and postcolonial nationalism are always already cosmopolitical sociocultural formations rather than determinate identities at their very inception, so too the writing and reading of postcolonial literature is always already an intellectual and cultural activity that forms a constellation of local, national, and global practicalities and political realities.

WORKS CITED

Abraham, Collin. *The Naked Social Order: The Roots of Racial Polarisation in Malaysia*. Subang Jaya, Selangor Darul Ehsan, Malaysia: Pelanduk Publications, 2004.

Adorno, Theodor. *Aesthetic Theory*. Trans. and ed. Robery Hullot-Kentor. Minneapolis: University of Minnesota Press, 1997.

———. "Beethoven's Late Style." In *Can One Live After Auschwitz? A Philosophical Reader*, ed. Rolf Tiedemann. trans. Rodney Livingstone et al. Stanford, CA: Stanford University Press, 2003. 295–98.

———. "Culture and Administration." In *The Culture Industry: Selected Essays on Mass Culture*. London: Routledge, 2001. 107–31.

———. "Cultural Criticism and Society." In *The Adorno Reader*, ed. Brian O'Connor. Oxford: Blackwell, 2000. 195–210.

———. "Culture Industry Reconsidered." In *The Culture Industry Reconsidered: Selected Essays on Mass Culture*. London: Routledge, 2001. 98–106.

———. "The Essay as Form." In *The Adorno Reader*, ed. Brian O'Connor. Oxford: Blackwell, 2000. 91–111.

———. *History and Freedom*. London: Polity, 2006.

———. "Lyric Poetry and Society." Trans. Bruce Mayo. In *Critical Theory and Society: A Reader*, ed. Stephen Eric Bronner and Douglas MacKay Kellner. New York: Routledge, 1989. 155–71.

———. *Minima Moralia: Reflections on a Damaged Life*. Trans. E. F. N. Jephcott. London: Verso, 2005.

———. *Negative Dialectics*. New York: Continuum, 1981.

———. "Negative Dialectics and the Possibility of Philosophy." In *The Adorno Reader*, ed. Brian O'Connor. Trans. E. B. Ashton. Oxford: Blackwell, 2000. 54–78.

———. "Subject and Object." In *The Essential Frankfurt School Reader*, ed. Andrew Arato and Eike Ebhart. New York: Urizen Books, 1978. 497–511.

Alatas, Syed Hussein. *The Myth of the Lazy Native*. London: F. Cass, 1977.

Amin-Khan, Tariq. *The Post-Colonial State in the Era of Capitalist Globalization*. New York: Routledge, 2012.

Andaya, Barbara Watson and Leonard Y. Andaya. *A History of Malaysia*. Basingstoke: Palgrave, 2001.

Anderson, Benedict. *Imagined Communities: Reflections on the Origin and Spread of Nationalism*. London: Verso, 1983.

Appadurai, Arjun. *Modernity at Large: Cultural Dimensions of Globalization*. Minneapolis: University of Minnesota Press, 1996.

Arnold, Matthew. *Culture and Anarchy and Other Writings*. Ed. Stefan Collini. Cambridge: Cambridge University Press, 1993.

Ashcroft, Bill, Gareth Griffiths, and Helen Tiffin. *The Empire Writes Back: Theory and Practice in Post-Colonial Literatures*. London: Routledge, 1989.

Bakar, Sharon. "Bibliobibuli: Preeta Samarasan Interview part 2." September 16, 2008. http://thebookaholic.blogspot.com/2008/09/preeta-samarasan-interview-part-2.html (accessed July 28, 2009).

———. "It's a BIG Book." Review of *The Gift of Rain* by Twan Eng Tan. *Star Online*, February 25, 2007. http://thestar.com.my/lifestyle/story.asp?file=/2007/2/25/lifebookshelf/16944110 (accessed July 28, 2009).

Benedict, Ruth. *The Chrysanthemum and the Sword: Patterns of Japanese Culture*. 1946. New York: Mariner Books, 2005.

Benjamin, Walter. *The Origin of German Tragic Drama*. Trans. John Osborne. London: New Left Books, 1977.

Berlatsky, Eric. *The Real, the True, and the Told: Postmodern Historical Narrative and the Ethics of Representation*. Columbus: The Ohio State University Press, 2011.

Bewes, Timothy. "Late Style in Naipaul: Adorno's Aesthetics and the Post-Colonial Novel." In *Adorno and Literature*, ed. David Cunningham and Nigel Mapp. London: Continuum, 2006. 171–87.

Bhabha, Homi. "DissemiNation: Time, Narrative, and the Margins of the Modern Nation." In *Nation and Narration*, ed. Homi Bhabha. London; New York: Routledge, 1990. 291–322.

Booker, M. Keith and Dubravka Juraga. *The Caribbean Novel in English: An Introduction*. Portsmouth, NH: Heinemann, 2001.

Borpujari, Utpal. "Indian, Yet Truly Malaysian." Interview with Preeta Samarasan. September 29, 2008. http://utpalborpujari.wordpress.com/2008/09/29/indian-yet-truly-malaysian (accessed July 29, 2009).

Bostonist. "Preeta Samarasan, *Evening Is the Whole Day*, Harvard Book Store." Interview with Preeta Samarasan. May 15, 2008. http://bostonist.com/2008/05/13/preeta_samarasa.php (accessed July 28, 2009).

Brennan, Timothy. "The National Longing for Form." In *Nation and Narration*, ed. Homi K. Bhabha. London; New York: Routledge, 1990. 44–70.

Breslin, Paul. *Nobody's Nation: Reading Derek Walcott*. Chicago: University of Chicago Press, 2001.

Brouillette, Sarah. *Postcolonial Writers in the Global Literary Marketplace*. New York: Palgrave Macmillan, 2007.

Brown, David. *The State and Ethnic Politics in Southeast Asia.* London and New York: Routledge, 1994.
Brown-Rose, J. A. *Critical Nostalgia and Caribbean Migration.* New York: Peter Lang, 2009.
Burton, Antoinette, ed. *After the Imperial Turn: Thinking With and Through the Nation.* Durham, NC: Duke University Press, 2003.
Butler, Judith. "Gender Is Burning: Questions of Appropriation and Subversion." In *Dangerous Liaisons: Gender, Nation, and Postcolonial Perspectives,* ed. Anne McClintock, Aamir Mufti, and Ella Shohat. Minneapolis: University of Minnesota Press, 1997. 381–95.
Césaire, Aimé. *Discourse on Colonialism.* New York: Monthly Review Press, 2000.
Cheah, Pheng. "Introduction Part II: The Cosmopolitical—Today." In *Cosmopolitics: Thinking and Feeling beyond the Nation,* ed. Pheng Cheah and Bruce Robbins. Minneapolis: University of Minnesota Press, 1998. 20–41.
———. *Spectral Nationality: Passages of Freedom from Kant to Postcolonial Literatures of Liberation.* New York: Columbia University Press, 2004.
Chicago Cultural Studies Group. "Critical Multiculturalism." *Critical Inquiry* 18.3 (Spring 1992): 530–55.
Chow, Rey. *The Protestant Ethnic and the Spirit of Capitalism.* New York: Columbia University Press, 2002.
———. *Sentimental Fabulations, Contemporary Chinese Films: Attachment in the Age of Global Visibility.* New York: Columbia University Press, 2007.
———. *Writing Diaspora: Tactics of Intervention in Contemporary Cultural Studies.* Bloomington: Indiana University Press, 1993.
Chu, Patricia P. *Assimilating Asians: Gendered Strategies of Authorship in Asian America.* Durham, NC: Duke University Press, 2000.
Chua, Beng Huat. "Racial-Singaporeans: Absence after the Hyphen." In *Southeast Asian Identities: Culture and the Politics of Representation in Indonesia, Malaysia, Singapore and Thailand,* ed. Joel S. Kahn. New York: St. Martin's, 1998. 28–50.
Clifford, James. *The Predicament of Culture: Twentieth-Century Ethnography, Literature, and Art.* Cambridge, MA: Harvard University Press, 1988.
———. *Routes: Travel and Translation in the Late Twentieth Century.* Cambridge, MA: Harvard University Press, 1997.
Cooppan, Vilashini. *Worlds Within: National Narratives and Global Connections in Postcolonial Writing.* Palo Alto, CA: Stanford University Press, 2009.
Dawson, Ashley. *Mongrel Nation: Diasporic Culture and the Making of Postcolonial Britain.* Ann Arbor: University of Michigan Press, 2007.
Donaghy, Gerry. "Review-a-Day: War and (Inner) Peace." Review of *The Gift of Rain* by Twan Eng Tan. Powells.com, May 3, 2008. http://www.powells.com/review/2008_05_03.html (accessed July 28, 2009).
Donnell, Alison. *Twentieth-Century Caribbean Literature: Critical Moments in Anglophone Literary History.* New York: Routledge, 2006.
Dowd, Vincent. "How Do You Win a Booker Prize?" *BBC News,* July 10, 2008. http://news.bbc.co.uk/2/hi/entertainment/7495663.stm (accessed April 14, 2013).
Drabble, Margaret. *A Writer's Britain: Landscape in Literature.* London: Thames and Hudson, 1979.
Edwards, Brent Hayes. "The Uses of Diaspora." *Social Text* 19.1 (2001):45–73.
Esty, Jed. *A Shrinking Island: Modernism and National Culture in England.* Princeton, NJ: Princeton University Press, 2004.

Fanon, Frantz. *Black Skin, White Masks*. Trans. Richard Philcox. New York: Grove, 2008.
———. *The Wretched of the Earth*. Trans. Richard Philcox. New York: Grove, 2005.
Fichte, Johann Gottlieb. *Addresses to the German Nation*. Trans. R. F. Jones and G. H. Turnbull. Chicago, IL: The Open Court Publishing Company, 1922.
Fleishman, Avrom. *The English Historical Novel: Walter Scott to Virginia Woolf*. Baltimore: Johns Hopkins University Press, 1971.
Foucault, Michel. "Society Must Be Defended": Lectures at the Collège de France, 1975–1976. Trans. David Macey. New York: Picador, 2003.
François, Pierre. "The Spectral Return of Depths in Kazuo Ishiguro's *The Unconsoled*." *Commonwealth Essays and Studies* 26.2 (2004): 77, 90.
Frey, Edward. *The Kris: Mystic Weapon of the Malay World*. Singapore: Oxford University Press, 1986.
Fumagalli, Maria Cristina. *Caribbean Perspectives on Modernity: Returning Medusa's Gaze*. Charlottesville: University of Virginia Press, 2009.
Geertz, Clifford. *Works and Lives: The Anthropologist as Author*. Stanford, CA: Stanford University Press, 1988.
Ghosh, Bishnupriya. *When Borne Across: Literary Cosmopolitics in the Contemporary Indian Novel*. New Brunswick, NJ: Rutgers University Press, 2004.
Gibson, Nigel. *Fanon: The Postcolonial Imagination*. London: Polity, 2003.
Gikandi, Simon. *Writing in Limbo: Modernism and Caribbean Literature*. Ithaca, NY: Cornell University Press, 1992.
Gilroy, Paul. *The Black Atlantic: Modernity and Double Consciousness*. Cambridge, MA: Harvard University Press, 1993.
Goodman, Allegra. "What Aasha Saw." Review of *Evening Is the Whole Day* by Preeta Samarasan. *New York Times*, July 27, 2008. http://www.nytimes.com/2008/07/27/books/review/Goodman-t.html (accessed July 29, 2009).
Gopinath, Gayatri. *Impossible Desires: Queer Diasporas and South Asian Public Cultures*. Durham, NC: Duke University Press, 2005.
Goulbourne, Harry. *Ethnicity and Nationalism in Post-Imperial Britain*. Cambridge: Cambridge University Press, 1991.
Haggas, Carol. Review of *Joss and Gold*. *Booklist* 97.1 (August 2001): 2087.
Hall, Stuart. "Conclusion: The Multi-cultural Question." In *Un/Settled Multiculturalisms: Diasporas, Entanglements, "Transruptions,"* ed. Barnor Hesse. London: Zed Books, 2000. 209–41.
———. "Cultural Identity and Diaspora." In *Identity: Community, Culture, Difference*, ed. Jonathan Rutherford. London: Lawrence & Wishart, 1990. 222–37.
———. "Negotiating Caribbean Identities." In *New Caribbean Thought: A Reader*, ed. Brian Meeks and Folke Lindahl. Jamaica: University of the West Indies Press, 2001. 24–39.
———. "The Question of Cultural Identity." In *Modernity: An Introduction to Modern Societies*, ed. Stuart Hall, David Held, Don Hubert, and Kenneth Thompson. Cambridge, MA: Blackwell, 1996. 596–634.
———. "When Was 'The Post-Colonial'? Thinking at the Limit." In *The Post-Colonial Question: Common Skies, Divided Horizons*, ed. Iain Chambers and Lidia Curtis. London: Routledge, 1996. 242–60.
Hamner, Robert D. *Epic of the Dispossessed: Derek Walcott's "Omeros."* Columbia: University of Missouri Press, 1997.

Hart, Michael and Jim Hansen. "Introduction: Contemporary Literature and the State." *Contemporary Literature* 49.4 (2008): 491–513.
Hayward, Helen. *The Enigma of V. S. Naipaul: Sources and Contexts.* New York: Palgrave Macmillan, 2002.
Heberle, Renée. "Introduction: Feminism and Negative Dialectics." In *Feminist Interpretations of Theodor Adorno,* ed. Renée Heberle. University Park: Pennsylvania State University Press, 2006. 1–20.
Herder, Johann Gottfried. "Essay on the Origin of Language." In *On the Origin of Language,* trans. John H. Moran and Alexander Gode. Chicago: University of Chicago Press, 1966. 85–166.
Hesse, Barnor. "Introduction: Un/Settled Multiculturalisms." In *Un/Settled Multiculturalisms: Diasporas, Entanglements, "Transruptions,"* ed. Barnor Hesse. London: Zed Books, 2000. 1–30.
Higgins, Andrew. "A Last Hurrah and an Empire Closes Down." *Guardian Online,* July 1, 1997. http://www.guardian.co.uk/world/1997/jul/01/china.andrewhiggins1/print (accessed November 28, 2010).
Horkheimer, Max and Theodor Adorno. *Dialectic of Enlightenment: Philosophical Fragments.* Palo Alto, CA: Stanford University Press, 2002.
Huang, Yunte. *Transpacific Displacement: Ethnography, Translation, and Intertextual Travel in Twentieth-Century American Literature.* Berkeley: University of California Press, 2002.
Huggan, Graham. *The Postcolonial Exotic: Marketing the Margins.* New York: Routledge, 2001.
Hutcheon, Linda. *A Poetics of Postmodernism: History, Theory, Fiction.* New York: Routledge, 1998.
Ishiguro, Kazuo. "An Interview with Kazuo Ishiguro by Brian Shaffer." *Contemporary Literature* 42.1 (2001): 1–14.
———. *The Remains of the Day.* London: Vintage, 1990.
———. *The Unconsoled.* London: Vintage, 1996.
———. *When We Were Orphans.* London: Vintage, 2000.
Ishiguro, Kazuo and Kenzaburo Oe. "The Novelist in Today's World: A Conversation." In *Japan in the World,* ed. Harry Harootunian and Masao Miyoshi. Durham, NC: Duke University Press, 1993. 163–76.
Jaggi, Maya. "Kazuo Ishiguro with Maya Jaggi." In *Writing across Worlds: Contemporary Writers Talk,* ed. Susheila Nasta. London: Routledge, 2004. 159–70.
Jameson, Fredric. *The Geopolitical Aesthetic: Cinema and Space in the World System.* Bloomington: Indiana University Press, 1992.
Jay, Martin. *Adorno.* Cambridge, MA: Harvard University Press, 1984.
———. "Adorno in America." *New German Critique* 31 (1984): 157–82.
Jordison, Sam. "Booker Club: *The Gift of Rain* by Tan Twan Eng." *The Guardian Online: Booksblog,* August 31, 2007. http://www.guardian.co.uk/books/booksblog/2007/aug/31/bookerclubthegiftofrainb (accessed April 16, 2013).
Kandiyoti, Deniz. "Identity and Its Discontents: Women and the Nation." In *Colonial Discourse and Post-colonial Theory: A Reader,* ed. Patrick Williams and Laura Chrisman. New York: Columbia University Press, 1994. 376–91.
Katrak, Ketu H. *Politics of the Female Body: Postcolonial Women Writers of the Third World.* New Brunswick, NJ: Rutgers University Press, 2006.

Keating, Michael. *Plurinational Democracy: Stateless Nations in a Post-Sovereign Era*. Oxford: Oxford University Press, 2001.
Keen, Suzanne. *Romances of the Archive in Contemporary British Fiction*. Toronto: University of Toronto Press, 2001.
King, Bruce. *Derek Walcott: A Caribbean Life*. Oxford: Oxford University Press, 2000.
———. "The New Internationalism: Shiva Naipaul, Salman Rushdie, Buchi Emecheta, Timothy Mo, and Kazuo Ishiguro." In *The British and Irish Novel since 1960*, ed. James Acheson. London: Macmillan, 1991. 192–211.
Klein, Ronald D. *The Other Empire: Literary Views of Japan from the Philippines, Singapore, and Malaysia*. Diliman, Quezon City: University of the Philippines Press, 2008.
Krider, Dylan Otto. "Rooted in a Small Space: An Interview with Kazuo Ishiguro." *Kenyon Review* 20.2 (Spring 1998): 146–54.
Lake, Ed. "Man Booker 2007 Prize: *The Gift of Rain*." Review of *The Gift of Rain* by Twan Eng Tan. *Telegraph*, August 18, 2007. http://www.telegraph.co.uk/culture/books/fictionreviews/3667300/Man-Booker-2007-Prize-The-Gift-of-Rain.html (accessed July 28, 2009).
Law-Yone, Wendy. "Casualties of War." Review of *The Gift of Rain* by Twan Eng Tan. *Washington Post*, December 21, 2008. http://www.washingtonpost.com/wp-dyn/content/article/2008/12/18/AR2008121803496_pf.html (accessed July 28, 2009).
Lazarus, Neil. *Nationalism and Cultural Practice in the Postcolonial World*. Cambridge: Cambridge University Press, 1999.
Leavis, F. R. "'English,' Unrest, and Continuity." In *Nor Shall My Sword: Discourses on Pluralism, Compassion, and Social Hope*. New York: Barnes and Noble, 1972. 103–33.
———. *The Living Principle: English as a Discipline of Thought*. London: Chatto and Windus, 1975.
Lee, Kuan Yew. *The Singapore Story: Memoirs of Lee Kuan Yew*. Singapore: Prentice-Hall, 1998.
Lee, Lisa Yun. "The Bared-Breasts Incident." In *Feminist Interpretations of Theodor Adorno*, ed. Renée Heberle. University Park: Pennsylvania State University Press, 2006. 113–39.
———. *Dialectics of the Body: Corporeality in the Philosophy of T. W. Adorno*. New York: Routledge, 2005.
Leong, Liew Geok. Afterword to *Joss and Gold*, by Shirley Geok-lin Lim. New York: Feminist Press, 2001.
Lim, Shirley Geok-lin. "Asians in Anglo-American Feminism: Reciprocity and Resistance." In *Writing S.E./Asia in English: Against the Grain: Focus on Asian English-Language Literature*. London: Skoob Books, 1994. 31–44.
———. "Bukit China." In *Monsoon History: Selected Poems*. London: Skoob Books, 1994. 3.
———. *Joss and Gold*. New York: Feminist Press, 2001.
———. "Learning to Love America." In *What the Fortune Teller Didn't Say*. Albuquerque, NM: West End, 1998. 74.
———. "Semiotics, Experience and the Material Self: An Inquiry into the Subject of the Contemporary Asian Woman Writer." In *Writing S.E./Asia in English: Against the Grain, Focus on Asian English-Language Literature*. London: Skoob Books, 1994. 8–30.
———. "The Source." In *Walking Backwards*. Albuquerque, NM: West End, 2010. 36.
Lowe, Lisa. *Immigrant Acts: On Asian American Cultural Politics*. Durham, NC: Duke University Press, 1996.

Lowenthal, David. *The Past Is a Foreign Country.* Cambridge: Cambridge University Press, 1985.

Ma, Sheng-mei. *Immigrant Subjectivities in Asian American and Asian Diaspora Literatures.* Albany: State University of New York Press, 1998.

Maniam, K. S. "Fiction into Fact, Fact into Fiction: A Personal Reflection." In *Malaysian Literature in English: A Critical Reader,* ed. Mohammad A. Quayum and Peter C. Wicks. Petaling Jaya, Malaysia: Pearson Education, 2001. 263–68.

———. "In Search of a Centre." http://www.ucalgary.ca/UofC/eduweb/engl392/492/maniam-cent.html (accessed April 16, 2013).

———. 1981. *The Return.* London: Skoob Books, 1993.

Manickam, Saras. "Malaysia through the Looking Glass." Review of *Evening Is the Whole Day* by Preeta Samarasan. *Star Online,* June 29, 2008. http://thestar.com.my/lifestyle/story.asp?file=/2008/6/29/lifebookshelf/21594289&sec=lifebookshelf (accessed July 29, 2009).

Mason, David. *Race and Ethnicity in Modern Britain.* Oxford: Oxford University Press, 1995.

Mauzy, Diane. "Malay Political Hegemony and 'Coercive Consociationalism.'" In *The Politics of Ethnic Conflict Regulation: Case Studies of Protracted Ethnic Conflicts,* ed. John McGarry and Brendan O'Leary. London and New York: Routledge, 1991. 106–27.

Nair, Sheila. "Colonialism, Nationalism, Ethnicity: Constructing Identity and Difference." In *Multiethnic Malaysia: Past, Present, and Future,* ed. Teck Ghee Lim, Alberto Gomes, Azly Rahman. Petaling Jaya, Malaysia: Strategic Information and Research Development Centre, 2009. 77–94.

Nazareth, Peter. Review of *Joss and Gold.* *World Literature Today* 76.1 (Winter 2002): 138–39.

O'Brien, Susie and Imre Szeman. "Introduction: The Globalization of Fiction / The Fiction of Globalization." *South Atlantic Quarterly* 100.3 (2001): 603–26.

O'Connor, Brian. *Adorno's Negative Dialectic: Philosophy and the Possibility of Critical Rationality.* Cambridge, MA: MIT Press, 2004.

O'Neill, Maggie, ed. *Adorno, Culture and Feminism.* London: Sage, 1999.

———. "Adorno and Women: Negative Dialectics, *Kulturkritik* and Unintentional Truth." In *Adorno, Culture and Feminism.* 21–40.

Ooi, Kee Beng. "Beyond Ethnocentrism: Malaysia and the Affirmation of Hybridisation." In *Multiethnic Malaysia: Past, Present, and Future,* ed. Teck Ghee Lim, Alberto Gomes, Azly Rahman. Petaling Jaya, Malaysia: Strategic Information and Research Development Centre, 2009. 447–62.

Piah, Harun Mat et al. *Traditional Malay Literature.* Trans. Harry Aveling. Kuala Lumpur: Dewan Bahasa dan Pustaka, 2002.

Pratt, Mary Louise. *Imperial Eyes: Travel Writing and Transculturation.* London: Routledge, 1992.

Publishers Weekly. Review of *Joss and Gold.* August 27, 2001, 52.

Puri, Shalini. *The Caribbean Postcolonial: Social Equality, Post-Nationalism, and Cultural Hybridity.* New York: Palgrave Macmillan, 2004.

Purushotam, Nirmala. "Women and Knowledge/Power: Notes on the Singaporean Dilemma." In *Imagining Singapore,* ed. Kah Choon Ban, Anne Pakir, and Chee Kiong Tong. Singapore: Marshall Cavendish, 2004. 328–64.

Quan, Shirley N. Review of *Joss and Gold.* *Library Journal,* August 2001, 52.

Quayum, Mohammad A. and Peter C. Wicks. Introduction to *Malaysian Literature in English: A Critical Reader.* Petaling Jaya, Malaysia: Pearson Education, 2001. x–xiv.

Reitz, Caroline. *Detecting the Nation: Fictions of Detection and the Imperial Venture.* Columbus: The Ohio State University Press, 2004.

Robbins, Bruce. "Very Busy Just Now: Globalization and Harriedness in Ishiguro's *The Unconsoled.*" *Comparative Literature* 53.4 (2001): 426–41.

Rose, Gillian. *The Melancholy Science: An Introduction to the Thought of Theodor W. Adorno.* New York: Columbia University Press, 1978.

Rosenberg, Leah. *Nationalism and the Formation of Caribbean Literature.* New York: Palgrave Macmillan, 2007.

Said, Edward. "Conversation with Bill Ashcroft." In *Interviews with Edward Said*, ed. Amritjit Singh and Bruce G. Johnson. Jackson: University of Mississippi Press, 2004. 84–103.

———. *Culture and Imperialism.* New York: Vintage, 1994.

———. *Humanism and Democratic Criticism.* New York: Columbia University Press, 2004.

———. "Introduction: Secular Criticism." In *The World, the Text, and the Critic.* Cambridge, MA: Harvard University Press, 1983. 1–30.

———. *Orientalism.* New York: Vintage, 1979.

———. *Reflections on Exile.* Cambridge, MA: Harvard University Press, 2000.

———. "Traveling Theory." In *The World, the Text, and the Critic.* Cambridge, MA: Harvard University Press, 1983. 226–47.

———. "Traveling Theory Reconsidered." In *Reflections on Exile.* 436–52.

Samarasan, Preeta. *Evening Is the Whole Day.* New York: Mariner Books, 2009.

Savory, Elaine. "Anglophone Caribbean Literature." In *The Cambridge History of African and Caribbean Literature.* Vol. 2, ed. F. Abiola Irele and Simon Gikandi. Cambridge: Cambridge University Press, 2004. 711–58.

Scott, David. *Conscripts of Modernity: The Tragedy of Colonial Enlightenment.* Durham, NC: Duke University Press, 2004.

Sim, Wai-chew. "Kazuo Ishiguro." *Review of Contemporary Fiction* 25.1 (2005): 80–115.

Solomos, John. *Race and Racism in Britain.* 3rd ed. New York: Palgrave, 2003.

Spencer, Robert. "Thoughts from Abroad: Theodor Adorno as Postcolonial Theory." *Culture, Theory, Critique* 51.3 (2010): 207–21.

Spivak, Gayatri Chakravorty. *A Critique of Postcolonial Reason: Towards a History of the Vanishing Present.* Cambridge, MA: Harvard University Press, 1999.

———. "Ethics and Politics in Tagore, Coetzee, and Certain Scenes of Teaching." *Diacritics* 32.3–4 (2002): 17–31.

———. *Nationalism and the Imagination.* Calcutta, India: Seagull Books, 2010.

———. "Position Without Identity—2004: An Interview with Gayatri Chakravorty Spivak by Yan Hairong." In *Other Asias.* Malden, MA: Blackwell, 2008. 239–55.

———. "Teaching for the Times." In *The Decolonization of the Imagination: Culture, Knowledge, and Power*, ed. Jan Nederveen Pieterse and Bhikhu Parekh. London: Zed Books, 1995. 177–202.

Stameshkin, Anne. "Interview with Preeta Samarasan, *Evening Is the Whole Day.*" *Fiction Writers Review,* October 4, 2008. http://fictionwritersreview.com/interviews/preeta-samarasan-evening-is-the-whole-day (accessed July 28, 2009).

Stein, Mark. *Black British Literature: Novels of Transformation.* Columbus: The Ohio State University Press, 2004.

Stevenson, Randall. *The Oxford English Literary History Volume 12: 1960–2000: The Last of England?* Oxford: Oxford University Press, 2005.
Su, John J. *Ethics and Nostalgia in the Contemporary Novel.* Cambridge: Cambridge University Press, 2005.
Swift, Graham. 1983. *Waterland.* London: Vintage, 1992.
Tam, Li Peng Michelle. "Labour of Love." *The Star Online,* September 14, 2012. http://thestar.com.my/lifestyle/story.asp?file=/2012/9/14/lifebookshelf/12010398 (accessed April 16, 2013).
Tan, Twan Eng. *The Gift of Rain.* New York: Weinstein Books, 2008.
Terada, Rei. *Derek Walcott's Poetry: American Mimicry.* Boston: Northeastern University Press, 1992.
Tham, Seong Chee. 1981. "The Politics of Literary Development in Malaysia." In *Malaysian Literature in English: A Critical Reader,* ed. Mohammad A. Quayum and Peter C. Wicks. Petaling Jaya, Malaysia: Pearson Education, 2001. 38–59.
Tölölyan, Khachig. "The Nation-State and Its Others: In Lieu of a Preface." *Diaspora* 1.1 (1991): 3–7.
———. "Rethinking Diaspora(s): Stateless Power in the Transnational Moment." *Diaspora* 5.1 (1996): 3–36.
Torres-Saillant, Silvio. *Towards an Aesthetic of West Indian Literature.* New York: Cambridge University Press, 1997.
Tsing, Anna Lowenhaupt. *Friction: An Ethnography of Global Connection.* Princeton, NJ: Princeton University Press, 2005.
Tu, Wei-ming. "Cultural China: The Periphery as Center." *Daedalus* 120.2 (1991): 1–32.
Varadharajan, Asha. *Exotic Parodies: Subjectivity in Adorno, Said, and Spivak.* Minneapolis: University of Minnesota Press, 1995.
Vorda, Allan and Kim Herzinger. "Stuck on the Margins: An Interview with Kazuo Ishiguro." In *Face to Face: Interviews with Contemporary Novelists,* ed. Allan Vorda. Houston, TX: Rice University Press, 1993. 1–35.
Walcott, Derek. *Another Life.* 2nd ed. Washington, DC: Three Continents, 1982.
———. "The Antilles: Fragments of Epic Memory." In *What the Twilight Says: Essays.* London: Faber and Faber, 1998. 65–84.
———. "The Caribbean: Culture or Mimicry?" *Journal of Interamerican Studies and World Affairs* 16.1 (1974): 3–13.
———. *Collected Poems: 1948–1984.* New York: Farrar, Straus and Giroux, 1986.
———. *Conversations with Derek Walcott.* Ed. William Baer. Jackson: University of Mississippi Press, 1996.
———. "An Interview with Derek Walcott by Leif Sjöberg." In *Conversations with Derek Walcott,* 79–85.
———. "An Interview with Derek Walcott by William Baer." In *Conversations with Derek Walcott,* 194–206.
———. "The Man Who Keeps the English Language Alive: An Interview with Rebekah Presson." In *Conversations with Derek Walcott,* 189–93.
———. "Meanings." In *Critical Perspectives on Derek Walcott,* comp. and ed. Robert D. Hamner. Washington, DC: Three Continents, 1993. 45–50.
———. "The Muse of History." In *What the Twilight Says: Essays.* New York: Farrar, Straus and Giroux, 1998. 36–64.
———. *Omeros.* New York: Farrar, Strauss and Giroux. 1990.

———. *The Prodigal*. New York: Farrar, Straus and Giroux, 2004.
———. "Reflections on *Omeros*." *South Atlantic Quarterly* 96.2 (Spring 1997): 229–46.
———. "The Schooner *Flight*." In *Collected Poems: 1948–1984*, 345–61.
———. "Sea Grapes." In *Collected Poems: 1948–1984*, 297.
———. "Society and the Artist." In *Critical Perspectives on Derek Walcott*, comp. and ed. Robert D. Hamner. Washington, DC: Three Continents, 1993. 15–17.
———. "To Return to the Trees." In *Collected Poems: 1948–1984*, 339–41.
Walkowitz, Rebecca. *Cosmopolitan Style: Modernism beyond the Nation*. New York: Columbia University Press, 2006.
———. "Ishiguro's Floating Worlds." *English Literary History* 68 (2001): 1049–76.
Williams, Eric. "Independence Day Address." In *Eric E. Williams Speaks: Essays on Colonialism and Independence*, ed. Selwyn R. Cudjoe. Wellesley, MA: Calaloux, 1993. 265–69.
———. "Massa Day Done." In *Eric E. Williams Speaks: Essays on Colonialism and Independence*, ed. Selwyn R. Cudjoe. Wellesley, MA: Calaloux, 1993. 237–64.
Williams, Raymond. *Marxism and Literature*. Oxford: Oxford University Press, 1977.
Žižek, Slavoj. "Multiculturalism, or, the Logic of Multinational Capitalism." *New Left Review* 225 (September–October 1997): 28–51.

INDEX

Abeng (Cliff), 88
Address to the German Nation (Fichte), 7
administration (political), 16–17, 81, 95–103, 126
Adorno, Culture, and Feminism (anthology), 122
Adorno, Theodor: *Aesthetic Theory*, 10–13, 24–27, 35–37, 56, 90, 93, 107, 159, 198–200; chiasmus and, 47, 50, 68, 76, 111–20, 159–60; constellations and, 13, 29–37, 50, 56, 60, 81, 101, 115, 121, 131, 175, 200; crystallization concept and, 12–13, 22, 26–29, 85–94, 101, 110, 157; "Culture and Administration," 16–17; *Dialectic of Enlightenment*, 16, 18–19, 22, 116, 173; gender and, 14, 121–22, 129–35; *Minima Moralia*, 1, 46–47, 77, 89–90, 107, 129–30, 134, 159; *Negative Dialectics*, 18, 21, 23–29, 37, 123; negative dialectics and, 1, 10–32, 49–60, 74, 90, 121–23, 129–37, 159–67, 198–200; nostalgia and, 44–46, 77, 158–59; poetry and, 31, 81, 103, 199–200

aesthetics: affect and, 122–24, 131–35, 157–61, 191–94; anthropological exotic and, 69–77, 162–66, 170–75, 186–97; constellations and, 13, 29–37, 50, 53–56, 60, 81, 101, 115, 121, 131, 175, 200; crystallization and, 12–13, 22, 26–29, 85–94, 101, 110, 157; formal structure and, 12–18, 21, 35–40, 48, 80–81, 89, 94, 115, 197; gender's relation to, 131–32; Ishiguro and, 49–60; modernity and, 11–15, 40, 50, 81, 87–89, 103, 114, 122, 129–35; national consciousness and, 82–95, 167, 170–75; negative dialectics and, 10–14, 51–60; nostalgia and longing and, 10–14, 38, 44–56, 66–68, 75–77, 84, 108, 118, 162, 189, 199; social justice movements and, 80–89, 103–20; style and, 18, 40, 44–60, 77, 87, 131–36, 162, 167–73, 189–91; truth and, 10–11; Walcott and, 81–83, 89–95. *See also* cosmopolitics; literature; national consciousness; painting; poetry

Aesthetic Theory (Adorno), 10–13, 24–27, 35–37, 56, 90, 93, 107, 159, 198–200
affect, 75–76, 114, 121–22, 124, 131–35, 157–61, 191–94. *See also* structures of feeling
aikido, 188–90
Amin-Khan, Tariq, 199–200
Anderson, Benedict, 8–9, 192
Another Life (Walcott), 91, 95–103, 111, 113, 116–18
anthropological exotic, 162–67, 170–97
anticolonialism, 1, 4–6, 15, 33, 80, 102, 116, 120, 200
"The Antilles" (Walcott), 82–89, 100–101
Appadurai, Arjun, 4–5
archives. *See* romances of the archive
Arnold, Matthew, 52–53
An Artist of the Floating World (Ishiguro), 39
Asian Americans, 130–35, 147–48, 194. *See also specific authors and works*
Auden, W. H., 81
authenticity (cultural or national), 6, 26, 38–39, 49–50, 63, 69–71, 76, 118, 131, 134, 194
Aw, Tash, 169

Beethoven, Ludwig van, 44–45, 48–50
Benedict, Ruth, 188, 192
Benjamin, Walter, 85, 192
Bennet, Louise, 74
Berlatsky, Eric, 164–65
Bhabha, Homi, 3–5
Bhagavad Gita, 34–35
Bildung (nation-culture bridge), 7–9, 26, 52, 61, 130, 136–38, 160
The Black Atlantic (Gilroy), 105, 107–8
Black Skin, White Masks (Fanon), 22
Brennan, Timothy, 8–9
Breslin, Paul, 90, 104
Britain: anthropological exotic and, 186–97; colonialism and, 14, 65, 69–77, 79–80, 84–85, 95–121, 125–29, 139, 167–70, 179–80, 182–86, 195, 198; essentialist nationalism and, 14, 38, 42, 47–50, 76–77, 189, 198–99; ethnic pluralism and, 39–40; Ishiguro's relation to, 38–77; landscapes of, 42–51, 60–73; multiculturalist discourses and, 39–40, 43–50, 74–77; romances of the archive in, 38, 43, 47, 49–60. *See also specific former colonies*
Brouillette, Sarah, 172, 197
bumioutera (ethnicity), 125, 141, 168–69, 194–95
Butler, Judith, 159–60
Byatt, A. S., 44, 51

capitalism: colonialism's relation to, 15–17, 24–25, 95–103; commodity culture and, 18–19, 38, 163–65, 170–75; geopolitical views of, 167, 174–75; globalization and, 1–3, 6–7, 9, 33, 98–99; neocolonial regimes and, 148–61. *See also* colonialism; commodification and commodities; modernity
Carribean identities: diasporas and, 81–82; global hermeneutics and, 78–80; modernity and, 87–89; postcolonial identities and, 4–5, 44, 84–85, 95–111; racial discourses in, 22–28, 81; Walcott and, 14, 78–79, 89–95
Césaire, Aimé, 15–17
Chakrabarty, Dipesh, 115
Cheah, Pheng, 9–10, 12
chiasmus, 47, 50, 68, 76, 111–20, 159–60
children. *See* filiation
China: diasporic belonging and, 122; gender and, 135–38; Hong Kong and, 69–74; Malaysia and Singapore politics and, 125–29, 139–61, 163–64, 180, 195
Chow, Rey, 6, 39, 134, 158, 165–66
The Chrysanthemum and the Sword (Benedict), 188
Chu, Patricia P., 130–31, 147
circulation discourses, 103–8, 123, 125
Cliff, Michelle, 88
Clifford, James, 3, 79
coercive mimeticism, 39, 124, 127, 134
Coetzee, J. M., 35–36, 172

cognitive mapping, 167, 174
colonialism: anthropological exotic and, 69–77, 166, 186–97; Britain and, 14, 65, 69–77, 79–80, 84–85, 95–121, 179–80, 182–86; capitalism and, 15–17, 24–25, 95–103; definitions of, 15–16; gender and, 129–47, 183–86, 192–94; hybridity and, 95–111, 183–84; Malaysia and, 121, 125–29, 139, 167–70, 179–80, 182–97; nationalisms and, 18–22, 73–77, 101–2; racialized discourses and, 22–28, 33–37, 141–42, 175–86; Singapore and, 121, 125–29, 139; subjectivities within, 22–30. *See also* anticolonialism; cosmopolitics; critical nationality; internal colonialism; modernity; neocolonialism; postcolonial theory
commodification and commodities: anthropological exotic and, 39–40, 50, 162–63, 170–75, 186–97; British heritage tradition and, 38, 61–69; Carribean tourism and, 116; instrumentalization of culture and, 46–50, 60–69, 123
Conan Doyle, Arthur, 71–72
Conrad, Joseph, 187
constellations, 10–13, 29–37, 50, 56, 60, 81, 101, 115, 121, 131, 175, 200
Contemporary Literature (journal), 198
contrapuntal analysis, 27–32, 74–75, 125
Cooppan, Vilashini, 9–10
cosmopolitics: aesthetics and, 1, 83–94; definitions of, 1–2, 122; ethnographic tactics and, 162–66, 170–97; filiation discourses and, 122–25, 135–38; gender and, 121–24, 129–38, 143–61, 183; global cosmopolitanism and, 2–3, 81–82, 197; literature and, 103–20; multicultural discourses and, 39–50, 74–77, 86–87; national consciousness and, 2–3, 69–77, 103–11, 199–200. *See also* critical nationality; instrumental rationality
critical nationality, 11, 14, 32, 37, 89, 111, 123, 135, 170–75, 181, 194, 199–200

critical theory. *See* Adorno, Theodor; aesthetics; cosmopolitics; instrumental rationality; negative dialectics
A Critique of Postcolonial Reason (Spivak), 32
crystallization, 12–13, 22, 26–29, 85–94, 101, 110, 157
"Culture and Administration" (Adorno), 16–17
Culture and Imperialism (Said), 30
cultures: affect and, 124, 131–35, 157–61; authenticity and, 6, 22–28, 76, 118, 131, 134, 194; *Bildung* concept and, 7–9, 26, 52, 61, 130, 136–38, 160; colonialism and, 16–18, 30, 123; commodification of, 162–63; definitions of, 3; essentializing role of, 81–83, 97–104, 121–29, 131–38, 148–61, 163–64, 167–70, 172–75, 177–78, 183–86, 190–97; global cosmopolitanism and, 2, 4–7, 98–99; hybrid identities and, 39, 78–79; identity thinking and, 1, 40–44, 51–60; nationalisms and, 3–6, 20, 22–28, 43–44, 49–50, 167–70, 183–86, 188; practices and, 192–97. *See also* colonialism; filiation; hybridity; language

Dawson, Ashley, 74
de Certeau, Michel, 165
decolonization, 20, 23–24, 31, 81, 117, 180
Derrida, Jacques, 32
de Sacy, Silvestre, 29
desire. *See* affect; nostalgia
Dialectic of Enlightenment (Horkheimer and Adorno), 16, 18–19, 22, 116, 173
Dialectics of the Body (Lee), 121–22
diaspora(s): critical analysis and, 38–77, 103–11, 139–40, 170–86; definitions of, 171–72; ethnographic tactics and, 163, 167–76, 178–97; gender and, 121–24, 131–35; hybrid subjectivities and, 3, 81–89, 103–11, 148–61, 170–86; national consciousness and, 32–37, 39–44, 147–61; native infor-

mant roles of, 32–37, 171; nostalgia and, 84, 108, 118–20; transnational cultures and, 4–6, 81–82, 131–35. *See also* cosmopolitics; hybridity; identity; national consciousness

discourse theory, 29–32. *See also* cosmopolitics; Foucault, Michel; national consciousness; racial discourses; transnationalism

Donnell, Alison, 119

double consciousness, 39–44, 47–48

Drabble, Margaret, 60, 64

Eckhart, Aaron, 51

Edwards, Brent Hayes, 171–72

Ee, Tiang Hong, 169

Elizabeth II (Queen), 80

English (language), 143–61, 177

Enlightenment, 19, 22–24, 81, 84, 97, 102, 115, 180

Essay on the Origin of Language (Herder), 7

essentialisms. *See* cultures; identity; landscapes and territory; racial discourses

Esty, Jed, 43, 50

ethnicity: commodification of, 162–63; economic status and, 125–29, 148–61, 168, 195; identity thinking and, 4–5, 103–11, 125–29, 176–80, 194–96; Ishiguro and, 14, 39–40; posed-, 60–69, 77, 189, 192, 194. *See also* cultures; identity; multiculturalist ideologies; national consciousness; racial discourses

ethnography: anthropological exotic and, 14, 40–43, 50, 69–77, 162–67, 170–76, 186–97; feminism and, 131–35; Lim criticism and, 136–38; scientific detachment and, 145–47; tactics and, 162–66, 170–97

Eurasians, 126, 128, 143, 152–53, 167–70

Evening Is the Whole Day (Samarasan), 163, 168–69, 175–86, 197

exoticism. *See* anthropological exotic

Falklands War, 69

Fanon, Frantz, 14, 17–18, 22–28, 30–31

feminism, 121–24, 126–61

Feminist Interpretations of Theodor Adorno (anthology), 122

fetishes and fetishization. *See* anthropological exotic; commodification and commodities; ethnography

Fichte, Johann Gottlieb, 7, 19, 53

filiation, 123–24, 126–29, 135–61. *See also* gender; national consciousness

Fleishman, Avrom, 164

Foe (Coetzee), 35–36

The Fortunate Traveller (Walcott), 90

Foucault, Michel, 7, 28–29

fragments, 81–89, 197

Frankfurt School. *See* Adorno, Theodor; Horkheimer, Max

Fumagalli, Maria Cristina, 88

The Fundamentalist (Mohsin), 199

the gaze, 22, 155, 179

Geertz, Clifford, 174

gender: affect and, 122, 124, 131–35, 153–54; filiation and, 121–25, 135–38, 148, 150–51; modernity and, 141–42; nation's connection to, 14, 121–22, 137, 139–61, 183–86, 192–94; Orientalism and, 143–47. *See also* colonialism; heroic masculinity; national consciousness

genealogy. *See* filiation

genre (literary), 112–14, 131. *See also* aesthetics; poetry; romances of the archive

geopolitics, 167, 174–75

Ghosh, Amitav, 176

Ghosh, Bishnupriya, 176

ghosts. *See* haunting

The Gift of Rain (Tan, T. E.), 163, 168, 186–97

Gikandi, Simon, 87–88, 174–75

Gilroy, Paul, 105, 107–8, 119

globalization, 2–6; capitalism and, 6, 33; modernity and, 11–15, 40

global moment, 14, 198; cosmopolitanism and, 2–6; definitions of, 1–2

Gopinath, Gayatri, 193

Gramsci, Antonio, 199

Hall, Stuart, 4–5, 20, 43–44, 81, 88, 171–74, 186
Hamid, Mohsin, 199
Hansen, Jim, 199
Hart, Michael, 199
haunting, 9–12, 191
Hegel, G. W. F., 10, 18, 22–24, 34
Herder, Johann Gottfried, 7, 53
heritage industry (in Britain), 38, 43–44, 47–50, 60–69, 76–77, 198
heroic masculinity, 14, 136, 147, 150, 167, 183
Hesse, Barnor, 44
Hikayat Hang Tuah (epic), 196
history: cosmopolitics and, 103–11, 131–35; literary realism and, 14, 163, 168–97; nationalisms and, 2, 4, 8–9, 13, 18–22, 28, 43–47, 51, 68–73, 85–89, 117, 142; postcolonial theories and, 28–35, 41, 74–81, 95–103; subject-object relation and, 26, 82, 158–59; temporality and, 113–15
Hokkien (language), 192–93
Hong Kong, 69
Hopkins, Gerard Manley, 136
Horkheimer, Max, 16, 18–19, 22, 116, 173
Houseman, A. E., 155–56
Huang, Yunte, 134
Huggan, Graham, 162–64, 167, 171, 176
hybridity: diasporic conceptions of, 3, 81–89, 103–11, 148–61, 170–71, 175–97; fascinations with, 152–53, 184; historical considerations in, 84–89; nationalist discourses and, 38–77, 103–11, 183–84; racial and ethnic discourses and, 78–79, 81. See also identity; national consciousness; racial discourses; subjectivities

idealized femininity, 139–61
identity: authenticity and, 6, 103–11, 118; definitions of, 18; essentialism and, 1, 7, 22–28, 31–32, 38–77, 81–83, 103–11, 117, 125–29, 163–65, 167–70, 183–86; gender and, 14, 121–22, 126–61; hybrid subjectivities and, 4–5, 81–89, 152–53; instrumentalization of, 11–40, 45–57, 61–62, 73–74, 78–79, 97–103, 121–35, 147–57, 181–82, 196–99; melting-pot assimilation and, 143–47; nationalisms and, 1–3, 6–10, 12, 20–37, 44–46, 170–72; patriotism and, 4–5, 14, 19–21, 27–32, 36–38, 48–51, 66–69, 96, 121, 180–82; self-fashioning and, 69–70; transnationalism and, 81–82, 108. See also filiation
Indians (ethnicity), 33–37, 141–42, 162–63, 175–86
insiderism. See authenticity (cultural or national); cultures; national consciousness
instrumental rationality, 11–40, 45–62, 97–103, 121–35, 147–57, 181–82, 196–99
internal colonialism, 115, 123–24
interpellation, 9, 34, 124, 127–30, 138–39, 145–47, 157–63
Ishiguro, Kazuo, 14, 38–77, 189–90, 192

Jamaica, 74, 83–84
Jameson, Fredric, 167, 174
Japan, 37–44, 68–69, 168, 186–97
Joss and Gold (Lim), 125, 127–30, 133, 135–61, 181
Journey to the West (Kingston), 153
The Joy Luck Club (Tan), 131, 157

Kandiyoti, Deniz, 129, 183
Katrak, Ketu, 123
Keating, Michael, 200
Keen, Suzanne, 43
King, Bruce, 90
Kingston, Maxine Hong, 131, 133, 153
Klein, Ronald D., 188, 196

landscapes and territory, 6, 44–51, 60–73, 178–79, 188–89
language: hybrid identities and, 37, 88–

89, 127–30, 142–49, 177–78, 187–93, 199; national-culture essentialism and, 7–9, 12, 26, 52, 61, 130, 136–38, 160–70. *See also specific countries and languages*
late style, 48–49, 53. *See also* style
Lawrence, T. E., 29, 116, 138, 156
"The Leaden Echo and the Golden Echo" (Hopkins), 136
"Learning to Love America" (Lim), 123
Leavis, F. R., 53, 138
Lee, Kuan Yew, 137
Lee, Lisa Yun, 121–22
Leong, Liew Geok, 157
Lim, Shirley Geok-lin: cosmopolitical perspective of, 139–61, 169; feminism and, 14, 121–24, 135–38; gender critiques of, 129–30; interpretations of, 136–38; Malaysian identity and, 121–22, 181; multicultural discourses and, 139–61, 177
literary tourism, 162, 164, 173–74. *See also* anthropological exotic; commodification and commodities; heritage industry (in Britain)
literature: affect and, 157–61; commodification of, 14, 37–39, 144–47, 162–63, 170–85, 187–97; cosmopolitics and, 1–2, 103–20, 164–66; critical nationality and, 31–32; crystallizing role of, 12–13, 22, 26–29, 85–94, 101, 110, 157; cultural discourse and, 6–10, 22–28, 131–35, 167–70; detective narratives and, 69–77; ethnographic exotic and, 39–40, 69–77, 164, 167, 186–97; feminism and, 121–24; gender and, 121–25, 129–35, 147–61; landscapes as devices in, 47–50, 69–73, 178–79, 188–89; language's representations and, 147–61; nationalism's relation to, 6–10, 34–37, 51–60, 78–79, 81–89; nostalgia and longing and, 10–14, 38, 44–56, 66–68, 75–77, 84, 108, 118, 162, 189, 199; style's effect on, 18, 40, 44–60, 77, 87, 131–36, 162, 167–73, 189–91. *See also specific authors and works*

longing, 11, 32–36, 45–49, 76, 91–92, 102, 108, 158–59. *See also* nostalgia
Lowe, Lisa, 194
Lyotard, Jean-François, 28

Ma, Sheng-mei, 133–34
Mahabharata, 34
Malays (ethnicity), 121–29, 139–61, 167, 180–81, 195–96
Malaysia: colonial period of, 164, 167–70, 186–97; ethnographic tactics and, 163, 166, 170–86; filiation narratives and, 125; Japan and, 187–97; landscapes of, 178–79; Lim's relation to, 121–23; official multiculturalism and, 14, 125–29, 139–61, 163–64, 168–69, 194–95; race riots of 1969 and, 135–36, 144–47, 151, 175, 180–81
Maniam, K. S., 177, 185
Marx, Karl, 10
masculinity, 14, 129–36, 143–48, 150, 157–61, 175–86
master-slave dialectic, 22–23, 30, 62, 79–80
memory, 9, 41–47, 53, 77, 82–85, 101–2, 112, 122. *See also* nostalgia
Midnight's Children (Rushdie), 162, 180
mimesis, 86, 124. *See also* coercive mimeticism
Minima Moralia (Adorno), 1, 46–47, 77, 89–90, 107, 129–30, 134, 159
Mishima, Yukio, 41
modernity, 11–13, 15, 40, 50, 81, 87, 89, 103, 114, 129–35, 141, 144
Monsoon History (Lim), 122
Morita, Akira, 41
mothers. *See* filiation
multiculturalist ideologies: Britain and, 39–40, 43–44, 47–50, 74–77; colonialism's relation to, 6; Malayasia and, 14, 125–29, 143–47, 163–64; state interests and, 85–87. *See also* colonialism; Malaysia; postcolonial theory; transnationalism
multilogicality, 131, 136–38, 177
"Muse of History" (Walcott), 83–85, 97

Muslims, 128, 141–42, 148–49

Naipaul, V. S., 86, 166
narratives: genre and, 112–13; historical writing and, 164–65; identity thinking and, 2; multilogical-, 131, 136–38. *See also* cosmopolitics; literature; *specific authors, genres, and works*
national consciousness: affect and, 59, 75–77, 112–14, 121–24, 131–33; *Bildung* concept and, 7–9, 26, 52, 61, 130, 136–38, 160; cosmopolitical perspectives on, 2–6, 69–77, 111–20, 123, 163, 170–75, 199–200; critical nationality and, 11, 14, 32, 37, 66–67, 89, 111, 123, 135, 162–67, 170–86, 194, 199–200; cultural essentialism and, 4–5, 7–9, 26, 51–60, 65, 69–79, 103–11, 131–61, 163–64, 188, 199–200; definitions of, 84; diaspora's effect on, 32–37, 39–44, 81–82, 121–23; Fanon on, 22–28; filiation discourses and, 121–24, 135–38; fragments and holisms and, 81–89, 197; gender and, 14, 121–24, 126–38, 143–61, 183, 192–94; heritage industries in, 40–44, 47–60; history's role in, 2–4, 8–9, 13, 18–22, 28, 43–47, 68–81, 85–89; identity thinking and, 1–10, 20, 38–41, 43–44, 69–79, 95–111, 118–20, 160–61, 167–70; instrumental nationality and, 11–40, 45–57, 61–62, 97–103, 121–35, 147–57, 181–82, 196–99; instrumental rationality and, 11–40, 45–57, 61–62, 97–103, 121–35, 147–57, 181–82, 196–99; landscapes and territoriality and, 6, 60–69; landscapes and territory and, 6, 42, 44–51, 60–73, 188–89; language's relation to, 7–9, 26, 52, 61, 127, 130, 136–38, 160–79, 187–93, 199; literature's underwriting of, 6–10, 34–37; nostalgia and longing and, 10–14, 38, 44–56, 66–68, 75–77, 84, 108, 118, 162, 189, 199; patriotic discourses and, 4–5, 14, 19–21, 27–32, 36–38, 48–51, 66–69, 96, 121, 180–82; postnational discourses and, 2–6, 16–19, 109; social formations and, 1–2, 79–80, 83–89, 123, 198–200; state concept's relation to, 3, 7, 9, 14, 19–22, 37, 83–84, 116, 198. *See also* cosmopolitics; ethnicity; filiation; neocolonialism; postnational discourses; racial discourses; transnationalism
Native Americans, 115
nativism, 27–32, 65, 86, 102. *See also* ethnicity; filiation; identity
Nazareth, Peter, 136–37
negative dialectics, 1, 10–32, 49–60, 74, 90, 121–23, 129–37, 159–67, 198–200
Negative Dialectics (Adorno), 18, 21, 23–29, 37, 123
neocolonialism, 95–103, 109, 112, 117, 129–35, 199–200
nostalgia, 10–14, 38, 44–56, 66–68, 75–77, 84, 108, 118, 162, 189, 199

objects and objectivity, 11–21, 35–40, 48–50, 80–81, 87–90, 103, 114, 121–23, 160. *See also* Adorno, Theodor; aesthetics; negative dialectics; subjectivities
Oe, Kenzaburo, 39, 41–43, 47, 68
Omeros (Walcott), 91, 103, 111–20
"On National Culture" (Fanon), 26
Orang Asli, 167, 169
Orientalism, 28–30, 126–29, 143–47, 152, 187–92
Orientalism (Said), 29

painting, 97–103
A Pale View of Hills (Ishiguro), 39
Paltrow, Gwyneth, 51
Pantomime (Walcott), 82–83
patriotism, 4–5, 14, 19–21, 27–32, 36–38, 48–51, 66–69, 96, 121, 180–82
Patten, Chris, 74
Penang (city), 186–97
Peranakan (ethnicity), 167

poetry, 31, 81, 85–111. *See also* Adorno, Theodor; aesthetics; *specific poems and poets*
politics. *See* cosmopolitics; national consciousness
posed-ethnicity, 60–69, 77, 189, 192, 194
Possession (Byatt), 44, 51
postcolonial theory: Adorno and, 28, 81, 103, 199–200; affective dimensions and, 112–14; anthropological exotic and, 14, 69–77, 162–66, 170–75; anticolonialism and, 1; contrapuntal analysis and, 27–32, 74–75, 125; gender and, 14, 121–24, 129–35, 143–61, 192–94; global culture narratives and, 2–3, 78–80; hybrid subjectivities and, 3–6, 81–89; literary form and, 1, 91–95; modernity and, 87; national consciousness and, 2–3, 6–10; nativism and, 27–32; negative dialectics and, 10–14; Said on, 27–32; social formation concept and, 1–2, 8, 79–80, 83–89, 123, 198–200. *See also* gender; hybridity; transnationalism; *specific theorists*
postnational discourses, 2–6, 33, 79, 82, 88
Pratt, Mary Louise, 166
The Prodigal (Walcott), 78, 103
psychoanalytical criticism, 49, 53
psychoanalytic criticism of, 44–45
Puri, Shalini, 82, 85
Purushotam, Nirmala, 129

queer theory, 192–96

racial discourses, 7, 12, 22–28, 40–44, 65, 71, 78–87, 103–11, 125–29, 167–80. *See also* ethnicity; filiation; identity
Ramayana, 85
rationality: affect and, 134–35; critical-, 11–13, 134; instrumental-, 11–40, 45–57, 61–62, 97–103, 121–35, 147–57, 181–82, 196–99
recognition, 22–24

Reitz, Caroline, 76
religion, 12, 115, 128, 142, 148–49
The Remains of the Day (Ishiguro), 40, 47–48, 51, 60–69, 72, 75–76, 189
Renan, Ernest, 29
representation(s). *See* aesthetics; literature; national consciousness
ressentiment, 24, 80, 117
The Return (Maniam), 185
romances of the archive, 38, 43, 47, 49–60. *See also* genre (literary)
Romanticism, 6–7, 9
Rushdie, Salman, 69, 162–63, 166, 172, 176, 180

Said, Edward, 14, 17–18, 22, 27–32, 74
St. Lucia, 78, 81, 83, 95–103, 111, 114, 116–17, 119
St. Omer, Dunstan, 99, 101
Samarasan, Preeta, 14, 163–65, 167–75, 197
Sartre, Jean-Paul, 22
"The Schooner *Flight*" (Walcott), 89, 91, 103–11
Scott, David, 112–14
Sea Grapes (Walcott), 91
"Sea Grapes" (Walcott), 91–92, 94
self-fashioning, 69–71, 134
sentimentality and sentiments, 44–45, 60, 68, 72, 82, 97, 118–24, 130–31, 158–60
Sim, Wai-chew, 50
Simmons, Harry, 97–103, 113
Singapore, 121, 125–29, 135–38, 147–61, 188, 193
The Singapore Story (Lee, K. Y.), 128
slavery, 35, 97–98, 101, 104, 107, 118
Smith, Charles Aubrey, 96
social formations: ethnographic tactics and, 162–65, 170–97; Fanon on, 22–28; gender and, 131–38; national consciousness and, 1–2, 198–200; postcolonial critiques and, 8; Walcott and, 78–79, 81–89, 103–20
"Society and the Artist" (Walcott), 83
"*Society Must Be Defended*" (Foucault), 7

somatic experience. *See* affect
"The Source" (Lim), 123
spectres and the spectral. *See* haunting
Spivak, Gayatri Chakravorty, 14, 17–18, 22, 27, 32–37
The Star-Apple Kingdom (Walcott), 103–11
state(s): cultural essentialisms and, 97–98, 101–2, 130, 136–38, 160; literary complicity in, 7–8; nation's relation to, 2–7, 9, 14, 19–22, 37, 83–84, 116, 198; neocolonialism and, 95–103, 127–30, 199–200; patriotic discourses and, 4–5, 14, 19–21, 27–32, 36–38, 48–51, 66–69, 121, 180–82. *See also* cosmopolitics; national consciousness
Stein, Mark, 48
strategy. *See* tactics
structures of feeling, 59, 75–77, 112–14
style, 18, 40, 44–60, 77, 87, 131–36, 162, 167–73, 189–91. *See also* tactics
subjectivities: Adorno's aesthetics and, 48–50; aesthetic theory and, 41–44, 52–60, 87–88; colonialism and, 15–16, 78–79, 82–89; diasporic- or transnational-, 4–6, 170–75, 186; gaze concept and, 22, 155, 179; gender and, 129–35; global cosmopolitanism and, 2, 12, 32–40, 78–80, 121; history and, 26; hybridity and, 3–6, 197; instrumental rationality and, 18–22; interpellation and, 9, 34, 124, 127–30, 138–39, 145–47, 159–63; objects and the objective and, 12–21, 35–36, 39–40, 48–50, 121–23
Swift, Graham, 179
symbolic violence, 84, 90

tactics, 163, 170–75, 177–97
Tan, Amy, 131, 133, 137, 157
Tan, Twan Eng, 14, 163–65, 167–76, 186–97
temporality, 2, 8–9, 13–20, 34–35, 47, 65, 84–85, 112–14, 160, 172, 183, 191–94
Thatcher, Margaret, 60

Tölöyan, Khachig, 42
"To Return to Trees" (Walcott), 91, 93–95, 101, 105–6
Torres-Saillant, Silvio, 88
tourism, 43–44
tragedy. *See* genre (literary)
transnationalism: anthropological exotic and, 14, 69–77, 162–66, 170–76, 178–97; British national identity and, 39–40; circulation metaphor and, 103, 105–8, 123, 125, 131, 170–75, 197; cosmopolitanism and, 2–6, 12, 32–37, 108, 121, 170–71, 198–99; gender and, 148–49; hybrid identities and, 81; languages and, 37, 78–79; Walcott readings and, 90–91. *See also* capitalism; diasporas; global moment; national consciousness
Trinidad, 80, 83, 85–86, 93, 97, 103–4, 109–13, 117
Tripmaster Monkey (Kingston), 131, 153
truth, 10–11, 123
Tsing, Anna Lowenhaupt, 165

uncanny, the, 9
The Unconsoled (Ishiguro), 49–60
United States: Adorno's exile in, 46; Asian Americans and, 123, 130–35, 147–48, 194; colonialism and imperialism of, 27–32, 115, 143–47, 152; commodity culture of, 18–19, 62–64; literary depictions of, 61–69; multicultural pluralism and, 87; nationalism and imperialism of, 27

violence, 24–25, 81, 90, 107, 112–13

Walcott, Derek: aesthetics of, 80–81, 87, 93–95, 104; biography of, 83–84; cosmopolitics of, 78–79, 84–90, 95–111, 121, 166; interpretations of, 90–91, 104, 119
Walking Backwards (Lim), 122
Walkowitz, Rebecca, 50

Waterland (Swift), 179
Weldon, Catherine, 115
What the Fortune Teller Didn't Say (Lim), 122–23
When We Were Orphans (Ishiguro), 51, 69–77
whiteness, 143–47
Williams, Eric, 80, 97, 103, 112–13, 117
Williams, Raymond, 75–76
Williams, William Carlos, 156

The Woman Warrior (Kingston), 134
women, 121–35, 139–61, 183–84
The Wretched of the Earth (Fanon), 23–26
A Writer's Britain (Drabble), 60

Yeats, William Butler, 31, 81

Žižek, Slavoj, 6

TRANSOCEANIC STUDIES
Ileana Rodriguez, Series Editor

The Transoceanic Studies series rests on the assumption of a one-world system. This system—simultaneously modern and colonial and now postmodern and postcolonial (global)—profoundly restructured the world, displaced the Mediterranean *mare nostrum* as a center of power and knowledge, and constructed dis-centered, transoceanic, waterways that reached across the world. The vast imaginary undergirding this system was Eurocentric in nature and intent. Europe was viewed as the sole culture-producing center. But Eurocentrism, theorized as the "coloniality of power" and "of knowledge," was contested from its inception, generating a rich, enormous, alternate corpus. In disputing Eurocentrism, books in this series will acknowledge above all the contributions coming from other areas of the world, colonial and postcolonial, without which neither the aspirations to universalism put forth by the Enlightenment nor those of globalization promoted by postmodernism will be fulfilled.

National Consciousness and Literary Cosmopolitics: Postcolonial Literature in a Global Moment
    WEIHSIN GUI

Writing AIDS: (Re)Conceptualizing the Individual and Social Body in Spanish American Literature
    JODIE PARYS

Learning to Unlearn: Decolonial Reflections from Eurasia and the Americas
    MADINA V. TLOSTANOVA AND WALTER D. MIGNOLO

Oriental Shadows: The Presence of the East in Early American Literature
    JIM EGAN